2

DIRT CHEAP, REAL GOOD

From the *Hometown Guides* series, books that offer lively and original regional history and travel for in and around Washington, D.C. Other titles include:

DIRT CHEAP, REAL GOOD

A Highway Guide to Thrift Stores in the Washington, D.C., Area

Chriss Slevin
and
Leah Smith

A Capital Hometown Guides Book

CAPITAL
BOOKS, INC.
Sterling, Virginia

Capital Books, Inc.
P.O. Box 605
Herndon, Virginia 20172-0605

ISBN 1-931868-68-9 (alk.paper)

Library of Congress Cataloging-in-Publication Data

Slevin, Chriss.
 Dirt cheap, real good : a highway guide to thrift stores in the Washington, D.C. area / Chriss Slevin and Leah Smith.—1st ed.
      p.   cm.
   "A Capital Hometown guides book."
   ISBN 1-931868-68-9 (alk. paper)
   1. Shopping—Washington Region—Guidebooks.   2. Thrift shops—Washington Region—Guidebooks.   3. Secondhand trade—Washington Region—Guidebooks.   4. Antique dealers—Washington Region—Guidebooks. 5. Washington Region—Tours.   6. Shopping—Middle Atlantic States—Guidebooks.   7. Thrift shops—Middle Atlantic States—Guidebooks. 8. Secondhand trade—Middle Atlantic States—Guidebooks.   9. Antique dealers—Middle Atlantic States—Guidebooks.   10. Middle Atlantic States—Tours.   I. Smith, Leah, 1975–   II. Title.

Printed in the United States of America on acid-free paper that meets the American National Standards Institute Z39-48 Standard.

First Edition

10   9   8   7   6   5   4   3   2   1

CONTENTS

ACKNOWLEDGMENTS

The authors would like to sincerely thank Noemi Taylor for her guidance and support.

Thank you also to Glenn Pudelka of Palmer & Dodge and the folks at Volunteer Lawyers for the Arts, Massachusetts.

Chriss sends thanks and smooches to Matt Palin, Frances McConihe, Amy Slevin, Shirly Camin, Heather Davis, Amy Nelson, Erin Blahut, Shawn Atkins, Sara McGrath, Tina and William Travis, Renee Piechocki, and Robert Olin, for your suggestions, support, and for letting us crash on your couch. Thanks to Melissa Potter, David Terry, Janice Shapiro, Priscilla Miner, Alan Gilbert, Edith Meeks, and all my pals at NYFA, for giving me your ideas and listening to me complain. A special debt to Ann Wagar for finding me a computer! Also to Jeanette Vuocolo, Natalie de la Paz, Glen Minasian, Elissa Swanger, Katherine Gleason, Laura Straus, Jennifer Feil, Michele Snyder, and Leah Kronenfeld for your hints, tips and ideas.

Leah would like to especially thank Andrew Thompson, Laurel Kirtz, Gabriel Boyer, and Roslyn Halper for their superior efforts and constant help. To Skip Elsheimer, for your words of wisdom. To Matt Gress, Mary Timony, Aunt Nancy, Amy Harmon, Philip Haut, Katherine Withers, Natalie Vinski, Krysta Spanier, and Michelle Lee for all of your helpful hints and recommendations. To Mara with the *Synonym Finder*. And many thanks to Frank Shea, Katya Gorker, and The Coolidge Corner Theatre for your moral support. To Robert Smith for putting up with me. And finally, to Ernest Longa for your timely and free advice.

Both authors thank the many owners and employees who offered driving directions, thrift store recommendations, and tons of juicy gossip. Last but not least, thanks to the Bedford County Visitors Bureau.

INTRODUCTION

How can you track down the best thrift, secondhand, and vintage shops across the United States? Well, we haven't covered the whole country (yet), but *Dirt Cheap, Real Good: A Highway Guide to Thrift Stores in the Washington, D.C., Area* delivers a piece of the action. *Dirt Cheap, Real Good* combines highway adventures and secondhand shopping into one jam-packed manual for thrift culture. We've searched high and low to bring you the best of the best and the oddest of the odd. This book will guide you to the stores with the cheapest prices, the widest selections, and the zaniest vibes. *Dirt Cheap, Real Good* is a directory of our most beloved thrift shops in the mid-Atlantic region.

Our hit list features a glittering variety of secondhand shops, ranging from the cavernous warehouse to the small-town church donation center. We give you the lowdown on locations, hours, prices, and most important, the goods. While this guide focuses mainly on the best places for dirt-cheap bargains, we've also included a number of reasonably priced antique and vintage shops, where dealers offer a great variety of retro merchandise—a bit pricier, but sometimes too good to pass up.

A road trip just ain't a road trip without unexpected places to stop and stretch your legs. In addition to secondhand shopping, this book points out one-of-a-kind pit stops and roadside attractions. Pull over and check out our favorite quirky bars, snack stops, cheap motels, and unusual entertainment venues. We've even included a smidgen of weirdo Americana and offbeat photo opportunities.

Dirt Cheap, Real Good covers the best of Washington, D.C., along with six travel routes that cover the best of the mid-Atlantic region, from the Chesapeake Bay to the Blue Ridge Mountains. Passing through the largest cities and the tiniest rural towns, the routes are designed so that you can connect the dots to create your own path or simply use the book as a reference guide to the best stores in one particular area. Put the pedal to the metal for a whirlwind tour, whichever route you choose!

This book is your on-the-go manual to the ultimate road trip and thrift shopping spree. Let *Dirt Cheap, Real Good* be your guide, and you're sure to find the cheapest thrills and frills throughout this corner of America. Happy trails, and always remember, dirt cheap *is* real good.

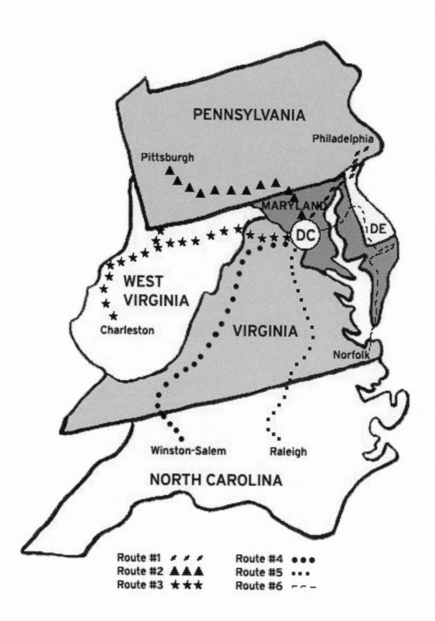

PENNSYLVANIA

Philadelphia

Pittsburgh

MARYLAND

DC

DE

WEST
VIRGINIA

VIRGINIA

Charleston

Norfolk

Winston-Salem

Raleigh

NORTH CAROLINA

Route #1 ✗✗✗
Route #2 ▲▲▲
Route #3 ★★★
Route #4 ●●●
Route #5 ▪▪▪
Route #6 − − −

HOW TO USE THIS BOOK AND ALL ABOUT OUR DIRT-CHEAP PHILOSOPHY

We've driven thousands of miles and visited hundreds of thrift and secondhand stores in the mid-Atlantic region, and this book is a compendium of our favorite stops. You can use this book to plan a penny-pinching road trip or keep it around as a reference for secondhand shops in your local area. Pack it in your overnight bag if you're taking a weekend trip away or leave it in the glove compartment for spur-of-the-moment thrifting.

The first chapter is dedicated to the Washington, D.C., metropolitan area, including shops within the Beltway that circles the city. The six routes are laid out roughly chronologically, beginning in D.C. and looping outward across seven states in the region. Along these, you'll encounter tiny quirky shops, huge warehouse thrifts, and everything in between. Be sure to bring along a decent map, some good tunes, and plenty of trunk space for all the stuff you'll probably find.

Dirt cheap *is* real good. In a nutshell, that is the philosophy behind this book. If you share the thrill of the hunt, you'll enjoy using it to chase down thrifty bargains without totally emptying your wallet. Thrifting is great for many reasons—you can recycle once-loved items, borrow from the world library of stuff, unearth the local cultural archeology, or play dress-up for cheap.

Road trips, like thrift stores, are not about the final destination. Exploring is more than half the fun. That said, there seems to be some universal law about thrift shopping with a particular purchase in mind. The stock is always changing, and there's no predicting what you might stumble across. You might just end up with something better instead.

Even with all our months of grueling work, we're sure to have missed some good spots during the course of our "research" . . . or maybe we're just keeping secrets from you, you paranoid freak.

Send us a postcard if you know about one that we missed. Chriss particularly likes vintage postcards of old motels.

Keep in mind that this book is based totally and unabashedly on our personal opinions. Sometimes we have completely different takes on a particular stop. Beauty and value are in the eyes of the beholders.

MAPS AND OTHER PLANNING, IN CASE YOU'RE INTO THAT

Thrift stores come and go. While the info in this book is accurate at the time of publication, hours of business change, stores change location (can you say "moving sale"?), and so on. We strongly recommend calling ahead if you have your heart set on visiting a particular shop.

For getting around, particularly in the large cities, you'll really need a detailed street map. Another tip is to visit one of several free Internet mapping services (see Resources, page xvi). You can punch in any address and print out a local map or driving directions, from anywhere to anywhere—for free! This is how cheap we really are.

TERMINOLOGY

The world of secondhand stuff is a complicated jungle. Different kinds of stores carry particular types of merchandise. In addition, location is a factor—rural areas often have better prices than big city thrifts, although sometimes the selections will be smaller. We have isolated the following species and have listed them here from cheapest to priciest. As you'd probably expect, stores in this book inhabit the lower rungs in terms of pricing.

Junk Shop:	junk—very cheap
Thrift Store:	clothes, furniture, and stuff—very cheap to cheap
Indoor Flea Market:	usually household stuff, collectibles, and furniture—cheap to fair prices
Antiques and Collectibles (often multidealer):	nicer household stuff, collectibles, and furniture—cheap to pricey
Vintage:	older clothing and accessories—fair to pricey
Consignment:	newer clothing and accessories—fair to pricey
Upscale Consignment:	high-quality clothing and accessories—pricey
Fine Antiques and Collectibles:	just plain expensive

WHERE TO STAY—SOME IDEAS

1. Drop in on all those friends that you haven't seen in ages. Crash on the couch.
2. Pajama party at a hostel. Overnight lodging is inexpensive, and if you have a little group you can even get private rooms for way cheaper than a city hotel. Hostel guides are available for free in—you guessed it, hostels!
3. Bring a tent and camp. The only downfall is that a tent in the trunk seriously diminishes your available storage space for new junk.
4. Cough up some cash and share a hotel room with all of your friends.
5. Sleep in your car. Usually not very fun.

RESOURCES

Mapquest:	www.mapquest.com
Superpages:	www.superpages.com
AnyWho:	www.anywho.com
Hostel Directories:	www.hostels.com
	www.hiayh.org
Camping Directories:	www.camping-usa.com
	www.woodalls.com (click on "where to tent")
	www.gocampingamerica.com

HOME BASE

Washington, D.C., Metropolitan Area

Ruff & Ready Furnishings,
Washington, D.C.

American Rescue Workers Thrift Store,
District Heights, Maryland

Rage Clothing,
Washington, D.C.

Your thrift adventures kick off with this chapter, devoted to everything dirt cheap inside the Beltway.

Quirky boutiques like **Meeps & Aunt Neensie's Fashionette** or the **Crystal Dove Gift Shop** are among the many you'll find around the nation's capital. Search out hip collectibles at **Ruff & Ready Furnishings** and **L & N Super Thrift** in Northwest. Detour for cheap eats at **Five Guys** burger joint, and after lunch swing by the massive **Value Village Thrift** in Hyattsville. Wrap up the tour with vintage scores at **Takoma Underground**.

As in all urban areas, D.C. thrifts can be subject to city prices. Nevertheless, there are loads of bargains along the way. Explore the city's secondhand treats and use it as a home base to begin any of the other six thrifting road trips in this book.

WASHINGTON, D.C.

Begin your D.C. thrift extravaganza at the **Georgia Avenue Thrift Store**, everyone's favorite and practically a local legend. Aisles are swarming with busy thrifters. The store is only average in size but has an upbeat atmosphere and is jam-packed with super bargains. Constantly replenished racks offer jeans, scarves, pants, skirts, dresses, and the like for men, women, and children. Clothing prices span from $2 to $20, with flashy formal wear at the upper end of the spectrum. Georgia Avenue Thrift also accommodates all of your household needs. Sheets, homespun afghans, and quilted bedspreads are neatly hung on hangars, and a hefty-size book section is located in the back, near stacks of furniture. You'll also find an electronics department with lamps and blaring TVs. Pick up some cheap-o designer dishes and colorful assorted housewares to take home.

Fourteenth Street in Northwest Washington also has some quality used furniture outlets, so stay hot on the trail with next-door neighbors **McKey's Antiques** and **Ruff & Ready Furnishings**. Pull over when you see the incredible furniture pieces hanging out on the sidewalk.

At **McKey's Antiques** weave your way through the shop to find high-quality items from the last century up to the 1970s. Check out the collection of stylish home furnishings as well as smaller objects like paintings, architectural details, and random nicknacks. Find a vintage leather suitcase, a set of vinyl kitchen chairs, or some brocade upholstered furniture. There are lots of quirky finds here, especially from the 1960s and '70s. The elongated shop isn't especially clean, and the prices aren't especially good, but you might have a hard time walking away from some of these goodies even so. McKey's has been open for business for more than six years and is tried and true, a solid choice if you're in the neighborhood.

The owner of **Ruff & Ready Furnishings** regards his store as a junk shop, but we think this huge antique haven deserves a loftier descrip-

---

GEORGIA AVENUE THRIFT STORE
6101 Georgia Avenue NW
Washington, D.C.
Phone: (202) 291-4013
Hours: Mon–Sat 9–9, Sun 11–7

MCKEY'S ANTIQUES
1902 14th Street NW
Washington, D.C.
Phone: (301) 452-0888
Hours: Thurs–Sun 12–6

RUFF & READY FURNISHINGS
1908 14th Street NW
Washington, D.C.
Phone: (202) 667-7833
Hours: Sat–Sun 11–6

tion. Try not to be overwhelmed by this unbelievable store as you squeeze by crammed-in merchandise and ponder whether to refurbish your living room, dining room, or patio. Have your pick of goodies from the enticing main floor, the half-price basement, or the additional garden area and furniture showroom out back. Find furniture stacked high with lots of pieces from the Deco era to the 1950s. Look for discount shelves of odds and ends like records, puzzles, curios, and clocks.

Test out an elegant divan on the sidewalk out front. Throughout the main floor, spot quality wood furniture like dressers, chairs, and writing desks. Romantic statuettes and paintings are dotted around. Tour the aisle of vintage kitchen appliances and utensils and don't miss the china, lamps, toys, and books. Find that deco Bakelite vanity set you've always wanted. In the basement, check out an assortment of retro furniture, from a leopard print office chair to a gold mod-style lamp. The garden area out back is loaded with planters, birdbaths, metal garden furniture, and rusty bicycles. Continue past the garden for a showroom of fancier furniture from the 1920s to the 1940s. These pieces are more expensive, but what finds! The prices at Rough & Ready are not the same as a thrift store's, yet you'll find them reasonable for an antique dealer. With all of Ruff & Ready's special sale items, anyone can leave with a good deal in hand.

SPARKY'S
1720A 14th Street NW
Washington, D.C.
Phone: (202) 332-9334
Hours: Mon–Fri 7am–11pm,
  Sat 8am–10pm, Sun 9am–10pm

Wander in for refreshments at **Sparky's** café. A passerby on a bicycle recommended Sparky's for the best coffee in town, and she just may be right! For atmosphere, this coffee shop definitely has that cool factor, without feeling pretentious. The menu offers all of your favorite coffee and tea concoctions as well as frozen and iced versions. Sparky's gets an award for best soy latte! For a quick meal, choose from bagels, hot and cold cereal, sandwiches, salads, and desserts. Sit indoors or at sidewalk tables or at the cozy booths with red vinyl seats. The checkerboard floor and stamped-tin ceiling add a retro feel. You can even check your e-mail at the one lonely computer.

Put **L & N Super Thrift** on your checklist of thriftworthy stops. This large store is chock-full of good castoffs like TVs, stereos, bicycles, and vacuum cleaners. Give the spinning rack of sunglasses a whirl. Men's, women's, and children's clothing is available, but there's little vintage action to report. Sift through and find a funny T-shirt or a new bra with the tags still on. Up front, spot some usable household items like coffeemakers, blenders, lamps, and telephones. Small furniture pieces like chairs and bar stools are also available. This store is cheap and has that fabulous thrift appeal.

L & N SUPER THRIFT
1830 14th Street NW
Washington, D.C.
Phone: (202) 588-0020
Hours: Mon–Sat 9–7

MEEPS & AUNT NEENSIE'S FASHIONETTE
1420 U Street NW
Washington, D.C.
Phone: (202) 265-6546
Hours: Tues–Thurs 4–7, Fri–Sat 12–8, Sun 1–6

MISS PIXIE'S
1810 Adams Mill Road NW
Washington, D.C.
Phone: (202) 232-8171
Hours: Thurs 12–9, Fri–Sun 12–7

Encounter two floors of retro wear at **Meeps & Aunt Neensie's Fashionette** and accessorize yourself in ultimate style. The cheery first floor sports a few racks of women's clothing and a whole wall of denim jeans. Get lucky with old school bathing suits, pretty dresses, skirts, and Bermuda shorts. Also look out for chic eyewear, handbags, cuff links, and artsy postcards up front. Climb the creaky stairs for another slice of vintage heaven. The two rooms on the second floor are divided up between men's and women's clothing. For the guys, there are plenty of vintage suits, plus an assortment of patterned shirts, shoes, and leather jackets. Gals will have a field day with the selection of formal to casual dresses and footwear. Seek out chiffon, glitter, and colorful prints in cottons, silks, and synthetics. This store is hip and laid-back, but still a fine place to bring your mom. Find city prices at Meeps & Aunt Neensie's. Expect to pay from $15 to $30 for the one-of-a-kind duds sold here.

In the Adams Morgan section of town, we recommend **Miss Pixie's** for its spacious, homey, and sparkling-clean environment. Look around the lofted shop for some stylish home furnishings and accessories. Find a handsome wicker couch, a coffee table, or a rustic wooden bench. Chests, mirrors, rugs, lamps, and chandeliers are also among the items in stock. Prices vary according to quality and antique value. Most larger furniture pieces are in the $100 to $300 range. Make for the nicknack and dishware areas of the shop for cheaper thrills. Pick up some old postcards or vintage canning labels for 25 cents or less. Cup and saucer sets, trays, glass bowls, and statuettes are readily available for $30 or under.

Snatch up the bargains in an upper-crust neighborhood—head over to P Street in Georgetown for **The Thrift Shop**. This sparkly clean and attractive shop carries lots of fine antiques, elegant furniture, and quality, almost-new clothes at prices that are often not thrifty at all. Hunt thoroughly and be pleasantly surprised with a few random vintage accessories. For clothing, get lucky with some feathery and gold-trimmed house slippers, hidden in among the boutique prices and conservative styles. Find a wrap or denim skirt for $10 to $12 among the racks of ladies' suits priced up to $50. Upstairs drool over huge cases of enticing jewelry with big colorful gems (priced into the hundreds) and scan the shelves for fine gift and household items. Silver platters, engraved jewelry boxes, and glass lamps are likely finds here. Don't miss the cheery side room of affordable toys, books, and records. Hardcover books are only $2 a piece, and Chriss found a groovy 1970s sewing book with lots of good pictures to take you back in time. We never saw a thrift that looked so much like an antique store.

> **THE THRIFT SHOP**
> 2622 P Street NW
> Washington, D.C.
> Phone: (202) 338-8714
> Hours: Tues–Sat 11–5
>
> **SECONDHAND ROSE OF GEORGETOWN**
> 1516 Wisconsin Avenue NW
> Washington, D.C.
> Phone: (202) 337-3378
> Hours: Mon–Sat 11:30–6

A few blocks away on bustling Wisconsin Avenue, climb the stairs to the upscale **Secondhand Rose of Georgetown**. Vintage clothing hangs in the hallway, in addition to the two rooms of retro to modern stylish wear. Snag a pair of silk pants and some Gautier or Prada from a few seasons back. Find a psychedelic designer dress by Emilio Pucci or some silver western boots. Get that unusual velour bathrobe you've always wanted or a sturdy fur-trimmed winter coat. Belts, shoes, hats, and scarves are all the rage. Prices are erratic; expect to pay up for most garments. If you're willing to throw down a little extra cash for your next formal occasion, you'll be the belle of the ball.

Farther down Wisconsin Avenue, located next door to a sex shop, groove to the pumping dance music at **Rage Clothing** and steer yourself through two floors of vintage apparel for men and women. Old Levi's jeans, cords, and slacks are the main attraction on the first floor. Find them in every size and color piled onto tables. Izod shirts, flamboyant polyester tops, and T-shirts are plentiful as well. Upstairs sift through glamorous and funky dresses, suits, and accessories like hats, belts, and ties. At Halloween time Rage plumps up the merchandise with costumes and even more vintage gear, including some "Bride of Frankenstein" wedding gowns. Prices tend to be $20 and up, but get lucky and make it in for one of the store's "stuff it all in a bag" seasonal sales.

RAGE CLOTHING
1069 Wisconsin Avenue NW
Washington, D.C.
Phone: (202) 333-1069
Hours: Mon–Thurs 11–8, Fri–Sat
   11–9, Sun 11–7

DEJA BLUE
3005 M Street NW
Washington, D.C.
Phone: (202) 337-7100
Hours: Mon–Sat 12–8, Sun 12–6

Around the corner on M Street, **Deja Blue** is another good place to pick up some used jeans. The atmosphere is much tamer here than the vibe at Rage. The store has the feel of a new clothing boutique and is a little on the sporty side. For pants, name brands like Lee, Wrangler, and Levi's are widely available. Select jeans or cords in many varieties, colors, and sizes. For jean shorts, why ruin your favorite pair when you can buy them here, precut and frayed for around $13 a pair? Surplus gear like army jackets, raglan T-shirts, and Hawaiian shirts are also in the mix. Overall, the deals at Deja Blue are just so-so.

Drop in on the peculiar **Prevention of Blindness Thrift Shop**, a small-ish, one-room house of thrift. Step inside to find a lineup of comfy couches and shelves of bric-a-brac. Clothing, books, and records make up the rest. Sort through a table of folded T-shirts or a rack of hanging dresses for a mere $3 to $8. Find a classic yellow velvet chair or a wooden coffee table. Flip through the vinyl collection of 1980s pop hits and assorted mood music. Take home an attractive candy dish, some kitschy shot glasses, or an outdated radio. Vaguely organized bookshelves include adult and teen fiction and some unique craft titles.

PREVENTION OF BLINDNESS
  THRIFT SHOP
2216 Rhode Island Avenue (Route 1)
Washington, D.C.
Phone: (202) 269-0203
Hours: Tues–Sat 9–4

ODD-EVEN THRIFT SHOP
3400 Rhode Island Avenue (Route 1)
Mount Rainier, Maryland
Phone: (301) 864-6755
Hours: Mon–Sat 10–7

MOUNT RAINIER, MARYLAND

If you're in the mood for a cluttered and dusty venture, take some time to dig around the **Odd-Even Thrift Shop** in Mount Rainier. When we visited this messy little one-room junk shop, the jovial owner boasted that the goods were selling cheap. Fiddling with gadgets while keeping an eye on the store, he is certainly ready to make you a deal. Take a look around to spot furniture piled up high. Don't be surprised to find quality vintage pieces, upholstered with satin and velvet, in the chaotic mix. Among the shelves and jumbled piles seek out books, electronics, old tools, a couple of stacks of records, and possibly a doll or two. Grab a set of encyclopedias, a retro cassette recorder, or a pink parlor chair. Come prepared with a feather duster.

TAKOMA PARK, MARYLAND

Takoma Park is a vintage clothing wonderland. That's about all you'll find there for secondhand goods, but who's complaining? **Polly Sue's,**

Odd-Even Thrift Shop, Mount Rainier, Maryland

Takoma Underground, and **Rerun** are all within walking distance from each other, so park the thriftmobile and get busy.

Hit up **Polly Sue's** sizable vintage closet. This shop is slightly less put together than Takoma Underground. Among the racks of brooding colors find a black velvet dress from the 1940s or a couple of Edwardian jackets hanging on the wall. Scan the rest of the room for classic ensembles and accessories. Find fluffy party dresses in the $20 or $30 range, or a man's smoking jacket with a satiny finish. The downstairs is a little funkier, offering a clutter of lower-quality bargains. Here you can pick up that hideous polyester you've been wanting or a slightly crinkled sweater. The basement selection is fun and full of patterns and interesting fabrics, certainly suitable for wearing out or for a costume party.

POLLY SUE'S VINTAGE SHOP
6915 Laurel Avenue
Takoma Park, Maryland
Phone: (301) 270-5511
Hours: Mon 3–7, Tues–Fri 11–7,
Sat 11–6, Sun 11–5

Rerun is a weird boutique carrying a mixture of styles—think Joan Baez posters, Ché Guevera T-shirts, long hippie skirts, and pink chiffon party dresses with rhinestone straps. The oddball collection includes lots of 1960s-era clothes, like suede fringed vests, tapestry coats, and hand-crocheted shawls. Prices are reasonable, but Rerun falls solidly in the vintage category. Score on trunks full of scarves and bins full of records. Check it out and decide for yourself.

Takoma Underground is probably the best place to go for vintage clothing and accessories in the D.C. area. Down in the basement store, you'll be greeted by welcoming displays of ladies' hats and exquisite dresses from the Victorian era to the 1920s. Find racks of silk slips and a wardrobe of satiny sleepwear, along with breathtaking formal dresses and daywear from the 1940s and 1950s. Spend some time figuring out how to incorporate a pink tulle ball gown with rhinestones into your wardrobe. Max out on cat's eye sunglasses and shiny jewels at the counter. Decorative collectibles and uncommon accessories can be found throughout. Although vintage prices are attached to these retro finds, 20 percent off and half-price seasonal sales mean you don't have to break the bank. Sing along to the sweet tunes of Peggy Lee on the Victrola as you comb through the exotic selection.

> **RERUN**
> 7001 Carroll Avenue
> Takoma Park, Maryland
> Phone: (301) 270-0360
> Hours: Mon–Fri 11–7, Sat 10–8, Sun 10–6
>
> **TAKOMA UNDERGROUND**
> 7000B Carroll Avenue
> Takoma Park, Maryland
> Phone: (301) 270-6380
> Hours: Tues–Fri 11–7, Sat 11–6, Sun 10–5
>
> **GLAD RAGS**
> 7306 Carroll Avenue
> Takoma Park, Maryland
> Phone: (301) 891-6870
> Hours: Tues–Sat 10–6, Sun 12–5

For a punkier vibe, visit **Glad Rags**. The shop carries a super selection of retro duds plus many hip fashion accoutrements like makeup, loud jewelry, and brightly colored feather boas. Snap up a finely made 1940s dress or a wild animal print from the 1980s. Glad Rags also stocks some retro fashions from reputable designers like Betsy Johnson. The prices are good, with clothes mostly in the $10 to $20 range, with a few worthy exceptions. Get some stellar footwear and handbags for around the same price. Take home one of Glad Rags' one-of-a kind paper shopping bags, colored with markers, with your purchase.

BETHESDA, MARYLAND

Bethesda is a green, tree-filled suburban town with a lively shopping area and a few secondhand stores to make it worth your while.

On Wisconsin Avenue, start out at **Mustard Seed**. At first glance, the merchandise looks brand-new and modern, but further investigations reveal plenty of used clothing and retro apparel. Scan a double rack of used jeans, wide belts, and gently worn urban footwear. You'll find lots of labels like Free People and Lux. Get a pair of low-rise pinstripe jeans for $12 or a retro suede tote for even less. There are also some psychedelic prints and peasant garb hanging about. Pick up a reconstructed T-shirt or a zippered hoodie at a fraction of their original cost. The selection also includes some new items by hip designers.

MUSTARD SEED
7349 Wisconsin Avenue
Bethesda, Maryland
Phone: (301) 907-4699
Hours: Mon–Sat 11–8, Sun 12–6

MONTGOMERY COUNTY THRIFT SHOP
7125 Wisconsin Avenue
Bethesda, Maryland
Phone: (301) 654-0063
Hours: Mon–Sat 9:30–4

Montgomery County Thrift Shop is set back off of Wisconsin Avenue, located next to Hadji Carpets. On the weekends, eager shoppers are lined up outside waiting for the store to open, and the buzz doesn't stop there. Upon entering, make for the clothing racks in the first room, before the cocktail dresses are snapped up by other ravenous thrifters. Jeans and $1 T-shirts are fully stocked, and you can also bag brightly patterned dresses on the cheap. Jewels are kept under glass, and $2 handbags reside nearby. The side room is brimming with nicer housewares and accessories, such as elegant brass lamps and framed paintings. Pick up a pair of ceramic flowered candlesticks for only $12. Snuggle up with a wintery quilt and a used book to read beneath it. Flip though the bins of classical records, plus musical oddities from Disney or Dionne Warwick.

Stop by the **Opportunity Shop** of Saint John's Episcopal Church, found right around the corner from the Montgomery County Thrift Shop. "Opp Shoppers," as they're called, will find only a rack or two of clothes, but the rest of the shop has plenty of thrifty finds to look over. Redecorate with an oriental-inspired screen, ceramic jars, or a new-to-you tea set. Or go the garden route with a birdcage or some unusual planters. Candelabras, crystal dishware, and fine table linens are attractively displayed about the shop. For inexpensive gift items, score on snazzy figurines, a dazzling golden necklace, or men's ties for 50 cents apiece.

> **OPPORTUNITY SHOP**
> 4710 Bethesda Avenue
> Bethesda, Maryland
> Phone: (301) 654-4999
> Hours: Tues–Sat 10–4
>
> **SECOND STORY BOOKS
> AND ANTIQUES**
> 4836 Bethesda Avenue
> Bethesda, Maryland
> Phone: (301) 656-0170
> Hours: Mon–Sun 10–10

If you're nuts about books and records, then **Second Story Books and Antiques** is the place for you. Used books, used books, and more used books are what's happening all around this place, and you can find them in just about every genre. Get lost searching for sci-fi and horror favorites, women's studies, and Civil War titles. Hidden on the shelves are 1950s children's books and comics collections like *The Addams Family* and *Peanuts*. There are many orderly stacks of jazz, classic rock, and country records as well as some unusual musical treats. Bins are crammed with vintage posters that go for around $20 each. Thankfully for misers like us, paperbacks are marked half off the original cover price. Leave with a heavy stack of dog-eared favorites.

FALLS CHURCH, VIRGINIA

Drop in on a little beige house on Broad Street, **Old Habits**. The store advertises itself as an antique *and* thrift store, but the fancy selection makes it a collectibles shop to us. At the front counter examine a pretty collection of glittery vintage pins and bracelets. Spot some kitsch collectibles on the mantle, like a pair of cherubic gold figurines with faux emerald eyes. Wander into another small room and gloat over old paper dolls and valuable craft books. Upstairs spot some inviting displays of vintage clothing—a 1950s cocktail dress and some fancy gloves, hats, and shoes to go with it. Stately looking antique furniture is also dotted around the shop, but typically sells at much higher prices than the rest of the merchandise. Smaller items aren't always dirt cheap either, but many can be found for $20 or less.

OLD HABITS
817 West Broad Street
Falls Church, Virginia
Phone: (703) 532-3090
Hours: Mon–Wed 11–6,
Fri–Sun 11–6

JOSEPH'S COAT
3022 Annandale Road
Falls Church, Virginia
Phone: (703) 538-6289
Hours: Mon–Sat 10–6

CLOCK TOWER THRIFT SHOP
2860 Annandale Road
Falls Church, Virginia
Phone: (703) 237-1910
Hours: Mon–Wed 10–6, Thurs–Fri
10–8, Sat 10–6, Sun 12–5

Continue the thrift tour of Falls Church with a couple of hot spots on Annandale Road. First, join the hoopla at **Joseph's Coat,** a shop overflowing with uncommon finds. Acquire a hilarious painting (like a portrait of a horse that stares back at you) or an armload of goofy mugs. Clothing is abundant, and the shoes are especially good—score on a pair of 1970s-style suede ankle boots. An entire ensemble could easily cost you less than $15. Test out the springs on some living room seating or browse the extensive collection of books and records against the wall. Junky jewelry and little baggies of hotel soaps can be picked up at the counter on your way out.

The **Clock Tower Thrift Shop** in Falls Church is a sizable store with a winning selection of lightweight items (meaning no furniture, unfortunately). Clothing is available for all ages and genders, and mirrors are strategically placed for trying things on. Find many clean and attractive sweaters, skirts, and jackets with a conservative edge. Retro bric-a-brac, odd videos, vinyl records, and a big bin of plastic toys are other attractions at Clock Tower. Score in these departments with 1970s serving ware, folk music, and B movies on VHS.

Snag some handsome and inexpensive furniture at the Falls Church **Goodwill**, in the Wilston Center shopping plaza. Nab a retro velvet couch for the shockingly low price of $70 and lounge chairs for around $30. But the bargains don't stop there. Vinyl, books, electronics, and bric-a-brac make up about a third of the store, and this branch doesn't skimp on clothing either. Vintage collectors should hit the dress racks for psychedelic prints and puffed sleeves. There is also plenty of casual wear, formal attire, and lingerie for *all* kinds of occasions. The prices on clothes are rock bottom, with many noteworthy finds at $3 to $7.

> **GOODWILL**
> Wilston Center
> 6136 Arlington Boulevard
>   (Route 50)
> Falls Church, Virginia
> Phone: (703) 533-1840
> Hours: Mon–Sat 10–9, Sun 12–6
>
> **THE ARLINGTON COMMUNITY**
>   **TEMPORARY SHELTER**
>   **THRIFT STORE (TACT)**
> 2729 Wilson Boulevard
> Arlington, Virginia
> Phone: (703) 807-2460
> Hours: Tues–Wed 12–6, Thurs
>   12–8, Fri–Sat 10–6, Sun 12–5

ARLINGTON, VIRGINIA

On Wilson Street, look out for **TACT: The Arlington Community Temporary Shelter Thrift Store**. Check out the crowded window display featuring striped plates, paintings, and darling figurines, only a sample of what's inside. There are just a few racks of clothing, but they hold a surprising variety. Pick up a wedding dress and maybe some hidden vintage wear as well. Unusually patterned dishes are plentiful, filling up an entire bookcase. Hard- and softcover books are available for all age groups. Scavenge through some bins of household linens, or if music is your passion, there are several stacks of records and shelves of CDs. There is a lot packed into this small shop, and who's to say what treasures await?

For a light snack, kick back at the **Java Shack** just down the street. Refuel with coffees, teas, and other beverages and replenish with bagels, croissants, scones, and muffins. The little café is clean and inviting and is a great place for an anytime snack. Relax and enjoy the atmosphere inside or out front, for as long as you can control the impulse to thrift.

JAVA SHACK
2507 North Franklin Road
Arlington, Virginia
Phone: (703) 527-9556
Hours: Mon–Thurs 7am–8pm,
 Fri–Sat 7am–10pm,
 Sun 8am–10pm

CORNER CUPBOARD
2649 North Pershing Drive
Arlington, Virginia
Phone: (703) 276-0060
Hours: Tues–Sat 11–6, Sun 12–5

ECLECTIC THREADS
2647 North Pershing Drive
Arlington, Virginia
Phone: (703) 276-0051
Hours: Tues–Sat 11–6, Sun 12–5

The final two stops in Arlington are both conveniently located on the corner of Pershing Street and Washington Boulevard. For a little of everything collectible from the past fifty years, visit the **Corner Cupboard**. The store has a sort of split personality between things elegant and kitsch. Find fancy brocade armchairs, dainty tea sets, and silver platters or rummage for a 1950s children's record player, an old rocking chair, tarnished candlesticks, or some scenic beer mugs. Wall hangings, books, and records are also plentiful. With many of these valuables between $10 and $20, good luck on deciding which of them to bring home.

Head next door to **Eclectic Threads** for a whirlwind of ladies' vintage clothing and accessories. Try on old-fashioned jackets and fancy flowing gowns. Rhinestone gems, boxy purses, feathery hats, and printed scarves are easily found. In addition, the shop offers old magazines and nostalgic LPs as well as some curious stuffed dolls. A fancifully dressed mannequin guards the door. Flash back to simpler times at this cozy dress shop.

A little business strip on Arlington's 23rd Street offers a few charming eateries and stores to add to your itinerary. A great place to go for brunch is the **Deluxe Diner** in the center of the block. Its appealing trapezoidal shaped storefront shines in chrome. Expect to be welcomed by cheery hosts and a sparkling-clean blue-and-white interior. Sit at cozy booths with blue vinyl benches or at the counter, where you can watch the chefs cook up scrumptious plates. For breakfast have your pick of fluffy Belgian waffles, pancakes, or a mean eggs Benedict. The menu also offers sandwiches, subs, fries, and onion rings. Take advantage of the heaping plates of food and friendly service at the Deluxe Diner, open round the clock for midnight munchies, too.

DELUXE DINER
539 South 23rd Street
Arlington, Virginia
Phone: (703) 920-2700
Hours: Open 24 hours

CRYSTAL DOVE GIFT SHOP
570 South 23rd Street
Arlington, Virginia
Phone: (703) 979-7001
Hours: Tues 10–6, Thurs–Sun 10–6

At the end of the block look for the **Crystal Dove Gift Shop.** This place is a trip! The energetic owner has quite a few jokes up his sleeve, making this stop all the more entertaining. Poke around for antique furniture and collectibles. In the first room you'll find shelves of curiosities, including vintage Avon bottles and some sparkly jewelry. In the back be prepared to walk single file. Hunt for vintage furniture like a set of matching mod leather chairs or a wooden dresser with mirror attached for $125. Score on kitschy mugs for $2 to $10 apiece, such as a super-cool "South of the Border" ceramic mug with swinging figurine. When Leah asked the price of a pink rhinestone ring, the owner replied that it used to belong to his mother and was worth $1,000, then went on to sell it for $3. We highly recommend the Crystal Dove Gift Shop for its oddball selection, reasonable prices, and sidesplitting sense of humor.

ALEXANDRIA, VIRGINIA

Travel to the heart of Alexandria, a quaint old town area, for a few note-worthy shops on King Street. Then discover a few solid choices for thrifting and one surprisingly good place to eat amid the shopping plazas on Route 1.

In the historic district of Alexandria, head over to King Street for the ever-popular **Prevention of Blindness Thrift Shop**. This memorable shop is crowded with narrow passageways and jam-packed with goodies. In the front room, you'll spot tables full of 50-cent and $1 glassware, as well as lamps, brass candlestick holders, and many nicknacks. Vinyl enthusiasts can be seen frantically flipping through the stacks of classic rock, blues, and pop music. Most of the clothing ($5 to $10) is in the crowded back room, where you'll find men's suits, tops, and pants and ladies' skirts and dresses. The rows and rows of shoes should not be overlooked. You can also get an array of ties, leatherette handbags, and utilitarian luggage.

> **PREVENTION OF BLINDNESS THRIFT SHOP**
> 900 King Street
> Alexandria, Virginia
> Phone: (703) 683-2558
> Hours: Tues–Sat 10–5,
>   Sun–Mon 12–5
>
> **ODDS & ENDS ANTIQUE SHOPPE**
> 1325 King Street
> Alexandria, Virginia
> Phone: (703) 836-6722
> Hours: Unavailable

Rows of small collectibles line the storefront windows at **Odds & Ends Antique Shoppe**. Inside, hunt around for mushroom-shaped salt 'n' pepper shakers, toy cars, shot glass sets, and dressed-up dolls. Pick up a fine crystal vase, a set of china, or a handsome wall clock. Clothing is missing from the stash, but you might be able to get some fine accessories like a sequin purse or a rhinestone brooch. Odds & Ends is high on the kitsch factor and on all things pretty as well.

Get some quality used items at **Select Seconds**, located in the Woodlawn Center Plaza on Richmond Highway. Here you can pick up basic clothing for the whole family and even some satiny and silky fabrics for special occasions. Bric-a-brac shelves are loaded with scenic pictures, glass ashtrays, and casserole dishes for $1 to $3. Flowery 1970s dishware is going cheap. On your way out, hit the counter at the register for "boutique" items and some colorful beaded necklaces. Keep your antennae up for Dollar Days and half-price days, too.

Revamp your wardrobe at the **Recycled Clothing Store**. This place is super-duper for clothes, not only for its vast selection, but for its hard-to-beat prices as well. You'll see many tags between $3 and $8, with fancier fare slightly higher. Find racks and racks of summer dresses, pants, jeans, and blouses. The selection is mainly cheap and trendy, with plenty of back-to-school favorites. Try on your finds in the little dressing rooms and leave with at least a few new additions to your closet.

In the same shopping plaza, you can find the **Back Porch of UCM** thrift store. The sizable shop carries everything from electronics and furniture to clothing and books. Scan the racks for a tweed suit or some lacey lingerie in prices ranging from $3 to $10. Plan ahead for Easter with some wicker baskets or take home a few decorative tins. Scan the many racks of household linens and the shelves full of vases, plates, and mugs. Dining room sets may be found for $150, and cushy couches go for $70. The book area is organized by category with labeled shelves, with everything from hard- and softcover fiction to travel books and cookbooks. When we visited, Back Porch was having an incredible record blowout sale at eight for only $1. LPs normally go for a buck each.

SELECT SECONDS
Woodlawn Center Plaza
8736 Richmond Highway (Route 1)
Alexandria, Virginia
Phone: (703) 780-4603
Hours: Mon–Tues 10–4, Wed 10–6,
    Thurs–Fri 10–4, Sat 10–2

RECYCLED CLOTHING STORE
Mt. Vernon Crossroads Plaza
7810 Richmond Highway (Route 1)
Alexandria, Virginia
Phone: (703) 619-6660
Hours: Mon–Sat 11–8, Sun 11–6

BACK PORCH OF UCM
Mt. Vernon Crossroads Plaza
7838 Richmond Highway (Route 1)
Alexandria, Virginia
Phone: (703) 799-7015
Hours: Mon–Sat 10–8, Sun 12–6

For tasty food that's fast, try the famous **Five Guys** burger joint. Step up to the counter and order freshly grilled burgers, with a dozen or so free toppings to choose from. Don't forget to order some fries—also out of this world. Check the daily bulletin board to find out what nationality of potatoes are being fried up today. While you wait, dip into a large cardboard box of roasted peanuts in the shell—for free! For vegetarians, a meatless sandwich with extra toppings is just as satisfying as the real thing. Locally loved Five Guys has been voted "Best Burger" by *Zagat's*, *Washingtonian* magazine, and many others.

SUITLAND, MARYLAND

The huge red lettering on the sign jumps out at you from the road, signaling you to pull over for a real showstopper. Suitland's **Value Village** is a huge shop, located barely outside of the Beltway. Shop for men's, women's, and children's clothes and scan the baggies of toys and craft items that hang above the racks. Scarves, pantyhose, slips, and socks are aplenty. There are aisles and aisles of bric-a-brac, with many wall pictures and frames, some for as little as 50 cents. Furniture and electronics are in the back of the store, along with lamps, peculiar light fixtures, and many varieties of lampshades. Records mixed in with laser discs are located at the front. This store is massive and could easily provide a whole afternoon's adventures.

FIVE GUYS
7622 Richmond Highway (Route 1)
Alexandria, Virginia
Phone: (703) 717-0090
Hours: Mon–Sun 11am–10pm

VALUE VILLAGE
4917 Allentown Road
Suitland, Maryland
Phone: (301) 967-0700
Hours: Mon–Sat 9–8

DISTRICT HEIGHTS, MARYLAND

In District Heights, swing by the **American Rescue Workers Thrift Store**. The racks are teeming with lucky finds that the friendly staff will be happy to share opinions on. There are many half-price colored-tags sales, and be on the lookout for all-encompassing 50 percent off sale days. Vintage wear is in the mix, like a 1980s movie star dress or some frilly lingerie. The clothing selection for men is more sparse. Check out the dolled-up furniture displays. For housewares, pick up some utensils, plates, and useful kitchen items. The prices here are great even without the special sales, with loads of items from $1 to $6.

> **AMERICAN RESCUE WORKERS THRIFT STORE**
> 7625 Marlboro Pike
> District Heights, Maryland
> Phone: (301) 516-5923
> Hours: Mon–Sat 9–5

> **VILLAGE THRIFT STORE**
> Bladensburg Shopping Center
> 4960 Annapolis Road
> Bladensburg, Maryland
> Hours: Mon–Fri 9–9, Sat 9–8, Sun 10–5
> Phone: (301) 864-4870

BLADENSBURG, MARYLAND

At the mega **Village Thrift Store** take a moment to gape at the 1970s arched storefront of what seems to have once been a supermarket. Then grab a shopping cart and plunge into bargain city! Clotheshorses beware of the many $1 to $3 items and half price deals lurking within. The store is jam-packed with racks of clothing, shoes, toys, and nicknacks. Brightly colored 1970s housewares, jewelry gems, and scarves are prominently displayed near the front. Mosey through the

Village Thrift Store, Bladensburg, Maryland

aisles and snatch up some funky sheets, bedspreads, or window dressings. Be sure to check the tags for the day's color-coded discounts. Enjoy the homey atmosphere at one of our favorite locations! For a side trip to the Wild West, check out the rodeo shop next door.

Step on the brakes for the phenomenal **Value Village Thrift**. Be prepared to spend at least an hour in this king-size warehouse, but try not to get lost inside. This is a thrifter's dreamland, and prices are dirt cheap to boot! Although the bulk of the store is clothing, find everything from 80-cent records to dollar toys and books. Camera geeks will want to pick over the massive selection of photo gear. Join the commotion and parade through the many aisles of assorted housewares. Five lanes of cashiers await you at the front of the store. Fill your trunk with lucky finds at this truly exceptional secondhand superstore.

VALUE VILLAGE THRIFT
Cherry Hill Shopping Center
6611 Annapolis Road
Bladensburg, Maryland
Phone:Unavailable
Hours: Mon–Sat 9–7:30

SALVATION ARMY
3304 Kenilworth Road
Bladensburg, Maryland
Phone: (301) 864-5645
Hours: Mon–Sat 10–6

Travel the back roads to arrive at the ultimate in family value thrift. Swing by the squeaky-clean and modern **Salvation Army** on Kenilworth Road. The white corporate exterior, reminiscent of a contemporary office building, makes this an unusual stop. The store is truly enormous, with thousands of neatly tagged items. Sift through the aisles of clothing on the main floor. Find a fur coat, a glittery ball gown, or almost any clothing item imaginable. Check out the mammoth furniture display, flip through dozens of records, and test out a variety of electronic gear. In the rear is a separate book room with overflowing floor-to-ceiling shelves. Don't miss "The General Store," the in-house boutique of antique nicknacks, china, and higher-quality furniture. Prices for most clothing are $6 to $15, but furniture prices can be pretty steep. This stop is a great introduction for any first-time thrifter and a sure shot for antiques collectors.

RIVERDALE, MARYLAND

Bookworms won't want to miss the **Riverdale Bookshop and Coffee Depot.** Browse through three rooms of conveniently organized used books. Find everything from classics and cookbooks to sci-fi, horror, and history. The books are in good condition, with many marked at less than $10. Take note of the little dolls and scenic displays that grace the bookshelves around the store.

After thumbing through the stacks, kick back with a few good titles at the eat-in café. Choose from a gourmet selection of coffees and teas and satisfy your sweet tooth with cookies and cakes. The knowledgeable owner will gladly tell you all about his store, including details on the Saturday night Music Junction series featuring live performers. Light reading in the rustically charming bathroom includes back issues of *National Geographic.*

RIVERDALE BOOKSHOP AND COFFEE DEPOT
4701 Queensbury Road
Riverdale, Maryland
Phone: (301) 277-8141
Hours: Tues–Friday 8:30–6,
   Sat–Sun 12–6

VALUE VILLAGE THRIFT
2277 University Boulevard
Hyattsville, Maryland
Phone: (301) 422-2406
Hours: Mon–Sat 9–7

HYATTSVILLE, MARYLAND

For the D.C. area finale we suggest yet another massive thrift warehouse experience. **Value Village Thrift** in Hyattsville carries tons of all things secondhand. Clothes are well organized by garment type and size, including plenty of dresses, jeans, sweaters, and more. For the daring (!) check out the neatly hung rows of bras and panties. A large collection of bicycles can be found out front. The furniture and electronics areas are just so-so, but take home some dirt-cheap kids' toys, from giant stuffed animals to a small army of Barbie dolls. In the housewares department find many serving and casserole dishes from the 1960s and '70s. Find yarns, trimmings, and crafting odds and ends, too. Admire the intriguing artwork and hit the fantastic book and record areas on your way out.

ROUTE #1

Washington, D.C., to Philadelphia, Pennsylvania

Galvanize,
Baltimore, Maryland

Jeane's Hospital Opportunity Shoppe,
Philadelphia, Pennsylvania

Value Village Thrift Store,
Baltimore, Maryland

Route #1 rambles along secondary highways in the shadow of Interstate 95, leaving D.C. and heading roughly north through a succession of smaller towns. Crossing into Delaware, the trip zigzags across the urban Wilmington area and winds its way into Pennsylvania. The tour concludes in Philadelphia and a few of its surrounding suburban towns.

Route #1 Driving Time: (stops not included) 4 hours

Heading northeast out of D.C., raid **My Friend's Closet** in Beltsville for miscellaneous clothing and housewares. The excitement has only just begun when you hit Laurel—sort through a bit of everything at the **Laurel Thrift Center** and **Village Thrift**. Snag some superior vintage finds at Baltimore's **Dreamland**, take home an old-fashioned loveseat from **David's Used Furniture,** and visit the shrunken heads and mermaids at the **American Dime Museum**. On the outskirts of Wilmington, visit the sprawling **Family Thrift Store Center** as well as three floors of mayhem and treasures at **Lee Jewelree & Thrift** in Marcus Hook. Finally, get silly in Philly, our favorite bargain city! Wonders never cease at the **Whosoever Gospel Mission** and the **Bargain Thrift Center**, two dirt-cheap Philadelphia favorites.

23

BELTSVILLE, MARYLAND

From D.C., head north along Route 1 to the little jewel in Beltsville, **My Friend's Closet**, found in the Beltsville Plaza Shopping Center. Swing by for some newish clothes and a particularly good housewares corner. Scan the overflowing shelves and find weird old candles, coffee mugs, tote bags, and toys. Rescue a crystal-esque plastic cake plate from the jumble of kitchenware. The linen area is full of homemade afghans and flowery bedspreads as well as sheets with butterfly or GI Joe patterns. Hit up the craft section for dress patterns, ribbons, and gift wrap. Inexpensive Polaroids and other old cameras are heaped into bins. The clothing racks include options for kids and adults, with a few exciting finds mixed in with the usual fare. Snag a jacket for around $6 or a dress for $14. If you don't make it in for "Surprise Savings Thursdays" be sure to investigate the bulletin board for 50 percent off specials.

MY FRIEND'S CLOSET—THE ARC OF PRINCE GEORGE'S COUNTY THRIFT SHOP
Beltsville Plaza Shopping Center
11000 Baltimore Avenue (Route 1)
Beltsville, Maryland
Phone: (301) 572-4241
Hours: Mon–Fri 10–8, Sat 10–6, Sun 12–5

TEEN CHALLENGE FLEA MARKET
13919 Baltimore Avenue (Route 1)
Laurel, Maryland
Phone: (301) 490-1667
Hours: Mon–Tues 10–7, Wed 10–6, Thurs–Fri 10–7, Sat 10–6

LAUREL, MARYLAND

The town of Laurel is blessed with a number of first-rate thrift options. Teen Challenge Flea Market and its next-door neighbor, Repeats Consignment, are both excellent places to lay your thrifty little paws on furniture. Both of these shops are located on the back side of a small shopping strip and are invisible from the road. In front of the entrance to **Teen Challenge Flea Market**, discover rows of chairs and other home furnishings, many priced at $10 or less. Inside, you'll stumble across coffee tables, bed frames, and couches, along with shelving units and 1970s office furniture of varying quality. Poke around in the housewares area, full of glassware, TV trays, and coffee mugs, and liberate a toucan-shaped vase for next to nothing ($3).

For home appliances, there are several washing machines and stoves as well as piles of personal care products like curling irons. There are masses of records to investigate, and a sprawling (although not well-lit) book corner with hundreds of odd titles, from *Self Hypnotism* to *Heartbreaker*. Clothes here are only $1 to $2, but the selection is nothing to crow about. Find bargain surprises every which way you turn, including hand-lettered Bible quotes on colored construction paper strategically posted throughout the shop.

Just next door, the merchandise at **Repeats Consignment** is a tiny bit cleaner and nicer, but with a similar flavor. A tiny clothing area has some run-of-the-mill threads, but the furniture department contains better choices. Take home an elegant oak dining room table or a huge curio cabinet with glass front for $225. You might see a fancy pair of matching brass lamps or a beautiful wooden headboard for your bed. Although the higher quality of merchandise here is reflected in the prices, they are still affordable compared to new or antiques shop purchases.

REPEATS CONSIGNMENT
13919 Baltimore Avenue (Route 1)
Laurel, Maryland
Phone: (301) 604-2400
Hours: Mon–Fri 10–7, Sat 10–6

VILLAGE THRIFT
Laurel Plaza
9644 Fort Meade Road
Laurel, Maryland
Phone: (301) 498-4628
Hours: Mon 9–7, Tues–Sat 9–9,
    Sun 10–6

Village Thrift in Laurel Plaza is a gigantic store of the "lost-your-friends-but-hope-to-meet-up-with-them-at-the-register" variety. There's no shortage of clothes here, and in fact that's probably the best reason to visit. The racks contain super dirt-cheap finds, with many for $2 or less. In addition, certain color tags give half-off discounts, and surprise sale days give half off everything! From suits, vests, and summer dresses, to play clothes and ski wear, you'll find prizes in almost every aisle. Look for socks in every shade of the rainbow hanging above the racks. For fancy housewares, bring home some Blue Heaven diner plates or an amber-colored iced tea pitcher with matching glasses.

Last, but definitely not least is **Laurel Thrift Center**, with its yellow, wild west-style sign. Hit the jackpot at this thrift extravaganza! Grab a shopping cart and head left to find inexpensive ladies' skirts for less than $5 and frilly gowns for $15 as well as racks of men's and children's clothing. In the housewares area, sets of mugs, glasses, and dishes are taped together in small bundles. Overflowing shelves of picture frames, small flowerpots, baskets, and spice racks round out the selection. Scrutinize several shelves of books and magazines. Past the electronics room, full of blaring televisions and audio equipment, you can tour the massive furniture area. Pick up a bureau for as little as $35. There's a wide selection of kitchen and bedroom sets to choose from as well as travel lockers and trunks. Make off with a blender, fan, or coffeemaker from the appliance aisle or nab some unusual light fixtures from this favorite shop.

LAUREL THRIFT CENTER
9880 Washington Boulevard North
 (Route 1)
Laurel, Maryland
Phone: (301) 953-0090
Hours: Mon–Sat 9–9, Sun 11–7

SALVATION ARMY
10350 Gilford Road
Jessup, Maryland
Phone: (301) 776-4888
Hours: Mon–Sat 10–7

JESSUP, MARYLAND

Like a mirage, the red and white **Salvation Army** sign peeks out from behind a stand of trees on the roadside. To get to the store, turn from Route 1 onto Gilford Road. More fabulous furniture awaits inside, where you'll discover aisles of dressers, desks, and living room couches. Don't miss the super selection of kitchen tables, from hardwood rustic finds to elegant dining room pieces, and many table lamps of unusual shape and style. Nicknacks, bud vases, and casserole dishes are the main attraction in the mini housewares displays. For clothing, there is plenty to choose from, including many basic and casual styles.

Consider making a detour to **Scooters** for dinner. At this seafood specialty house, the waitstaff serves up giant overflowing trays of crabs, along with mallets and other tools of destruction (for the crabs)—order some beer and get crackin'! Toss all the shells into a giant bucket. The décor at Scooter's hasn't changed in years. Enjoy some savory crab cakes while you admire the light-up model ship in the smoking section or dine outside at picnic tables near the volleyball sandpit. Expect to find the slightly rowdy crowd chain-smoking and heckling the waitresses. A full-on seafood dinner and some beer at Scooters might set you back about $20, but it's worth it.

MILLERSVILLE, MARYLAND

Diverging a bit from Route 1, at the **Goodwill** in Millersville you can pick up some corporate attire, like a crisp shirt or a two-piece suit for only $4 or $5. Ladies' clothes are also good deals. Grab a short winter jacket for $8 or a full-length wool coat for $12. Find a few racks of evening wear, plus shoes, bags, and accessories. The book room holds shelves of great titles for kids and adults, including lots of classic fiction, plus newer and trashier finds. Many book prices are rock-bottom, like a paperback copy of *Native Son* for 12 cents. Scan the luggage collection for a powder blue carrying case or raid the housewares aisles for sherbet bowls and glasses priced around $1 each.

SCOOTER'S
7615 Washington Boulevard
Elkridge, Maryland
Phone: (410) 799-5432
Hours: Mon–Fri 10:30–10,
    Sat 11–10, Sun 12–10

GOODWILL
674A Old Mill Road
Millersville, Maryland
Phone: (410) 987-9740
Hours: Mon–Sat 9–9, Sun 12–5

OBJECTS FOUND
2302 Frederick Road
Catonsville, Maryland
Phone: (410) 744-9000
Hours: Mon–Sun 10–6

CATONSVILLE, MARYLAND

Visit **Objects Found**, a small antique shop in Catonsville, for a peculiar mixture of thrifty and fancy goods. Out front, bargain price tags flutter in the air. Investigate the array of unique furnishings for a vintage office chair, a curving bench, cushioned stools, old cabinets, and wire shelving. For $15, you can take home a large unicorn painting on black velvet. Inside the shop, every tabletop and other surface is covered with plates, vases, and other small objects. Grab a set of daisy-flowered drinking glasses from the stash. Carved picture frames, elegant scarves, and old marbles are squished in as well. A vintage toy section in the back offers old storybooks, ceramic piggy banks, and bedside lamps. While not rock-bottom, most of the prices at Objects Found are moderate.

BALTIMORE, MARYLAND

Baltimore is packed full of thrifty hot spots. This town is home to a number of great vintage clothing shops, at least one amazing bargain outlet for home furnishings, a super used record store, and a hodge-podge of other inexpensive gadgets and trinkets.

SALVATION ARMY
2700 West Patapsco Avenue
Baltimore, Maryland
Phone: (410) 644-9705
Hours: Mon–Sat 9–8

DREAM LAND
1013 North Charles Street
Baltimore, Maryland
Phone: (410) 727-4575
Hours: Wed–Sat 12–6

Great furniture can be had for a song at the **Salvation Army** on West Patapsco Avenue, on the outskirts of Baltimore. The enormous tan brick building is sparkling clean and spacious inside, with tidy racks of neatly hung clothing and orderly rows of home furnishings. Couches, easy chairs, and matching sets of living room furniture are plentiful here. Redo your pad on a shoestring with a new brown loveseat and a kidney-shaped coffee table. Find styles from every era, from 1970s dinette sets to art deco wooden cabinets. This Salvation Army also carries televisions and stereo components, along with larger home appliances. Take home a cut-glass candy dish or fruit bowl from the inexpensive housewares aisle. You might also find a cookie jar in the shape of a pig or other such rarities. Acquire a pair of nouveau-inspired figurine lamps for the den. Penny-pinchers should be sure to look over the day's special deals, listed near the entrance. Between the hours of 9 and 4, drop into the As Is Sales area for slightly beat up, fixer-upper furniture.

Vintage bathing suits! Flowing scarves! Tutus! Descend into **Dream Land**, the basement-level vintage clothing shop on Charles Street. Dream Land offers a wealth of classy and quirky apparel for both men and women. Try on men's leather jackets, dressy trousers, and fancy button-down shirts. Look over the collection of Chinese silk pajamas and robes and sort though bins of scarves and shoes. Hats are lined up in neat rows along the shelves, and the jewelry case is full of colorful plastic bangles, rhinestone finery, glittery pins, bracelets, and necklaces. A multitude of dress styles are squeezed together into the ladies' clothing racks, packed to the gills with super scores between $10 and $35. Get a beaded cardigan from the 1950s for $12 or a tapestry handbag for around the same price. Tim, the owner, is a vintage clothing expert, who often strikes some great bargains for friendly shoppers.

Check out more faded elegance at **The Zone**, another vintage shop farther down Charles Street. The ornate chandelier and hardwood floor set the tone for the sophisticated merchandise. A bit fancier and a bit more expensive than Dream Land, The Zone carries everyday clothing for $15 to $30 and evening dresses ranging from $30 to $70. The men's wear selection includes trousers, shirts, sweaters, amazing silk ties, and quality suit jackets, marked around $40. There are a few new fashion-y garments, like tube tops, for sale as well. Expect to find both new and vintage jewelry in gaudy to tasteful styles.

THE ZONE
813 North Charles Street
Baltimore, Maryland
Phone: (410) 539-2817
Hours: Mon–Sat 12–6

VALUE VILLAGE
5013 York Road
Baltimore, Maryland
Phone: (410) 433-9090
Hours: Mon–Sat 9–9, Sun 11–7

Drop by the **Value Village** on York Road at Winston Avenue. Shelves overflowing with home items can be glimpsed through the large storefront windows. Find pitchers, mugs, glassware, and plates for just a few dollars apiece. Some specialty items, like a crouching lynx sculpture for $20, are stored behind the register. The electronics aisle carries lights and lamps, fax machines, television sets, and a handful of computer components. The clothing racks hold a variety of styles, from J Crew to sporty 1970s. For practically pennies, nab some flowery newish curtains from the linens department. The book area is rewarding, too—find plenty of old school mini encyclopedia sets and tons of hardcover titles.

Goodwill Surplus Store is a smallish, dark, two-room affair. There are few good clothing options here, but as always, it never hurts to look. Housewares are jumbled and tossed, but in the disarray you might find pots and pans, silverware, and some oddball lamps and lampshades. Records are probably the best reason to stop in—tall shelves along the back wall of the shop offer any number of albums, all musical types and styles.

An even better location for vinyl addicts is right around the corner at **Normals**. Browse the impressive variety of used records and books, from old favorites to imports and rarities. Music lovers can find anything from jazz to soul to new wave and punk. Prices range from $6 to $25, with many options on the lower end of the scale. Bookshelves are in the next room, neatly catalogued by topic, with their contents often going for less than half of the cover price. There is also a great offering of 'zines, hard-to-find magazines, and other offbeat press.

GOODWILL SURPLUS STORE
3101 Greenmount Avenue
Baltimore, Maryland
Phone: (410) 467-7505
Hours: Mon–Wed 10–6,
   Thurs–Sat 10–7

NORMALS
425 East 31st Street
Baltimore, Maryland
Phone: (410) 243-6888
Hours: Mon–Sun 11–6

SALVATION ARMY
903 West 36th Street
Baltimore, Maryland
Phone: (410) 243-5916
Hours: Mon–Sat 10–6

There are a number of good spots clustered along West 36th Street, so make an afternoon of it and hit them all. The **Salvation Army** seems picked clean of interesting merchandise; however, in every thrift store, there are a few exceptions lurking in the aisles. As a hard-core thrifter, it is your mission to uncover them. Although marked "professionally cleaned," some of the furniture items look as though they've been through the wringer. Clothing is not so thrilling either. A small area for antiques can be found near the register—we saw a set of Danish modern dishware and a chocolate pot, but both were priced at around $30. Look over the outdoor furniture for a few decent bargains. Find a glass-top wicker table and set of four chairs for the backyard, marked at $110. Keep in mind that selections are always changing.

Galvanized is an appealing vintage shop on the same street. Clothing is on the main floor, with tons of old hats and vintage bell-bottoms for $10 to $20. Pick up special costumes and clothes for everyday dress-up, from outerwear to underwear. At Galvanized, men can find offbeat ties, straw hats, Hawaiian print shirts, and other fun clothes. Some fashionable acces- sories include a bassinet full of gauzy and silky scarves as well as handbags, glamorous sunglasses, old-fashioned hatboxes, and vintage suitcases. Pick out some neat-o items for the home, like ashtray stands, coffee tables, and mod hanging lamps. More house- wares, antiques, books, and records can be found in the basement.

> **GALVANIZED**
> 927 West 36th Street
> Baltimore, Maryland
> Phone: (410) 889-5237
> Hours: Fri 11:30–5, Sat 11–6,
>   Sun 11–5
>
> **CJ'S EMPORIUM**
> 3553 Roland Avenue
> Baltimore, Maryland
> Phone: (410) 467-4510
> Hours: Mon–Sat 10–6

CJ's Emporium, on the corner of Roland Avenue and West 36th Street, is a small flea market-style store with lots of miscellaneous junk to exam- ine. On the sidewalk out front, you might find old wooden rockers or a cedar chest. A few more furniture items are located within as well as smaller-size oddities. Look over shelves of old crockery and china and a few tangled boxes of antiquated jewelry. Find skinny and fat flower vases, ceramic candy dishes, and miniature teapots. While there are plenty of furnishings and nicknacks at CJ's, you'll find little to no clothing, books, or records. The "random factor" in this little shop is high, so you could stumble across anything from an old painted wooden school desk to a se- quined evening bag.

Hit the jackpot at **David's Used Furniture**, the jewel of West 36th Street, offering what is arguably the best selection of furniture for miles and miles around. One large room is spread with lots of quality choices, all in excellent shape. Relax on a stylish, seven-foot olive leather couch from the 1960s, a great value at around $100. A stylin' wrought iron table and chairs set is in a similar price range. Reasonable furniture deals abound, from couches to cabinets, dinette sets, and vanities. The friendly staff is always ready to help, but also willing to let you browse freely. If you live locally, David's can set up delivery to your home. If you live far away, rent a U-Haul, because there are oodles of great finds here.

From West 36th Street, it's just a short drive to **Always Different**, a tiny, oddball junk shop on Falls Road. Full of mostly small-size odds and ends, the shop carries things like old combs, wall hangings, embroidered pillows, or quirky little figurines with cutesy sayings for just 50 cents. Pick up a few eccentric greeting cards or an electric shaver. The super-cheap goods are spread on tables around the store with no particular rhyme or reason. Equally erratic are the hours—the shop is closed on Tuesdays, but is otherwise open at random times. Like the merchandise, the hours of business are Always Different.

DAVID'S USED FURNITURE
914 West 36th Street
Baltimore, Maryland
Phone: (410) 467-8159
Hours: Mon–Thurs 10–5,
    Fri–Sat 10–6

ALWAYS DIFFERENT
3716 Falls Road
Baltimore, Maryland
Phone: Unavailable
Hours: Unavailable

VOGUE REVISITED
4002 Roland Avenue
Baltimore, Maryland
Phone: (410) 235-4140
Hours: Mon 11–5:30, Tues 11–6:30,
    Wed 11–5:30, Thurs 11–6:30,
    Fri 11–5:30, Sat 10–5

Although the name makes it sound like a vintage shop, **Vogue Revisited** is actually a small consignment boutique full of clothes and accessories for women. Most items are $40 or less, with prices slashed on older stock. The jewelry offering is extensive, and you might also find scarves, belts, and bags to dress up your image. Shoes are displayed singly in the back room—you need to ask to try on both. Clothing styles are contemporary, yet conservative, and all the garments are crammed onto racks according to size and garment type.

A greater variety for clothing can be found at the **Goodwill**. The men's clothing section is smaller than the women's, but you can find plenty of good deals in either. Most of the clothing is up to date, with a few frocks from the 1960s hiding in the aisles. Pick up a cropped leopard-style jacket or a white faux fur coat for $12 each. Slacks and tops are priced around $4. In the housewares area, stacks and stacks of clear glass bowls, cups, platters, and dishes can be purchased for around a dollar apiece, along with shimmering colored glass and ceramic mugs. Pick up some weirdo sculptures and nicknacks, too. Don't overlook the easily missed basement, where you can grab books and records at astonishing deals, especially if they are still running the Monday Special (hardcover books for $1 apiece and vinyl at three for $1). Also downstairs, check out a few furniture items, exercise equipment, and overflowing shelves of stuffed toys.

> **GOODWILL**
> 5644 The Alameda
> Baltimore, Maryland
> Phone: (410) 323-6638
> Hours: Mon–Sat 9–8, Sun 12–5
>
> **HELPING UP MISSION THRIFT STORE**
> 4515 Harford Road
> Baltimore, Maryland
> Phone: (410) 254-2500
> Hours: Mon–Fri 10–8, Sat 10–5

Helping Up Mission Thrift Store is still another super-fantastic spot for used furniture, from stylishly upholstered couches to easy chairs and side tables. Pick up a pair of blue glass globe lamps with silver feet for $40. They also carry TVs, coffee tables, and small rugs. Priced anywhere between $35 and $150, the home furnishings offer a large selection, tremendous deals, and good quality. In the front room, choose from nicknacks, dishes, and old wrapping paper and browse through a small collection of clothing. Snap up tall stacks of books for 50 cents each and look over the assortment of old *National Geographic* and *Life* magazines. Climb the steep creaky stairs for even more furniture options in the attic.

Helping Up Mission Thrift Store, Baltimore, Maryland

The tiny **Community Thrift Store** is notable for an unusual selection of beautiful saris, caftans, and silk scarves, mixed in with a more typical thrifty clothing selection. Several shelves are stacked with neatly folded textile remnants of fine dyed cottons, embroidered silks, and other uncommon fabrics. Other than apparel and fabric, the store carries just a little jewelry and a few books. Prices are very inexpensive here, and the stock rotates weekly.

COMMUNITY THRIFT STORE
4305 Harford Road
Baltimore, Maryland
Phone: (410) 426-7401
Hours: Mon–Sat 10–7

AMERICAN DIME MUSEUM
1808 Maryland Avenue
Baltimore, Maryland
Phone: (410) 230-0236
Hours: Wed–Fri 12–3, Sat–Sun 12–5

Take an educational field trip to Baltimore's famous **American Dime Museum**, showplace for artifacts of novelty Americana. The offbeat exhibits feature flying squirrels, bearded ladies, sword swallowers, circus props, and tattoos. Check out mermaids, unicorns, and mummified giants here. You don't even have to pay the $5 admission price to see the World's Largest Ball of String, visible from the street at the Museum's front entrance. Measuring in at 837.5 miles, surely this sight is one of the cheapest thrills to be had for miles around.

Stop in for a wee drink at **The Club Charles**, another offbeat pit stop in town. Ring the buzzer at the door, and if you're cool enough, they'll let you in. (Just kidding, because obviously they let us in, and have you ever *seen* us?) Anyway, enjoy the super-chic red deco interior and the great jukebox in this hipster joint. Murals of red devils and flames grace the bathroom walls. 'Fraidy cats beware—the Charles is reportedly haunted.

The Fell's Point **Goodwill** is located inside an old church building, on the corner of South Broadway and East Pratt Street. Though not huge, the shop carries a good sampling of books, records, housewares, and a surprising clothing selection. Get a stylish wool blazer or a corduroy jacket for around $5. Grab some mismatched dishes, plates, and coffee cups or an unusual light fixture and some funny old candles. Also peek through the jewelry and accessories, where you can get bright and shiny trinkets for next to nothing.

THE CLUB CHARLES
1724 North Charles Street
Baltimore, Maryland
Phone: (410) 727-8815
Hours: Mon–Fri 5pm–2am,
    Sat–Sun 3pm–2am

GOODWILL
200 South Broadway
Baltimore, Maryland
Phone: (410) 327-2211
Hours: Mon–Thurs 9–6, Sat 9–7,
    Sun 12–5

KILLER TRASH
602 South Broadway
Baltimore, Maryland
Phone: (410) 675-2449
Hours: Mon–Sun 11:30–6:30

Killer Trash, the tiny Fell's Point vintage shop, is stuffed from floor to ceiling with hanging racks of clothes. Find men's and ladies' clothes here, from seersucker slacks to flowery A-line dresses. Cuddle up with a hand-crocheted shawl for $15 or less. Grab a green floor-length evening gown with rhinestone waistband or a red and white gauzy dress, either for around $40. Rifle through the bin of colorful cummerbunds. You can also find tons of totes and handbags around the shop, and leather jackets and suit jackets are in abundance, as well.

One final stop in Baltimore is **Value Village Thrift** on Eastern Avenue, a dirt-cheap favorite. Men's and children's clothing is on the first floor, along with a massive linens department full of striped sheets, gauzy curtains, and flower-shaped bathmats. A room of random finds is full of funky dish sets, gleaming decanters, "crystal" bowls, and pitchers, along with small armies of collectible figurines (small elves, owls, etc.). Choose from lots of books, some records, and tons of picture frames and decorator baskets. On the second level, find ladies' clothing, almost always priced at $5 or under. Sleepwear, sweaters, scarves, shoes, and wigs can all be found on this floor. Snap up the last bargains in Baltimore before heading on to new thrifty horizons.

VALUE VILLAGE THRIFT
3424 Eastern Avenue
Baltimore, Maryland
Phone: (410) 327-5300
Hours: Mon–Sun 9–9

VILLAGE THRIFT STORE
10 Stemmers Run Road
Essex, Maryland
Phone: (410) 238-7306
Hours: Mon–Sat 9–9, Sun 10–5

ESSEX, MARYLAND

Heading out of Baltimore, Route 40 winds through the smaller towns of Essex, Edgewood, and Aberdeen. Along the way, stop by two large thrift centers and one small but unusual antiques shop.

Drop in our beloved **Village Thrift Store** in Essex, a short distance off the direct path of our road trip along Route 40—but fully worth the extra mile or two! Village Thrift is gigantic, with tons of clothing deals and steals at every turn. Men can find flannels, jackets, belts, and trousers. The ladies' section is also full to the brim, with sweaters, coats and blouses. Don't miss the sleepwear aisles, with lots of frilly slips, camisoles, and silky pajama sets ($6). Unfortunately there are no dressing rooms or mirrors around to model your finds, so you'll have to rely on the opinions of your pals. There are some books, along with inexpensive housewares, but you have to search closely here for the best goodies. Take home a punch bowl set for under $10. As cooler weather approaches, Village Thrift is excellent for woolen mittens (50 cents) and fuzzy scarves ($1). In addition to the color tag specials, inquire about any markdowns for the day—on the afternoon that we visited, if you waited until after 2 p.m., everything in the store became half off!

EDGEWOOD, MARYLAND

Edgewood Thrift Store Center is yet another extra large favorite on Route 40 between Baltimore and Philly. Choose from lots of small appliances and electronics as well as exercise equipment and bicycles. Clamber through tons of toys and games and bring home an Easy Bake Oven or Lite Brite, still in their original boxes, for around $4. Softcover books are only 33 cents, and the shelves are full of cookbooks, crafting books, and fiction. Apparel racks in the clothing section are full of hidden treasures, with most items selling at $3 to $5. Find a vintage, fur-cuff winter coat for $10 to $30. Score in the housewares and furniture departments, too.

> **EDGEWOOD THRIFT STORE CENTER**
> 1900 Pulaski Highway (Route 40)
> Edgewood, Maryland
> Phone: (410) 679-7750
> Hours: Mon–Sat 9–9, Sun 11–7
>
> **SOMETHING UNUSUAL ANTIQUES**
> 3502 Churchville Road (Route 22)
> Aberdeen, Maryland
> Phone: (410) 734-6911
> Hours: Mon 9–3, Tues 9–5,
>   Wed 9–3, Thurs–Sun 9–5

ABERDEEN, MARYLAND

Next stop, Aberdeen, Maryland. Find **Something Unusual Antiques** on Churchville Road (Route 22) a few miles north of the intersection with Route 40. The front yard is lined with concrete garden sculptures and furniture and inside you can find mass quantities of antiques, furniture, and plenty of silver and turquoise jewelry. Look for all kinds of small, dusty collectibles, from ancient medicine bottles to brass bookends to glass lampshades and iron skillets. Rescue a pair of elegant deco wall sconces. Though many of the antiques are *not* sold at huge bargains, don't pass up the chronologically catalogued library of old

*Playboy*s and other magazines from the 1960s through the 1980s, each priced at only $4.

HAVRE DE GRACE, MARYLAND

Situated just off Route 40 on the bank of the beautiful Susquehanna River, Havre de Grace is a small-town USA-type spot, charming to the point of being possibly annoying. Washington Street functions as the main drag in the touristy section of town. There are several large multi-dealer antique malls within walking distance of one another, all carrying a similar selection—retro kitchen wares, fancy vintage clothing and linens, collectibles, and furniture. Each of the shops is good to hunt through, offering very wide varieties of oddball collectibles. The prices at area shops are generally moderate—for truly dirt-cheap prices you'll have to head to the next town. Meanwhile, there's plenty to investigate at **Thorofair Antiques Center**, **Seneca Cannery**, and **Bayside Antiques**. Add to your jadeite or Fiestaware collections here.

Bookworms may spend many fascinating hours at **Washington Street Books & Antiques**. Find stacks of fiction, American history, cookbooks, and art books, all at middle range discounts. The massive biography section will satisfy most curious readers. The only stumbling point here is the sealed plastic that covers each and every book in stock. You can

THOROFAIR ANTIQUES CENTER
220 North Washington Street
Havre de Grace, Maryland
Phone: (410) 939-5455
Hours: Mon–Sat 10–5, Sun 12–5

SENECA CANNERY, INC.
201 St. John's Street
Havre de Grace, Maryland
Phone: (410) 942-0701
Hours: Mon–Sat 10–5, Sun 11–5

BAYSIDE ANTIQUES
230 North Washington Street
Havre de Grace, Maryland
Phone: (410) 939-9397
Hours: Mon–Fri 10–5, Sat 10–6,
    Sun 11–5

**WASHINGTON STREET BOOKS
    AND ANTIQUES**
131 North Washington Street
Havre de Grace, Maryland
Phone: (410) 939-6215
Hours: Mon 11–6, Wed–Thurs
    11–6, Fri–Sat 11–8, Sun 12–6

ask the staff for help, but this aspect seriously limits your ability to browse. In a side room, the store carries thousands and thousands of old comic books, along with a few antiques. Check out the glass cabinets full of Star Wars and X-Men toys and collectible action hero figurines.

For suppertime, the Italian restaurant **La Cucina** in Havre de Grace is a fine place to eat. More on the "real good" side than on the dirt-cheap one (dinner plates priced at around $13), La Cucina serves delectable home-cooked pastas, salads, and Italian seafood specialties. Or just order a pizza. The atmosphere is casual, making La Cucina a top spot for dinner with the gang.

> **LA CUCINA**
> 103 North Washington Street
> Havre de Grace, Maryland
> Phone: (410) 939-1401
> Hours: Mon–Thurs 10:30–9:30,
>   Fri–Sat 10:30–10:30,
>   Sun 12–8:30

ELKTON, MARYLAND

It's back to real deal thrifting with a quick stop at **Kingdom Come Thrift Store** in Elkton. Stop in at this tiny shop to poke through the front aisles of clothing or try the back room's

> **KINGDOM COME THRIFT STORE**
> 104 Landing Lane
> Elkton, Maryland
> Phone: (410) 620-2355
> Hours: Mon–Tues 3–8,
>   Thurs–Fri 3–8, Sat 9–8

shelves of dishes, glassware, and smaller kitchen gadgets. Check over the tiny book racks for a few quirky titles. Clothes are priced from $3 to $5, and there are also small numbers of shoes, hats and gloves. Kingdom Come is relatively new to the thrifting scene, but Patricia, the owner, says that word of mouth is spreading quickly, and the little shop is picking up steam.

BEAR, DELAWARE

Even more secondhand stuff can be found at the **Goodwill** in Bear. Tucked away at the far end of the enormous Fox Run Shopping Center, located at the intersection of routes 40 and 72, the Goodwill has lots of $3 to $5 clothing options for sale. Coasters, glasses, ceramic boxes, and bud vases cram the housewares shelves along the far wall, with most price tags under $3. Investigate a decent cache of vinyl as well as some cheap and funky luggage. Score on a $5 super-8 film projector, if you get that lucky.

WILMINGTON, DELAWARE

In Wilmington, with its mix of urban decay and suburban greenery, find thrift and secondhand stores of all stripes. The Wilmington area also boasts an unusual concentration of fruitful Goodwills.

First, drop into the **Family Thrift Store Center** on the outskirts of Wilmington, another *Dirt Cheap* favorite. All departments are well stocked with thrilling deals—shoes, clothes, seasonal decorations, electronics, music, and even a separate room for household linens. Pants, jeans, and slacks are priced around $5, while dresses are $6 to $10. Scarves, mittens, hats, and gloves are all under $5. Men can find racks of ties, belts, and shoes, too. The housewares offerings are out of this world—for only $2, you can acquire a toilet bowl-shaped ashtray with the slogan, "Rest your ash here." Or pick up a giant mushroom-shape cookie jar ($5), candle holders, playing cards, and sugar and creamer sets. You name it, and you can probably find it here.

Family Thrift Store Center keeps all the furniture items in a separate shop front, a few doors down in the same shopping plaza. Look over many headboards and bed frames, dining room tables, and dinette sets for under $100. Also browse around in the weirdo art department, where you might happen upon a warped clown portrait or a homemade

GOODWILL
Fox Run Shopping Center
334 Fox Hunt Drive
Bear, Delaware
Phone: (302) 834-6780
Hours: Mon–Fri 8:30–9,
    Sat–Sun 10–5

FAMILY THRIFT STORE CENTER
2012 West Newport Pike
Wilmington, Delaware
Phone: (302) 996-0661
Hours: Mon–Sat 9–9, Sun 9–6

embroidery project. Also available are chairs, dressers, chests, and curio cabinets on the cheap.

Visit another **Goodwill** along Route 2 for lots and lots of clothes. You'll find many racks of separates priced at $5 or less and winter coats for under $10. Men can find a large selection of trousers, T-shirts, and full suits. Books, puzzles, and board games are also for sale, along with a good offering of classical music on vinyl. Bring home some new gauzy curtains from the linens racks, full of colorful sheets and pillowcases. Find new-to-you robes and PJs in a nearby aisle.

You can make off with everything but clothes at **Grandma's Treasures Resale Shop**. Look for the fluttering red awning over the door. Grandma's is jam-packed with kitchen goods and random collectible objects, all at super prices. With everything from overflowing shelves of glassware to furniture and vintage accessories, there are plenty of deals to go around. Snap up a tiny hand-beaded change purse ($3), an old Polaroid Square Shooter ($5),

GOODWILL
4315 Kirkwood Highway (Route 2)
Wilmington, Delaware
Phone: (302) 993-0413
Hours: Mon–Fri 9–8, Sat 9–6,
 Sun 9–4

GRANDMA'S TREASURES
 RESALE SHOP
1709 Philadelphia Pike
Wilmington, Delaware
Phone: (302) 792-2820
Hours: Tues–Sat 10–5

BLUEBERRY HILL RESALE SHOP
1015 Brandywine Boulevard
Wilmington, Delaware
Phone: (302) 765-2047
Hours: Tues–Sat 11–5, Sun 1–5

or several shelves of records from the 1960s. You can find tons of mixing bowls, linen napkins and tablecloths, and even furniture here. The back room is "the warehouse," a confusion of dishes, old paintings (some paint by number), lamps, and family photos. Grandma prices almost everything fairly, and there is a nice mix of quality and cheap-o goods scattered around.

Blueberry Hill Resale Shop is a tiny bit more highbrow, but it offers an interesting mix all the same. The super-charming, flower-bedecked brick house displays a profusion of garden furniture out front. Step inside to see lots of creatively arranged and nicely priced antiques. The front rooms carry heaps of vintage jewelry, collectible toys, and small figurines. Find a red ceramic toreador sculpture or a vase in the shape of a lady's head. As you proceed through the house, peek into the kitchen room for old electric mixers, glass cake plates, drinking glass sets, and unusual wall hangings for the kitchen. In the far back, a small room contains a few racks of vintage dresses, gloves, and belts. Try on dressy hats, velvet or covered with tulle flowers. Even with such high-quality merchandise, you'll find many fair prices throughout the shop.

Fearless thrifters can venture to **Catholic Charities Catholic Thrift Store** next. There's very little here in the way of housewares or nicknacks, but the back room is lined with many inexpensive furniture deals.

CATHOLIC CHARITIES CATHOLIC THRIFT STORE
1320 East 23rd Street
Wilmington, Delaware
Phone: (302) 764-2717
Hours: Mon–Fri 9–4, Sat 9–3

SALVATION ARMY
107 South Market Street
Wilmington, Delaware
Phone: (302) 654-8808
Hours: Mon–Sat 9–6

Sofas are priced between $25 and $50, with some stylish options, on up to fancier sideboards and cabinets for closer to $200. Clothing in the front room is very inexpensive at around $2, and many complementary accessories can be found at the counter display. Find the secret stash of vinyl LPs, but as always, check the quality and condition before you pay up.

Rows and rows of clothes are the main attraction at the **Salvation Army** on South Market Street. Find long- and short-sleeve T-shirts for $3 to $5 and dresses for $5 to $9. A few fancier things are priced a smidgen higher, and you might find assorted vintage clothing in the mix. The nicknacks area carries tons of cheap decorative objects, like flower vases, curios, bizarre figurines, and Avon perfume bottles. The shop boasts records for $1 and books at four for $1 as well as neatly folded, inexpensive linens.

Find more clothing at another **Goodwill** in the Wilmington area. Technically located over the state line in Chadds Ford, Pennsylvania, this shop is very big, with hundreds of apparel choices for women, men, and children, almost all priced at around $3.50. You won't find much vintage action here, but root around for the oddball striped ski jacket, denim western wear skirt, or black tuxedo trousers. The back shelves are covered with plastics, water pitchers, old candles, and other housewares for a few bucks apiece. Furniture is pretty blah, but there's not much to see in that department anyway. Instead, try the record collection, a mixed bag of classical musical and quirky finds.

CLAYMONT, DELAWARE

From Wilmington, hop onto Route 13, making stops in Claymont and Marcus Hook. Drop by Claymont's **Goodwill**, where you can lay your mitts on more good clothes at more good prices! A very wide selection of men's clothing is notable here. The sections for women's and children's clothes are also full of many steals and deals at $5 or less. You're sure to find something good in the overfull racks of sheets, quilted bedspreads, flouncy curtains, and tablecloths. Find some interesting books, records for 25 cents, and don't forget to check out the dishes and kitchenware, too.

> **GOODWILL**
> 255A Wilmington Westchester Pike (Route 202)
> Chadds Ford, Pennsylvania
> Phone: (610) 558-3722
> Hours: Mon–Fri 9–8, Sat 9–6, Sun 12–5
>
> **GOODWILL**
> 2701 Philadelphia Pike
> Claymont, Delaware
> Phone: (302) 798-9047
> Hours: Mon–Fri 9–8, Sat 9–6, Sun 12–5
>
> **LEE JEWELREE & THRIFT**
> 1004 Market Street
> Marcus Hook, Pennsylvania
> Phone: (610) 485-7974
> Hours: Mon–Sat 10–6

MARCUS HOOK, PENNSYLVANIA

If miscellaneous goodies are what you seek, you'll have a ball browsing three whole floors of assorted stuff at **Lee Jewelree & Thrift** in Marcus Hook. Investigate many little booths, squished full of nicknacks, jewelry, vintage linens, old cameras, pictures, and framed artwork. Upstairs, pick your way through even more, with many bookshelves, fabric remnants, spoon rests, coasters, and other oddities. Hunt around to find crazy lamps, lacy napkins, or a giant orange ceramic ashtray. Furniture is stored in the basement, where you might unearth a wooden bench, a chest, or some rickety-but-cool chairs with fair price tags all around. If you enjoy sifting through mass quantities of random things, you'll love Lee's Jewelree.

BROOKHAVEN, PENNSYLVANIA

Leaving Marcus Hook, take a short drive along Route 352. The town of Brookhaven should be proud of **New To You Hadassah Thrift Shop**, an eccentric little thrift located in the Plaza 352 Shopping Court. Follow the concrete walkway toward the back of the plaza and stumble on a garage sale-style spread of baking pans, Tupperware, glasses, or a flowery plastic tissue box cover. Heaps of linens and other disheveled goodies await. The key word here is random. Find an oversize white plastic Louis XIV wall clock for $25, a marble-top side table with built-in cherub lamp for $110, or a John Deere baseball cap for 50 cents. The thrift art section in the back is assuredly worth a peek—find some great art school paintings and 1970s needlework for just a few dollars. Don't miss this oddball spot.

NEW TO YOU HADASSAH THRIFT SHOP
Plaza 352 Shopping Court
Brookhaven, Pennsylvania
Phone: (610) 874-9392
Hours: Mon 9–4, Tues 11–3, Wed–Fri 9–4, Sun by chance

SERENDIPITY SHOP
Chester Crozer Medical Center
1 Medical Center Boulevard
Brookhaven, Pennsylvania
Phone: (610) 872-2428
Hours: Mon–Fri 10–4

To locate the **Serendipity Shop**, turn off Upland Drive into the main entrance of the Chester Crozer Medical Center. Keep your eyes peeled for the beige-colored house on the right (across from parking garage #2), home to our next thrifting destination. Though the shop seems small upon entering, explore to find a string of rooms on the main floor, full of housewares and furniture. Though this place falls solidly into the thrift shop category, you can pick up loads of fine antiques here at better-than-reasonable prices. Nab a pair of golden yellow velvet headboards, priced at $5 each, or a large Chinese cloisonné jar for $15. In the back, find table and study lamps, light fixtures, and electronics. A so-so furniture selection still offers many good prices—don't miss the furniture overflow on the front porch, too. The second floor holds mostly mature clothing and shoe styles, priced from $3 to $5. Better deals are downstairs with the household goods.

MEDIA, PENNSYLVANIA

Continue past Brookhaven on Route 352 to Route 1. Enjoy the mixed bag of finds that you'll encounter at two little shops in Media. Start with **Riddle Thrift Shop** at Riddle Memorial Hospital. On the main floor, clothes for men and women take up much of the space, with a separate room for children's items. Brand-name jeans (Mudd and Calvin Klein) are a steal at $6 to $10. Dresses, sweaters, slacks, and jackets are also available. The shoe racks are full of footwear in great condition and more recent styles. Don't miss the belts and scarves near the counter—some have never been worn. Try on your finds in a microscopic communal dressing room.

RIDDLE THRIFT SHOP
Riddle Memorial Hospital
1068 West Baltimore Pike
Media, Pennsylvania
Phone: (610) 627-4074
Hours: Mon–Fri 9:3–4, Sat 9:3–3

THE ATTIC THRIFT STORE
13 East State Street
Media, Pennsylvania
Phone: (610) 566-1502
Hours: Mon–Fri 10–4, Sat 11–3

The easily overlooked basement is full of kitchen items and household linens, like print tablecloths from the 1950s. Sewers should investigate the fabric remnants for unusual patterns and textures. A small room carries a tad bit of furniture as well. A swarm of ladies dressed in pink smocks operate the cash registers and fitting room.

The Attic Thrift Store is smaller but still has armloads of good stuff. Vintage ladies' gloves and scarves can be found in the glass case. Snag some unusually patterned dish sets and pick up a funky new pair of salt and pepper shakers. A brown coffee pitcher, set of six mugs, and matching tray circa someone's office, 1962, can be obtained for the dirt-cheap price of $15. Trays of cooking implements can also be had. The super book area includes many great titles on cooking and baking. Clothing is inexpensive ($4 or less for most items), but there are just a few racks to look over. Grab a bright red quilted book bag for the low, low price of $3.

PHILADELPHIA, PENNSYLVANIA

Take Philly by storm! With lots to see, do, and eat, you could spend at least a few days here if you wanted. Have a famous cheesesteak while you're here, then head off to check out the thriftiest spots around town.

Investigate the smallish but cute **Sort of New Thrift Shop**, the first stop on the outskirts of Philadelphia. The store is located on Haverford Avenue, near its intersection with Route 1. Find furniture here, including cabinets and tables from $100 to $150. Pick up a newish area rug, a serving tray, or a piece of thrifty artwork. Nicer home furnishings like silver platters and crystal vases are available as well, such as a brass globe lamp for $40. Look through the stack of 25-cent vinyl and the rows of costume jewelry up front. There's a moderate clothing selection to choose from, with many clean-cut styles for both men and women priced at $5 to $10. Don't miss the spinning rack of quirky vintage postcards, from Victorian valentines to scenes of deer hunting vacations, circa 1971.

SORT OF NEW THRIFT SHOP
7592 Haverford Avenue
Philadelphia, Pennsylvania
Phone: (215) 473-5590
Hours: Mon–Fri 9:30–5:30, Sat 11–5, Sun 11–3

IT'S NEW TO YOU THRIFT STORE
5648 Lancaster Avenue
Philadelphia, Pennsylvania
Phone: (215) 473-6996
Hours: Mon–Sat 10–5

At **It's New To You Thrift Store** find a secret hoard of furniture as well as quality housewares and antiques. Most of the goods here are older, with many items from the 1970s and earlier decades. Redecorate the sitting room with finds plucked from the narrow aisles of It's New To You. Acquire a couch or loveseat, Victorian dresser sets, and folding screens. Unusual table lamps, original artwork, rocking chairs, and wicker furnishings are also on the menu. Pick up a yellow vinyl chair with casters for $10 or a pair of orange velvet living room chairs for $75. Close inspection of the merchandise will reveal a small offering of antique books and smaller nicknacks throughout the shop.

Take a break at teatime for delicious desserts at the **Pink Rose Pastry Shop**. The pink flowery décor and stamped-tin ceiling create a tranquil atmosphere. Choose from the practically endless list of delectable pastries, frosted cakes, fresh-baked pies, and cookies. Tea is served in tiny pots with mismatched cup-and-saucer sets. Coffee kids can get their fix here, too. Breakfast and lunch menus are available for sandwiches and lighter fare.

Down the road at **Greasy Waitress Vintage**, nab some "vintage finds for today's discerning hipsters." Pick up an old-school rock band T-shirt, with iron-on pictures of your favorite pop icon. Find some cute luggage, bags, shoes, and retro sneakers. The styles here range from mod to early 1970s, with a little bit of glam mixed in. Investigate the sales racks for steals of $10 and under and cruise away on a brand new pair of roller skates.

Pick up some quality vintage goodies at **Decades Vintage**, which offers clothing and accessories for men and women. Most apparel is priced in the $15 to $40 range here, although there are generally a few sale racks of $10 items. Try an old-fashioned grandpa pajama set on for size or

PINK ROSE PASTRY SHOP
630 South 4th Street
Philadelphia, Pennsylvania
Phone: (215) 592-0565
Hours: Mon–Thurs 8–10:30,
    Fri 8–11:30, Sat 9–11:30,
    Sun 8–10:30

GREASY WAITRESS VINTAGE
701 South 3rd Street
Philadelphia, Pennsylvania
Phone: (215) 627-5464
Hours: Mon–Thurs 12–7,
    Fri–Sun 12–8

DECADES VINTAGE
615 Bainbridge Street
Philadelphia, Pennsylvania
Phone: (215) 923-3135
Hours: Wed–Sat 1–8

model one of the glitzy gowns from the racks. Pick up a tapestry overnight bag for only $20. Handsome jewelry, watches, and accessories are in a glass case near the register. Find scores of beautiful leather handbags, artfully displayed with coordinating silk scarves, and plenty of footwear to choose from.

Hope on 7th is not enormous, but you're sure to find some nifty treasures at this little thrift store in the South Street area. One side of the store is devoted to clothes, the other to housewares and miscellany. In the racks, find hippie gear and everyday castoffs but very few vintage items. Look through several rows of shoes, men's slacks, and a box of ties priced at 50 cents to $2. Over in the housewares section, the random factor makes for a quirkier selection. Grab some inexpensive kitchen implements, woven place mats, dishes, and hardcover cookbooks. A few pieces of furniture are for sale—get a cheap futon, a small couch, or a dining table here. Rifle through a few boxes for a new addition to your record collection.

HOPE ON 7TH
Corner of 7th and Bainbridge Street
Philadelphia, Pennsylvania
Phone: (215) 413-2301
Hours: Mon–Sun 12–7

SECONDS ON SOUTH (THE SOSNA THRIFT STORE)
1635 South Street
Philadelphia, Pennsylvania
Phone: (215) 732-8151
Hours: Mon–Fri 11–6, Sat 12–5

Drop into the SOSNA Thrift Store, otherwise know as **Seconds on South**, for plenty of well-priced clothes. Men can find fancy suits, trousers, and business-like neckties. Get a printed tank top from the 1960s for $3 or some broken-in khakis for $6. There's little vintage clothing, but the few pieces there are reasonably priced, such as a cream-colored, nubby-textured, full-length coat for $65. Get a new shoulder bag or backpack from the stash. Look over several bookshelves of interesting titles and scan the household goods for cookie jars, striped drinking glasses, and flowery glass pitchers. The prices at this shop are sure to please.

Yet another local outlet for clothes can be found at **Goodwill** on South Front Street. Come to this large, tidy store for woolen hats, scarves, and mittens to keep your paws warm. Dress-up clothes will set you back around $20, but everyday items such as button-up shirts or denim are priced lower, from $3 to $8. Find a huge selection of jeans including lots of name brands like FUBU and Calvin Klein. The housewares section in the back is full of good loot, with vividly colored dishware and sparkly glasses at the bargain rate of 19 cents apiece. Household goods also include seconds and new remnants from large department stores.

Bargain Thrift Center on Germantown Avenue is tops on our hit list of area favorites. The front corner of the store is devoted to fabulous vintage finds, while the rest of the shop offers more mainstream thrift gear. The retro area is full of amazingly priced goodies, from clothing to accessories and decorative home items. Find brightly patterned dresses, polyester print shirts, and one-of-a-kind vintage gloves and hankies, almost all priced at $10 or less. Pick up hats, purses, candy dishes, perfume bottles, and jewelry boxes in this area, too.

GOODWILL
2601 South Front Street
Philadelphia, Pennsylvania
Phone: (215) 463-5054
Hours: Mon–Sat 10–7

BARGAIN THRIFT CENTER
5261 Germantown Avenue
Philadelphia, Pennsylvania
Phone: (215) 849-3225
Hours: Mon–Sat 9:30–6

EKLECTIC TREASURES
5251 Germantown Avenue
Philadelphia, Pennsylvania
Phone: (215) 844-9272
Hours: Mon–Fri 10–5, Sat 10–6

Other sections of the store offer more clothing, kitchen goods, and linens. A small electronics room is full of curling irons, alarm clocks, and old toaster ovens. From the housewares shelves, take home a pair of macramé owls for $2 or a decorative plate for your wall for $4. Check the discount board at the shop entrance for special deals that change daily.

Just a few doors down, drop in for collectibles and more at **Eklectic Treasures**. The shop is packed full of interesting home items and furnishings. In the kitchen department, find vintage electric mixers, cookie jars, and pots and pans. Unearth some cute mixing bowls, old cookie cutters, and 1950s-style table linens, too. Cruise the narrow aisles and discover a pair of ceramic kitten salt and pepper shakers or a covered cake plate, both priced at $12, or take home a matching set of pastel casserole dishes. The tables and shelves are stacked neatly with milk pitchers, vases, and cutesy decorative items. With prices on many goods here between $10 and $20, collectors can find plenty of goodies on the cheap side.

Another beloved area stop is the **Whosoever Gospel Mission** in Germantown. This two-floor thrift extravaganza carries a colorful array of secondhand merchandise. On the ground floor, find clothes at dirt-cheap prices of $1 to $3, with the exception of men's tuxedos and suits at around $10. Housewares, records, and appliances can also be found downstairs. Check out shelves of old stereos, speakers, televisions, and alarm clocks and plunge into bins of vinyl, priced at $1 each or four for $5. Find inexpensive sugar and creamer sets, funky and elegant lamps, and lots of plates and dishes on the house-wares shelves. The second floor of the Whosoever Gospel Mission, where they keep the masses of furniture, is an old church, complete with a loft for the choir. Where the altar should be, find long rows of bargain basement secondhand chairs. A small book section is located in a chapel at the rear. The center area is stacked with credenzas, kitchen tables, curio cabinets, and nightstands, all at exceptional prices. Find an oddball set of turquoise vinyl bar stools, or a stylish vanity for cheap. The very reasonable price tags and varied selection make Whosoever Gospel Mission a "don't miss" in Philly.

WHOSOEVER GOSPEL MISSION
101 East Chelten Avenue
Philadelphia, Pennsylvania
Phone: (215) 438-3096
Hours: Mon–Thurs 9–4, Fri 9–5:30,
      Sat 9–4

VILLAGE THRIFT STORE
40 East Chelten Avenue
Philadelphia, Pennsylvania
Phone: (215) 844-3780
Hours: Mon–Fri 9–9, Sat 9–6,
      Sun 10–5

Just a block away, venture into the enormous **Village Thrift Store** for a massive display of clothes. Find lots of options on sweaters, tagged from $2 to $6, as well as trousers, cords, and jeans for around $3. Hunt through racks and racks of linens: sheets, curtains, pillowcases, and coverlets, almost all priced under $5. A large children's area has plenty of toys to keep the kiddies busy. The shelves of household goods are full of tiny nicknacks and random and mysterious kitchen goods.

If you're into costumes and dress-up, try **Past & Present Vintage Clothing** for offbeat garments and Halloween getups. Try on a silky dress for $30 to $40, with some exceptional items ranging as high as $110. There are tooled leather and 1960s fringed handbags to choose from as well as beaded clutches and silky evening bags. Flip though a rack of vintage slips, dressing gowns, and other frilly intimates. Also check out the hats, from flowery numbers to svelte cloches, generally in the $20 range. An under-$10 sale rack offers a decent selection, too. The back half of the store carries costumes, props, and accessories like face paint, wigs, boas, and fake swords.

Head down a small alleyway off of Germantown Avenue to find **Monkey Business,** a small thrift shop that carries mainly clothing, plus a few small housewares and accessories. Take home some fine silk scarves for $5 to $8 or a fancy leather belt for $15. Snag an embroidered Chinese silk dressing gown for $25. Most of the merchandise here is of high quality, and you can locate some unusual finds. Here and there, unearth some hardcover books, a crystal bowl, or fancy umbrella. Admire the case full of earrings and bangles, priced from $8 to $20, before you make your purchase.

PAST & PRESENT VINTAGE CLOTHING
7224 Germantown Avenue
Philadelphia, Pennsylvania
Phone: (215) 242-2909
Hours: Tues–Sat 11–5:30

MONKEY BUSINESS
8624 Germantown Avenue
Philadelphia, Pennsylvania
Phone: (215) 248-1835
Hours: Tues–Fri 9:30–4, Sat 10–4

ENCORE THRIFT SHOP
7616 Ogontz Avenue
Philadelphia, Pennsylvania
Phone: (215) 927-4110
Hours: Mon–Sat 11–5

At **Encore Thrift Shop,** find consignment quality selection and prices in a thrift store décor. Carrying mostly clothing for women, the funny little shop offers a small quantity of good-condition shoes and hand-bags, including the odd hipster find. Grab a suede courier bag with metal fasteners or a canvas tote with fuchsia sequins. Pick up a sweater for $5 to $15 and ladies' suits and dressy ensembles for around $40. The shop has new items coming in all the time—good news for frequent thrifters.

The quirkiest pit stop in Philly is **Carman's Country Kitchen**, a tiny South Philly breakfast joint. Carman reigns supreme over her bright luncheonette, offering coffee refills along with her delightfully sassy tableside manner. On weekends, the crowds flock here for spectacular brunch dishes, miraculously gourmet and down-home at the same time. Fill up on a "cornbread and collard greens omelette" or "peanut butter chocolate banana waffles." Don't miss the homemade jams and jellies, either. At around $12 per dish, the plates are generous enough to share. Or just be greedy and order your own.

> **CARMAN'S COUNTRY KITCHEN**
> 1301 South 11th Street
> Philadelphia, Pennsylvania
> Phone: (215) 339-9613
> Hours: Thurs–Mon 8am–2pm
>
> **SALVATION ARMY**
> 6427 Torresdale Avenue
> Philadelphia, Pennsylvania
> Phone: (215) 624-9487
> Hours: Mon–Sat 9–6

Stumble into yet another second-hand clothing warehouse at the **Salvation Army** on Torresdale Street, where you can find lots of apparel for men, women, and children. The variety here is impressive, and you can find it all at good thrift prices. Unearth numerous offbeat clothing finds, from funky 1980s dresses to colorful quilted blazers, as well as sleek scarves, hats, and leather shoes. Make off with a woolen sweater or newish top for under $5. Try on your finds in the tiny corner dressing room, the only place in the store where you can find a mirror. In the back, there's a selection of cheap, although slightly unexciting, furniture, with many tags ranging from $50 to $100. If nothing else looks appealing, give the televisions, lamps, and kitchen appliances a once over.

Find a bigger variety at the **St. Vincent de Paul Thrift Store**. In the furniture area up front, get yourself a $25 chair covered with green velvet flowers or a cushy striped ottoman. Snag a *"That 70's Show"* brown plaid couch and matching chair for $100. Find kitchen tables, bureaus, and end table/lamp combos at bargain prices. The front corner of the shop is home to a small vintage area, too. Browse a few racks of luscious evening finery, gauzy capes, and rhinestone-belted dresses. Clothing racks toward the back of the store carry a bit more vintage and some knockoff retro gear as well. Prices are super, with many items tagged at $5 or under. Raid the used record corner for classical, 1980s pop, and Broadway musicals and leaf through the small library of $1 books. Don't forget the housewares aisles, either, full of good, cheap kitchen goods and decorative nicknacks.

> **ST. VINCENT DE PAUL THRIFT STORE**
> 6247 Frankford Avenue
> Philadelphia, Pennsylvania
> Phone: (215) 624-4860
> Hours: Mon–Sat 9–4:45

St. Vincent de Paul Thrift Store, Philadelphia, Pennsylvania

Find a bit of this and a bit of that at **Lighthouse Thrift Shop**, smaller by comparison, but also brimming with bargains. If tiny figurines, dishes, platters and kitchenware are what you're after, head over to the housewares area on the left-hand side of the shop. Cut-glass candy dishes, drinking glasses, and punch bowl sets are among the many finds. Glance through a small collection of records, some used tapes, and a few CDs as well. Several clothing racks on the other side of the shop hold dresses, suits, jackets, and coats. Pick up a few nifty ties for $1.50 each.

Another area **Salvation Army** on Rising Sun Avenue carries more clothes, both sporty and dressy. Find lots of great bargains on apparel, with most items tagged at less than $5. Winter coats are a bit more, from $10 to $25. Snag a tan 1970s ski jacket or a quality vintage overcoat. In the men's department, grab some dress slacks or sportswear for around $5. Footwear fiends will want to snoop through the long rows of shoes for some stylish sneakers. This store carries a few housewares and some furniture, too, but the real deals are happening on the racks.

Get more cheap thrills at Beehive Thrift Shop and its across-the-street sister, Beehive Too. **Beehive Thrift Shop** is full of clothes, accessories, and smaller items for the home. Take home a silver tea set or a green glass vase for less than $20. Sort through baskets of silverware, shelves of kitchen items, and a bookshelf crammed with cookbooks. Lucky thrifters could score with a 1940s desk fan or an old clackety typewriter. In the linen area, find a chenille bedspread, a patchwork print coverlet, and some slightly used curtains. Sporting equipment and children's toys may be found in the back cor-

LIGHTHOUSE THRIFT SHOP
398 East Godfrey Avenue
Philadelphia, Pennsylvania
Phone: (215) 745-8780
Hours: Mon–Sat 10–4:30

SALVATION ARMY
6432 Rising Sun Avenue
Philadelphia, Pennsylvania
Phone: (215) 728-9616
Hours: Mon–Sat 9–6

BEEHIVE THRIFT SHOP
7136 Rising Sun Avenue
Philadelphia, Pennsylvania
Phone: (215) 742-5060
Hours: Mon–Fri 10–5, Sat 10–4

ner, along with a section for seasonal decorations, like Halloween costumes and Christmas gear. Nab some sturdy kitchen chairs for $30 each or a small wooden writing desk with porcelain knobs for the dirt-cheap price of $25! More furniture can be found across the street.

Full to the brim with used furniture, **Beehive Too** also carries a few televisions and pieces of old stereo equipment. It offers a mishmash of both high- and low-end home furnishings in a variety of styles, from old-fashioned school desks to huge antique curio cabinets. Uncover some good finds here, like a tall, finely crafted chest of drawers for only $125 or a nice rocking chair for $65. Snag an odd light fixture or one of several unusual lamps for $25 to $35. Bring home a new conversation piece for the living room, but expect to refinish or refurbish the cheapest bargains.

Another pair of thrifty siblings are located just a few doors apart on Oxford Avenue. Find a small but very inexpensive selection of clothing at **Jeane's Hospital Opportunity Shoppe**. Drop into the store for men's and women's apparel, with many separates priced between $3 and $5. Try on a dashing tweed suit jacket or grab a cute leather clutch or canvas shoulder bag from the

BEEHIVE TOO
7138 Rising Sun Boulevard
Philadelphia, Pennsylvania
Phone: (215) 728-1130
Hours: Mon–Fri 10–5, Sat 10–4

JEANE'S HOSPITAL
   OPPORTUNITY SHOPPE
7963 Oxford Avenue
Philadelphia, Pennsylvania
Phone: (215) 342-8444
Hours: Mon–Fri 10–5, Sat 10–4

OPPORTUNITY SHOPPE II
7971 Oxford Avenue
Philadelphia, Pennsylvania
Phone: (215) 742-0698
Hours: Mon–Fri 10–5, Sat 10–4

assortment in the back of the shop. A small section of the store is also devoted to children's clothes. Before you head down the street, look over neat little rows of costume jewelry and shiny baubles in the case—almost all are priced at $3. The pretty hatboxes that line the shop are unfortunately not for sale.

Opportunity Shoppe II is the happy ending of the thrift tour in the Philadelphia area. Though not enormous, this store is chockablock with quirky finds and rarities. Check out the rack of vintage greeting cards and 25-cent stationery. Decorate your walls with curious shell and macramé hangings, needlepoint projects, and framed prints. A few pieces of furniture, like a dresser or coffee table, are on sale for bargain rates. Snoop around in the linen area to find clean, bright, and neatly folded blankets and bedspreads. A small back room contains toys, sporting goods, and a not-to-be-missed crafting section. Snap up yarns, fabric remnants, patterns, and a stash of how-to crafting manuals on knitting and sewing. Look through a few stacks of records and books and head over to the housewares shelves for tons of sparkling-clean $1 glassware. A bargain bin near the counter is full of 25-cent orange-tagged junk, like a dusty jewelry box or slightly battered figurine. Exit with an armload of goodies on your way out of thrifty Philadelphia.

ROUTE #2

Washington, D.C., to Pittsburgh, Pennsylvania

Red White & Blue Thrift Store,
Pittsburgh, Pennsylvania

Giant Building Shaped Like a Coffee Pot,
Bedford, Pennsylvania

Goodwill,
Pittsburgh, Pennsylvania

From the suburban outskirts of Washington D.C., point your compass toward the northwest. Destination: Pittsburgh. Route #2 meanders along the westernmost edge of Maryland, cruising through small towns like Frederick, Everett, and Hagerstown before crossing the border into Pennsylvania. Along the way, you'll find an array of interesting places hawking the full range of secondhand stuff, from glitzy vintage threads to used books and collectable vinyl.

Route #2 Driving Time (stops not included): 5 hours

Highlights on the trip include the colorful historic district in Frederick, where you can root around in **Alice's Attic** and try on a glittering ball gown at **Venus on the Half Shell**. Make a special stop at the **National Pike Flea Market**, a dusty and slightly chaotic adventure. The Bedford area boasts **Yours & Mine** and **Julia's Resale**, two favorites for clothing and miscellany at low-down bargain rates. Defy the laws of physics (for free) at **Gravity Hill** and have a $32 slumber party at the colorful **Traveler's Rest Motel**. Wrap things up in Pittsburgh, which steals the show for inexpensive fun and games, as well as dirt-cheap deals on furniture, household goods, clothes, and music at favorite places like **Red White & Blue Thrift Shop**, **Yesterday's News**, and **Jerry's Records**.

WHEATON, MARYLAND

Begin by heading north on Route 97, aka Georgia Avenue, making a quick stop in Wheaton, Maryland, a suburban tangle that lies just outside the Beltway (Interstate 495). Say a prayer for your wallet upon entering the **St. Andrew's Lutheran Church Thrift Shop**. This love-able church basement shop, clearly marked with the bold "Thrift Store" sign, is petite but full of goodies. A quick glance around the tiny store will reveal 1960s suitcases, flashy art-work, and big beaded jewels. Many bargain wares may be found, but St. Andrew's *does* recognize the value of a good retro item (plaid bowling ball bag, $15), so expect to pay up for those. Just consider your purchase a donation and leave with a guilt-free conscience.

> **ST. ANDREW'S LUTHERAN CHURCH THRIFT SHOP**
> 12247 Georgia Avenue
> Wheaton, Maryland
> Phone: (301) 933-9340
> Hours: Tues–Fri 10–4, Sat 9–2

FREDERICK, MARYLAND

To escape the city traffic, continue toward the northwest and drop in on the hopping historic town of Frederick, Maryland, a laid-back commu-nity that attracts hipsters, connoisseurs, and visitors of all stripes. Founded in the late 1700s, this picturesque town makes for a great af-ternoon filled with antiques and thrift shops galore. Stroll the bustling roads amid the brightly colored townhouses and historic homes.

If you're looking for an assortment of antique furniture, secondhand clothing, or one-of-a-kind housewares, then Frederick is the town for you: At least ten secondhand hot spots can be found, dotted around the intersection of Market and Patrick streets. You'll find one fabulous shop after another as well as small cafés and restaurants serving up mouth-watering treats. In the summertime the birds twitter in the trees, and the sidewalks are humming with people. Forge ahead and spend some cash in Frederick without breaking the bank.

First, make a quick stop at the **Frederick Union Rescue Mission** on Market Street. This thrift store offers a nice selection of furniture and bric-a-brac as well as an assortment of electronics and records. Nothing fancy here, but you'll be able to find some practical home furnishings, like a couch or filing cabinet. Prices generally start at $10 and up, and the sales staff is happy to tell you about other bargain stops in the area.

Take a stroll around the corner onto Patrick Street and get ready! **Select Seconds**, run by some nice elderly ladies, is a huge floor-through with three adjoining rooms carrying mostly clothing for men, women, and children. Between an entire clothing rack devoted to plaid and another of wedding attire, you'll find an odd assortment of objects and accessories, from a beaded purse to a salad spinner. Although there is not much vintage in sight, the goods are neatly organized, with many finds for the mature lady. Prices range from $3 to $10, with plenty of half-price tags fluttering in the air. Lucky visitors may even encounter one of Select Seconds' "throw it all in a bag" sales.

**FREDERICK UNION
    RESCUE MISSION**
200 South Market Street
Frederick, Maryland
Phone: (301) 662-5219
Hours: Mon–Fri 10–6, Sat 10–4

SELECT SECONDS
8 East Patrick Street
Frederick, Maryland
Phone: (301) 662-8280
Hours: Tues–Fri 10–4, Sat 10–2:30

ENCORE INTERIOR CONSIGNMENTS
24 East Patrick Street
Frederick, Maryland
Phone: (301) 694-9390
Hours: Tues–Fri 10–6, Sat 10–5,
    Sun 12–5

Encore Interior Consignments is a marvelous place to pick up a few handsome curios or household furnishings. Tea sets, platters, and other fancy housewares are beautifully displayed on wide oak dining tables and varnished shelves throughout this spacious shop. You'll find intriguing artwork, retro dining room sets, lamps, china, remarkable dishware, and many small novelty items at prices you can handle. Double-check the dates on the price tags to get the real deal here. The longer the item remains on the shelf, the lower the price will go—if you're willing to gamble.

A few doors down the street investigate the **Antique Cellar and the Vintage House.** This store has great taste! A shabby chic wine-colored Victorian chair guards the front entrance. Bop to the beat of your modern rock favorites over the loudspeaker, while cruising through the showroom of funky and elegant furniture. You'll find tables and chairs, divans, lawn furniture, and accessories as well as ornate lamps and chandeliers dating from the Victorian era to the 1970s. In our opinion, this boutique is on the upside of the budget scale for the die-hard thrifter.

ANTIQUE CELLAR & THE VINTAGE HOUSE
38 East Patrick Street
Frederick, Maryland
Phone: (301) 620-0591
Hours: Mon–Thurs 10–5, Fri–Sat 10–6, Sun 12–5

BEANS, BAGELS AND MORE
49 East Patrick Street
Frederick, Maryland
Phone: (301) 620-2165
Hours: Mon–Fri 6:30–5, Sat 7–6, Sun 7–5

EMPORIUM ANTIQUES
112 East Patrick Street
Frederick, Maryland
Phone: (301) 620-7099
Hours: Mon–Sat 10–6, Sun 12–6

When we visited the Antique Cellar, Leah was sad to leave behind a nouveau-inspired 1970s garden chair made of weathered wrought iron. Much of the furniture here has been carefully refinished or refurbished, and yet retains its original charm. These forgotten treasures will surely be the hit of your next garden party.

Refuel at **Beans, Bagels and More**, a lively eat-in café offering bagel sandwiches and scrumptious snacks. The saucy counter staff serves up delicious gourmet coffee drinks, either steaming hot or iced, making this a choice spot to rest your weary legs. For dessert try one of their super-duper ooey-gooey chocolate chip cookies. The quick service will get you back on the thrift trail in no time.

Next, step into the world of **Emporium Antiques**, where over 130 dealers stockpile collectible favorites and finery from the last century.

Take some time to hunt around, and you're sure to find invaluable treasures in quantity, from exquisite antique furniture, to piles of costume jewelry, to table spreads of silverware and other curious relics. The prices here are not always the thriftiest, but a careful search of this enormous indoor antique mall may reveal special bargains hiding in the aisles.

The flaming pink storefront of **Alice's Attic Consignment** is easily spotted on Market Street. Weirdly, Alice's Attic is attached to a bridal gown shop. Upon entering the doorway on the right, you'll be startled to emerge into a wonderland of fancy ball gowns and veils. But not to fret, the owner is a friendly lady who will steer you gently back into the thrift department. Though small, Alice's can be highly recommended for its dirt-cheap appeal. You'll no doubt want to throw down some pennies on a few stylish trinkets here. Fill up your shopping bag with clothing and accessories, books and records, and an assortment of other rarities. Don't pass up Alice's great scarf and jewelry collection as well as miscellaneous items for about a buck a piece. Items are jam-packed into tight corners and scattered about the floor, yet the space is sparkling-clean and inviting. Shop to your heart's content in this oasis of fun.

> **ALICE'S ATTIC CONSIGNMENT**
> 301 North Market Street
> Frederick, Maryland
> Phone: (301) 631-6779
> Hours: Mon–Sat 10–5
>
> **JUNKTION THRIFT SHOP**
> 302 North Market Street
> Frederick, Maryland
> Phone: (301) 698-5811
> Hours: Call ahead for hours

Almost directly across the street from Alice's Attic is **Junktion Thrift Shop**, a tiny hippie shop with a "world beat" flavor. While Junktion is not strictly a thrift store, it offers an interesting mix of goodies. Along with the usual hippie fare of incense, beads, and candles, you'll find several racks of used denim jeans as well as vintage dresses and skirts, with prices ranging from $2 to $8. Poke around at Junktion for used books, wall hangings and household goods from the 1960s and 1970s.

Don't drop while you shop. Take a break for a treat and scarf down some homemade sweets at **The Candy Kitchen**, which has been cranking out confections since 1902. Rot your teeth with homemade chocolates, caramels, creams, fudge, and other sugary morsels, guaranteed to induce feelings of euphoria. Try one of Leah's favorites, chocolate-covered pretzels with sprinkles, and keep your eyes peeled for free samples.

Down the street, the hipsters all flock to **Venus on the Half Shell** for an incredible selection of retro duds. Enjoy the lounge atmosphere and flash back a few decades to the tune of alternative music favorites while scouring the racks. The spacious red-carpeted room is mainly devoted to threads of the 1950s and '60s for guys and gals alike. Find glitz and glitter, fake fur coats, fuzzy mohair sweaters, handbags, and suits in stripes, plaids, and polka dots. Chill out on the velvet couch in the back while your friend tries on fashions for the mod ball. This store has a real uptown flair—clothing is in immaculate condition, reflected by boutique prices of $20 and up. Venus on the Half Shell is overflowing with lucky finds and is an absolute must for the vintage clothing enthusiast! Leave with an armful of timeless trends and garments worth showing off to your friends.

THE CANDY KITCHEN
52 North Market Street
Frederick, Maryland
Phone: (301) 698-0442
Hours: Mon–Sat 10–6

VENUS ON THE HALF SHELL
151 North Market Street
Frederick, Maryland
Phone: (301) 662-6213
Hours: Mon 12–6, Tues–Sat 12–9,
Sun 12–5

TINY'S TWICE AROUND
410 North Market Street
Frederick, Maryland
Phone: (301) 694-2999
Hours: Mon–Sun 9:30–5
(opens later when it rains)

Farther up Market Street, be prepared for the opposite end of the secondhand spectrum. **Tiny's Twice Around** is wall-to-wall nicknacks for the curiosity collector. A little zoo of animals inhabits the outdoor table display, while shelves of pint-size oddities peek out the storefront window. The shop's magnetic quality will lure you in to scan aisles crowded with a unique assortment of all things small, such as vintage salt and pepper shakers, flowery dishes, slogan cups, darling figurines, and china. Tiny's is the place to find that 1980s rainbow mug you threw out twenty years ago (silly you). Also, don't miss the clothing piles, crates of LP and 45 rpm records, and other junk spread out in the back room, garage sale-style. Just to note, some items might need a good rinsing out before use, unless you prefer your salt and pepper circa 1972. Prices hover from $1 to $15. The store is open every day at 9 a.m., but call ahead if it's raining, when it tends to open up a bit later than usual.

On your way out of Frederick, hightail it over to the **Way Station Thrift Shop** on West Patrick Street. This fair-size shop has a moderate selection of men's and women's clothing, housewares, accessories, and bric-a-brac. The store is pleasant, clean, and nicely arranged, with great prices. The location, a few miles from the main drag, as well as limited hours, make Way Station a well-kept secret in Frederick, not to be passed up.

WAY STATION THRIFT SHOP
217 West Patrick Street
Frederick, Maryland
Phone: (301) 695-1583
Hours: Mon–Fri 10–2

BARBARA FRITCHIE CANDY STICK RESTAURANT
1513 West Patrick Street (Route 40)
Frederick, Maryland
Phone: (301) 662-2500
Hours: Mon–Sun 7–10

Patrick Street soon turns into Route 40 West, a thrift and antique lover's dream route. Scan the roadside for unique examples of local culture and Americana. Between strip malls and green pastures, flea markets and resale shops pepper the countryside.

Screech into the parking lot of the **Barbara Fritchie Candy Stick Restaurant**. The eatery is named after Barbara Fritchie, a daring Civil War heroine from Frederick who waved her flag in defiance of Confederate troops and became an American legend. You can't miss the giant candy cane sign out front, in all its 1950s glory, and the interior décor is just as fun. Inside, order your fill of homemade cooking, like country ham, charcoal steaks, and barbecue, or just the good old sandwich. Everything here is made from scratch, and the homemade pie is destined to become its own American legend.

Farther along Route 40 on the way into Hagerstown, expect to dig deep on a real treasure hunt at the **National Pike Flea Market**. The Flea Market is set far back on a small dirt drive on the south side of the highway—keep your eyes peeled for the Sheetz Gas Station next door. The sign says, "Everything Under the Sun," and that's no joke! From the road, the building appears as a tiny spot at the top of the hill—but don't be fooled. Roughly the size of an airplane hangar, this two-story madhouse is really large and stuffed to the brim with musty attic treasures, with goods piled up outdoors as well.

Drive past the outdoor "yard sale" of bargain relics to fill your house and shed and enter in the rear of the building. You might find anything at National Pike: old post cards, collectible toys, racks of clothes, a pile of embroidery hoops, shelves of videotapes, and even a back room full of blaring televisions. Head downstairs to find books and magazines. The prices here are already rock-bottom, but you might try haggling for an even better steal. Hold up your numbers for auctions that take place every third Friday of the month. The National Pike Flea Market is chaotic fun for the adventurous.

Just a hop, skip, and a jump down Route 40 is a cluster of giant multi-dealer antique malls, such as Antique Crossroads, Antiques Market, and A&J Antiques, all large enough to get lost in. A better option is to follow the little footpath to the smaller shops in the back, where you can find our favorite among the giants, **Marsha's Closet**. This pleasant, medium-size shop carries high-quality vintage apparel for women. Ooh and ahh over the beautiful collection of classy, almost mint-condition garments from the 1920s, '30s, and '40s, along with a few exquisite Victorian pieces. Surprisingly, casual dresses are moderately priced at around $15, and you'll spend a little more on beautifully crafted bridal and formal attire. Marsha's has a great collection of

NATIONAL PIKE FLEA MARKET
20717 National Pike (Route 40)
Boonsboro, Maryland
Phone: (240) 420-5003
Hours: Tues–Fri 12–5, Sat 9–5, Sun 12–5

MARSHA'S CLOSET
Shops at Beaver Creek
20136 National Pike (Route 40)
Hagerstown, Maryland
Phone: (301) 582-1212
Hours: Thurs–Mon 10–5, Sun 1–5

hats and accessories, and if rhinestone gems suit your fancy, you'll find a lovely selection in the glass cabinet up front. You'll leave wishing Marsha's Closet was *your* closet.

Just before you reach Hagerstown on Route 40, drop in on **Memory Lane Antiques & Flea Market,** a large bazaar where over 150 dealers offer up a hodgepodge of collectibles. Memory Lane is sectioned into booths, and prices vary according to each dealer. Explore thoroughly and you may just bump into a good deal or two. Check out the expansive selection of housewares and nicknacks, with a few pieces of furniture mixed in. Collectors of toys and superhero action figures will have a ball! Unfortunately, clothing mavens are out of luck.

HAGERSTOWN, MARYLAND

Hagerstown offers several destinations for the hard-core thrifter. Secondhand shoppers should be prepared to venture into dingy corners to find the scores in this town. A good starting point is the **Union Rescue Mission Thrift Shop.** This drowsy store has a decent selection of clothing for men, women, and kids. Pick up a couch or bedroom set and thumb through the small array of books and records. Options are sparse for the housewares aficionado. One-of-a-kind oddities are few and far between here, but if basic clothing or furniture is what you need, you can surely find it at the Rescue Mission. Super rock-bottom prices make it worth the dreary atmosphere.

MEMORY LANE ANTIQUES & FLEA MARKET
1350 Dual Highway (Route 40)
Hagerstown, Maryland
Phone: (301) 773-7491
Hours: Mon–Sun 10–6

UNION RESCUE MISSION THRIFT SHOP
125 North Prospect Street
Hagerstown, Maryland
Phone: (301) 739-1114
Hours: Mon–Sat 9–5

SUMMIT BARGAIN SHOP
32 Summit Avenue
Hagerstown, Maryland
Phone: (301) 739-7810
Hours: Mon–Sun 9–5

The **Summit Bargain Shop** is also not for the faint of heart. Small, dark, and cluttered, it offers a *very* random collection of inexpensive gadgets, strewn over the shelves of two narrow rooms. You might find some interesting doodads in the $1 to $5 range as well as many use-for-parts items. It has little or nothing to offer for clothes or furniture, but it does carry an oddball selection of wall clocks and table lamps. Another dusty shop for the daring! Good luck! The shop also repairs vacuums, just in case you were wondering.

If you're bored with bleak, a sunnier spot to browse is **World Treasures Re-Uzit**, an itty-bitty place run by friendly women who will happily share their opinion on that flowered polyester dress you're trying on. World Treasures is top-notch for used clothing. Although there's not much vintage in sight, apparel for men and women is priced between $2 and $6. Nicknacks and jewelry go for $1 or less. Dirt cheap! Great prices! Goodies galore!

> **WORLD TREASURES RE-UZIT**
> 22 West Franklin Street
> Hagerstown, Maryland
> Phone: (301) 797-8624
> Hours: Mon–Sat 10–4
>
> **GOODWILL**
> 151 North Burhans Boulevard
>   (at Salem Avenue)
> Hagerstown, Maryland
> Phone: (301) 665-1044
> Hours: Mon–Sat 9–9, Sun 12–5

If Hagerstown thrifting has made you feel a bit dusty, don't worry, because we've saved the best for last! The **Goodwill** is an especially good place to recreate your wardrobe. You'll find a vast selection of apparel for the whole family and especially good stuff for the girls (aww, yeah). Roughly the size of a high school gym, this sunny store has lots of great merchandise to sort through. Snatch up blouses and slacks for $3 to $4 and rescue a nearly new winter coat for $8. You'll probably be too distracted by the racks and racks of shoes to notice that this Goodwill is a tiny bit short on furniture or housewares. Take advantage of these remarkable prices for a chain thrift store.

GREENCASTLE, PENNSYLVANIA

Just a twenty-minute drive north of Hagerstown on Route 11 is Greencastle, Pennsylvania. There's a little rumor going around that the town was named after Greencastle, Ireland. We have no idea whether or not that's true. Either way, there are a few places that you should plan to visit while passing through.

If you're looking for a neat and orderly secondhand boutique, wander into the **Nearly New Shoppe**. It's a great place to dig around for stylish, quality clothing, especially for women and children. Search the racks for name brands, like Gap, priced mostly under $10. The cheery store owner told us that with the exception of furniture, she carries a little bit of everything, and it's all sold on consignment. Find a gently used set of dishes, a pretty necklace, or a sturdy pair of shoes. Thumb through the books and records and snag some handsome luggage or an oddball curio. The Nearly New Shoppe is also a great place to pick decorations or crafts for the home. The store is restocked seasonally, culminating with special blowout half-price sales that happen every six months or so. Items that aren't sold or returned to consigners are donated to various local charities.

Situated just down the street from the Nearly New Shoppe is **Home Towne Antiques**, a top-notch spot to shop for collectibles such as vintage kitchenware, small furniture pieces, and fine linens. Find a set of striped drinking glasses or an elegant vase and check out the dressed-up mannequins in the back room. Merchandise is attractively scattered throughout the length of the store. Though items are a bit on the pricey side (tiny turquoise gooseneck desktop lamp, $18), it is possible to exit with a great buy in hand.

Swoon over the rich aroma as you approach **Greencastle Coffee Roasters** on East Baltimore Street. This place deserves raves for providing the

NEARLY NEW SHOPPE
18 South Carlisle Street
Greencastle, Pennsylvania
Phone: (717) 597-8883
Hours: Mon–Tues 9–4, Thurs–Fri
9–5, Sat 9–4

HOME TOWNE ANTIQUES
103 South Carlisle Street
Greencastle, Pennsylvania
Phone: (717) 597-5051
Hours: Mon–Tues 10–5, Thurs–Fri
10–5, Sun 12–4

GREENCASTLE COFFEE ROASTERS
164 East Baltimore Street
Greencastle Pennsylvania
Phone: (717) 597-1900
Hours: Mon–Thurs 10–6, Fri 10–7,
Sat 10–5, Sun 11–5

freshest and tastiest coffee for miles around. Watch through the window as exquisite Victorian-era coffee roasters spin and toast coffee beans from all over the world. Inside, you'll find over 200 varieties of blends and flavors, all freshly roasted and packed within the week. Try one of the "specialty blend" brews or choose from an international selection of beans, from South America to the Far East. The flavored varieties are something to talk about, with concoctions like Almond Joy, Brandy Alexander, and Danish Pastry, and others that you won't be able to find anywhere else. On Wednesdays and Sundays Greencastle Coffee Roasters changes the game—don't pass up its legendary jumbo Virginia peanuts, fresh-roasted to taste for only a buck a pound.

A highlight of true thrifting in Greencastle is the old standby, the **Goodwill**, located in the shopping center on North Antrim Way. What at first glance may seem like your average Goodwill chain store actually deserves a longer look. You'll find great clothing for men, women, and children, along with books, sunglasses, housewares, and toys for the kiddies. This medium-size secondhand shop sells many articles of clothing for under $5. Fancy dresses are priced at around $10. Get toasty with woolen hats and mittens from its seasonal collection. Browse the baubles, model a silk scarf, and acquire a new set of dishes all in a single stop.

> **GOODWILL**
> 524 North Antrim Way
> Greencastle, Pennsylvania
> Phone: (717) 595-0868
> Hours: Mon–Sat 9–9, Sun 12–5

EVERETT, PENNSYLVANIA

For further thrift and pit stops, continue along Route 11 for another fifteen miles or so beyond Greencastle, then turn west onto Route 30. Another forty-five minutes down the road, you'll pass through Breezewood, a neon-adorned trucker haven whose proximity to the interstate means lots of business for the fast-food chains. There are plenty of old-school, cheap motels along the flashing, electric main drag, but an even better option lies just a few miles farther down the road.

Adventure seekers looking for a comfy, kitsch place to spend the night will adore the **Traveler's Rest Motel**, located on Route 30 between Breezewood and Everett, Pennsylvania. The price for sleeping over is a super-dirt-cheap bargain at $32 a night—whether you're traveling solo or having a pajama party for four. The motel check-in and the matching restaurant next door are both bright yellow and orange A-frame structures, built according to popular fashion of the mid-1960s. The rooms are small, clean, and bursting with charm, decorated with groovy patterned bedspreads and 1960s-style furniture in quirky-mod fashion. The grounds are tidy and cheery—it's entirely possible that happy roosters will wake you in the morning. A cozy cottage out back is available for guests on an extended stay. Say hello to Karen, owner and veteran thrifter, and her cuddly dog, Gypsy. The motel has been owned by the family since 1947. In the quilty and colorful lobby, look for the framed picture of Gypsy's predecessor, Traveler, the original dog-hero of Traveler's Rest, and check out other old photos that chronicle the history of this amazing place.

Three bucks will get you a full-on, sunny-side up breakfast at the **Traveler's Rest Restaurant** next door. Perch on one of the green vinyl and chrome stools at the counter or enjoy your morning coffee overlooking the traffic meandering along Route 30. Feel the magic! We hope they never change a thing!

TRAVELER'S REST MOTEL
On Lincoln Highway (Route 30)
Everett, Pennsylvania
Phone: (814) 652-6263

**COUNTRY COTTAGE
    CONSIGNMENT SHOPPE**
342 West Main Street
Everett, Pennsylvania
Phone: (814) 652-9502
Hours: Mon–Fri 10–5, Sat 10–2

In the tiny business district of Everett, Pennsylvania, stop by **Country Cottage Consignment Shoppe**, located right on Main Street past the Rite-Aid. You'll find this small resale shop to be clean and orderly. The selection here runs towards the conservative, with some blue ribbon fashion finds from the 1960s and '70s mixed in. The long, narrow space offers racks of secondhand apparel, mostly for women. In addition, the store carries a trove of never before worn socks and other new and reasonably priced merchandise. Try on a silk dress or a "new to you" belt in the dressing rooms near the back.

A quirkier, more cluttered thrift experience can be found around the corner at **Deb's Resale**, which can be recognized as the blue house with a red roof. Deb's is located slightly off the main drag, across from the HOHA Laundry on East South Street Extension. Here you'll find jumbled racks of clothing priced from $2 to $8, with some men's items available as well. Fancy dresses can be found for $15. Small displays of housewares are scattered throughout this happily untidy shop, along with a hodgepodge of handbags, modern jewelry, and footwear for under $5. Snag some mini bottles of nail polish from a basket near the register.

DEB'S RESALE
8 East South Street Extension
Everett, Pennsylvania
Phone: (814) 652-9500
Hours: Mon–Fri 10–4:30, Sat 10–2

THE IGLOO
Route 30 East Business, just outside
 of Everett
Everett, Pennsylvania
Phone: (814) 652-2442
Hours: Summer season,
 Mon–Sun 11–10

On your way out of Everett, schedule an ice cream appointment for yourself at **The Igloo**, an ice cream hut shaped like a sundae, covered with chocolate sauce, and topped off with a cherry. Use the drive-thru window if you're in a rush or enjoy your treat on the deck out front. The Igloo serves up a decadent selection of shakes, sundaes, banana splits, and waffle cones using hand-dipped exotic flavors like rainbow, teaberry, and moose tracks as well as old standby favorites. You'll surely want to stop for this one of a kind attraction.

BEDFORD, PENNSYLVANIA

Route 30 will bring you directly into Bedford, Pennsylvania, where antique shops and galleries dot the ivy- and brick-lined avenues of the main shopping quarter. While in town, don't miss out on the budget finds at **Yours and Mine Consignment Shop**. Deceptively larger than it appears from the street, Yours and Mine occupies the entire first floor, with a string of crowded rooms off the main area. The front room stocks clothing for people of all ages. Explore further and you'll find an assortment of afghans, bed linens, and curtains, along with a mishmash of cutesie household items. Footwear fetishists will be happy to find that shoes have their very own department. Where else can you pick up a canvas tote bag or some funky 1970s greeting cards for under a dollar? There aren't many large furniture pieces for sale; however, it is possible to snag smaller furnishings such as shelves and folding tables at this shop. Bridal ensembles and prom finery can be found all the way in the back, near stacks of toys and games for the wee ones. Try on a swanky gown behind the purple plastic shower curtain in the itty-bitty dressing room. Yours and Mine carries a wide-ranging assortment of curiosities and useful items, so investigate every corner! The prices here are hard to beat.

YOURS & MINE CONSIGNMENT SHOP
120 West Pitt Street
Bedford, Pennsylvania
Phone: (814) 623-3321
Hours: Mon–Tues 10–6, Wed 10–7, Thurs–Fri 10–6, Sat 10–4

ST. JAMES EPISCOPAL CHURCH THRIFT SHOP
210 East John Street
Bedford, Pennsylvania
Phone: (814) 623-6649
Hours: Mon–Sat 10–3

Another favorite in Bedford is the **St. James Episcopal Church Thrift Shop**, a pint-size shop in the basement of the gray brick church annex. St. James is situated in a residential neighborhood, and the church is surrounded by lovely tall trees and green, shady lawns. At the side entrance you'll find a brick pathway that leads to the basement steps. The thrift shop is on the small side, but good things come in small packages. St. James mainly offers clothing for women, with many items priced at $3 or less. The lovely church ladies who run the shop will point the way to the makeshift dressing room under the stairs. Browse through the small collection of handbags and vintage jewelry or pick up some odd curios and kitchen items at really super prices. Clothing for tots occupies the back room.

Wrap it up in Bedford at a very special place for cheap clothes, **Julia's Resale Shop**. Julia's is housed in a not-so-clearly marked maroon and white building, located on Route 30 (Lincoln Highway), past the fairgrounds west of Bedford. Inside, the space is a bit dark and disorganized, but the selection is huge, varied, and inexpensive, with clothing price tags ranging from $2 to $8. In the spring, coats are a steal at $5. The cluttered and confused racks of apparel hold fashions for every taste, some unworn and with the original tags still attached. Ladies will find a wealth of styles, and there is a large toy and clothing section for children as well. Home items include serving dishes, mugs and glasses. Julia's Resale Shop offers a much larger selection than other area thrift shops, with boxes of new merchandise coming in every day. Put Julia's on your list of stores to frequent.

JULIA'S RESALE SHOP
7246 Lincoln Highway (Route 30 Business, past the fairgrounds west of Bedford)
Bedford, Pennsylvania
Phone: (814) 623-7576
Hours: Mon–Fri 10–5, Sat 9–5

GRAVITY HILL
Bedford County, Pennsylvania
www.gravityhill.com
Phone: 1 (800) 765-3331
 (Bedford County Visitor's Bureau)

Not so far from Julia's, check out the **Giant Building Shaped Like a Coffee Pot**, a classic roadside oddity. This weathered and abandoned structure is situated on Route 30 Business west of the shopping district. Get out your camera for this unique photo opportunity. Rumor has it that plans are afoot to disassemble the structure, so get your clicks while you can.

A truly out-of-this-world pit stop is **Gravity Hill**. Take a quick detour and witness unnatural forces as water flows uphill, and your car rolls backward up the incline. This mystery spot's claim to fame is its sheer defiance of earthly gravity. The only indicator of this natural wonder is the letters "GH" spray-painted onto the pavement. Disney World it is not. However, the pure freakishness of this experience will leave you questioning everything that you ever learned in physics. We're sure that someone out there can explain the Gravity Hill phenomenon, but we hope we never find that person. You're welcome to call the Bedford County Visitors Bureau (1-800-765-3331) for the Gravity Hill brochure, in case you think we made this up.

To experience Gravity Hill for yourself, follow these special directions, which only take about fifteen minutes. From Route 30 in Schellsburg, Pennsylvania, turn north onto Route 96 toward New Paris. Drive approximately four miles, and just before you get to the tiny metal bridge, turn left onto Bethel Hollow Road/SR 4016. Drive six-tenths of a mile and bear left at the Y in the road. Continue another 1.5 miles and bear right at the turnoff (a road with no sign). Proceed two-tenths of a mile and look for the first "GH" spray painted on the road—keep driving! Gravity Hill is located at the second GH on the pavement. Carefully check your rearview mirror for traffic and prepare to experience a freak of nature. Put the car in neutral and witness the car roll backward up the hill! You can also try it out with water or a tennis ball. Bizarre.

Tired yet? Roadside adventurers need soft beds on which to rest their weary heads. If you're ready for a good night's sleep, we think the **Jean Bonnet Tavern** is out of sight. The fieldstone and chestnut-beamed tavern has been around since 1760 and has managed to keep loads of colonial charm. Grab a bite or have a beer in the tavern, which buzzes with local character and occasional live music. Take your pint out to the porch in nice weather. The bed and breakfast up-

> **JEAN BONNET TAVERN**
> 6048 Lincoln Highway
> Bedford, Pennsylvania
> Phone: (814) 623-2250

stairs offers a decent price on spacious rooms featuring fluffy four-poster beds and views of the neighboring countryside. A cushy suite for four people goes for around $100 and includes a hearty breakfast to help you get your groove on in the morning.

PITTSBURGH, PENNSYLVANIA

Pittsburgh! Pittsburgh! Pittsburgh! This city ranks among our favorites in the region for cheap thrills. Known as the Golden Triangle, Pittsburgh's downtown district is situated at the confluence of the Allegheny, Monongahela, and Ohio rivers, with residential neighborhoods extending up the slopes and hills that surround the city. Formerly the heart and soul of the steel industry, postindustrial Pittsburgh has plenty of cultural and entertainment options for the visitor—not to mention super thrifting! A fascinating history, a huge variety of interesting architecture, and a vibrant creative community all lend themselves to Pittsburgh's certain kind of "je ne sais quoi."

East Carson Street, the hipster strip in Pittsburgh, is a great introduction to the South Side of our favorite city. Here you'll find a range of thrift stores, vintage boutiques, music shops, and booksellers. After dark the street hums with nightlife in bars and cafés up and down the road.

For thrifting, the biggest selection and arguably the best prices can be found at the **Salvation Army**, located on South 9th Street, a side street just off East Carson. Here you'll find an interesting mix of clothes, furniture, and items for the home, all at great bargain rates. Ladies' jackets go for $6, skirts for $4, and men's button-up shirts can be had for right around $3. Sift through the racks for your very own treasures. Furniture is upstairs, with the selection leaning toward the mass-produced. The housewares section is more fruitful—look for retro kitchen goods in Martha Stewart shades like mint, sky blue, and chocolate.

SALVATION ARMY
44 South 9th Street
Pittsburgh, Pennsylvania
Phone: (412) 481-7900
Hours: Mon–Sat 9–6

DIVA'S BY MONICA
1100 East Carson Street
Pittsburgh, Pennsylvania
Phone: (412) 481-5001
Hours: Mon–Thurs 11–7, Fri–Sat
  11–9, Sun 12–3

On the other end of the spectrum is **Diva's by Monica**, just up the road. Quality retro threads are the main fare here, and almost every vintage item at Diva's sells for under $20. Works by local designers share the stage. You can also find a colorful medley of crafty handmade bags, jewelry, and accessories for gettin' pretty. Diva's is also the place to go for great shoes! The vibrantly painted, lounge-like atmosphere is made complete by hand-decorated diva-esque furniture scattered throughout the space. Penny-pinchers should not miss the half-price room in the back.

Just down the street, **Yesterday's News** is a must for vintage collectors and aficionados. This small boutique is charmingly cluttered with a stylish collection of hip outfits for the girls, offering both everyday wear and glittery dresses for extra-special occasions. Try on fur-trimmed cardigans, jackets and coats, and funky formal wear from every era. Along with an extensive apparel selection, Yesterday's News is crammed with goodies such as one-of-a-kind vintage accessories, hats, handbags, old-fashioned umbrellas, and chic luggage for your travels. All of this and more under one beautifully stamped-tin ceiling—you'd be hard-pressed *not* to find something cool to take home with you.

There is no place on East Carson Street more worthy of a pit stop than **The Beehive**, a true Pittsburgh classic. This busy (as a beehive, ha ha) coffeehouse boasts a cheery mismatched 1950s décor, with funky Formica tables and chrome chairs in bright red and sunny yellow. Murals and offbeat local artwork cover the walls. Computer stations with Internet access do nothing to detract from the retro ambience. Choose from an assortment of teas and coffee beverages, pastries, and snacks, including the universe's best egg salad sandwich, which will set you back $1.50. Cool out in the courtyard or pick up something for your art collection at the Art-O-Mat, an ex-cigarette vending machine that has been refurbished to distribute small original artworks, all exactly the size of a box of cigarettes, at the dirt-cheap price of $4 per masterpiece. Another machine dispenses Zippos, paperback novels, and other unconventional treats. Work on your pinball game in the back room.

Two hot spots for bookworms are **El Jay's Used Books** and **City Books**. It's a great adventure to browse the stacks at either. At El Jay's, you'll find an enormous number of choices for used titles, both hard- and

> **YESTERDAY'S NEWS**
> 1405 East Carson Street
> Pittsburgh, Pennsylvania
> Phone: (412) 431-1712
> Hours: Mon–Tues 12–5,
>   Thurs–Sat 12–5
>
> **THE BEEHIVE**
> 1327 East Carson Street
> Pittsburgh, Pennsylvania
> Phone: (412) 488-4483
> Hours: Sun–Thurs 8:30am–1am,
>   Fri–Sat 8:30am–2am

Beehive, Pittsburgh, Pennsylvania

softcover, all in prime condition. The friendly and knowledgeable staff can help you navigate aisles and aisles of inexpensively marked fiction titles, including a superb science fiction section. Tacked onto a towering column inside the store, don't miss El Jay's mini-museum of oddball notes, postcards, and photographs that have been rescued from used books over the years. El Jay's *seems* appealingly disheveled, but, in fact, it is efficiently organized according to topic, with excellent prices to boot.

EL JAY'S USED BOOKS
1309 East Carson Street
Pittsburgh, Pennsylvania
Phone: (412) 381-7444
Hours: Mon–Thurs 12–8, Fri 12–10,
Sat 11–10, Sun 12–8

CITY BOOKS
1111 East Carson St
Pittsburgh, Pennsylvania
Phone: (412) 481-7555
Hours: Mon–Sat 11–6, Sun 1–5

A better option for art books, classic fiction, and rare titles is just down the road at **City Books**. Bring your top picks up the spiral staircase to the library on the second floor for a closer examination. Literary types and book collectors will feel warmly welcomed at City Books.

Before leaving the neighborhood, check out one of Pittsburgh's two inclined railroads, or funiculars, which scale the almost vertical heights overlooking the downtown area. The thrills are cheap—$1.75 for a one-way ticket, or $3.50 if you'd like to come back down again. Board the **Duquesne Incline** just across from Station Square, not far from East Carson Street. Disembark at the top and be dazzled. The sparkling skyline, particularly lovely after dusk, can be viewed from one of the lookout points along Mt. Washington's Grandview Avenue.

Next stop is Shadyside, where you can investigate the **Junior League Wear After Thrift Shop**, a gold mine of "gently worn clothing." Mannequins in the front window model conservatively fashionable ensembles, offering a taste of what's in store. Located along bustling Liberty Avenue, the Junior League is a neat and tidy shop that carries apparel for both men and women, along with hats, belts, handbags, and some classy jewelry pieces. Find decorative objects for your home or apartment as well as videotapes, luggage, and other necessities. Here you'll uncover a handful of vintage bargains mixed in with lots of merchandise for the mature shopper.

> **DUQUESNE INCLINE**
> 1220 Grandview Avenue
> Pittsburgh, Pennsylvania
> Phone: (412) 381-1665
> Hours: Mon–Sat 5:30am–12:45am,
> Sun 7am–12:45 am
>
> **JUNIOR LEAGUE WEAR AFTER THRIFT SHOP**
> 4707 Liberty Avenue
> Pittsburgh, Pennsylvania
> Phone: (412) 687-2600
> Hours: Mon–Wed 10–4, Thurs
> 10–6, Fri 10–4, Sat 10–3
>
> **GOODWILL**
> 5210 Liberty Avenue
> Pittsburgh, Pennsylvania
> Phone: (412) 687-8840
> Hours: Mon 9–8, Tues 9–9,
> Wed–Thurs 9–8, Friday 9–9,
> Sat 9–8, Sun 10–5

While not as sparkling clean as the Junior League, the **Goodwill** in Shadyside is a much larger space with a wondrous amount of clothing. Scan the racks for some great deals, like coats for $10, skirts and jackets at $5, and men's and ladies' shirts for even less. Especially fine bargains can be found according to seasonal clearance sales—our visit in the spring found the remainder of winter sweaters heading out the door for a buck each. Don't forget to check out the large household section in the

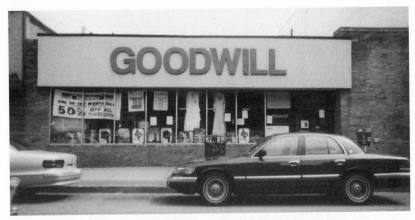

Goodwill, East Ohio Street, Pittsburgh, Pennsylvania

rear, where you can rummage through the shelves of dishes, mugs, picture frames, and baskets.

Not far from the Goodwill, make it a point to stop at **Consignments on Center**. This "resale boutique" offers quality goods at slightly-higher-than-thrift prices. The shop carries an array of dressier clothing, including several racks of well-made suits and other fine garments. Those in search of classy, grown-up accessories should stop in. Find a string of faux pearls, a stylish leather handbag, and a matching belt, all for far below full price. If you can't cough up the cash right away, no worries—they have a layaway plan!

Spruce up your wardrobe at **Eon's Fashion** boutique on the corner of College Street and Ellsworth Avenue. Look for the punk rock neon sign over the door. A half-hour and a few bucks at Eon's can transform you into the belle of the ball. The

CONSIGNMENTS ON CENTER
5503 Centre Avenue
Pittsburgh, Pennsylvania
Phone: (412) 682-3932
Hours: Mon–Tues 11–5, Wed–Thurs
11–7, Fri 11–5, Sat 10–4

EON'S FASHION
5850 Ellsworth Avenue
Pittsburgh, Pennsylvania
Phone: (412) 361-3368
Hours: Mon–Fri 12–6, Sat 11–6,
Sun 12–5

aisles are packed to the gills with classy vintage treasures—scarves, robes, fans, kimonos, and exotic finery. Boys can surf the racks of Hawaiian print summer gear, button-down dress shirts, bowler hats, and more. Old-fashioned hatboxes are stacked to the ceiling, and twinkling disco balls set the stage for groovy deals. Some sale dresses were spotted for $5 to $10, with full-price frocks going for around $25. But what's really special about Eon's is the tasty selection of styles, which runs from funky to psychedelic to luxuriously elegant, all in the blink of a false eyelash.

While you're in the neighborhood, drop in on **Hey Betty!** a three-floor spectacle of stunning vintage goods, offering stylish garments and objects for the home. The ground floor offers tons of options for the stylish man: smoking jackets, hats, shoes, and suit jackets, all very dapper. A lovely collection of boudoir threads for ladies includes slips, teddies, and silk pajama sets from the 1930s, '40s, and '50s. A case in the front displays row upon row of swanky vintage eyeglass frames as well as an assortment of dazzling rhinestone jewels and accessories. Downstairs, select from voguish shoes and ritzy dresses at slashed prices. Glamorize your pad with colorful examples of twentieth-century design from Hey Betty!: retro-mod table lamps, wall clocks, and bolts of bar cloth. No bachelor or bachelorette will be able to resist the selection of martini shakers, shot glasses, and collectible cocktail stirrers found on the top floor.

> **HEY BETTY!**
> 5892 Ellsworth Avenue
> Pittsburgh, Pennsylvania
> Phone: (412) 363-0999
> Hours: Mon–Sat 12–6, Sun 1–5
>
> **THE CLOTHES LINE**
> 256 South Highland Avenue
> Pittsburgh, Pennsylvania
> Phone: (412) 441-7577
> Hours: Mon–Sat 11–4

The Clothes Line on Highland Avenue is a small, tidy secondhand shop offering dirt-cheap deals on ladies clothing. Pants and shorts are priced at $3 to $4, T-shirts are only $1, and jackets and nicer outfits go only as high as $10 or $12. Special deals of the day are posted at the checkout counter. There is a very small bookshelf and housewares section and some costume jewelry and other trinkets, but the main trade at The Clothes Line is no-frills attire for women.

One of our most beloved Pittsburgh pit stops is the **Quiet Storm**, a combination coffeehouse, restaurant, and music venue. The patchwork linoleum floor and homegrown art adorning the walls give this place a laid-back, thrift-friendly vibe. Lounge around with a sorbet soy shake or a gingerade at a table out front or come inside for panini, salads, burritos, and tofu dishes served by the friendly, hip waitstaff. Choose from a plentiful menu of delicious and inexpensive vegetarian fare, and on weekends, a completely vegan brunch menu. Quiet Storm is open late into the evening and offers live music almost every night. Pick up a music calendar at the coffee counter.

QUIET STORM
5430 Penn Avenue
Pittsburgh, Pennsylvania
Phone: (412) 661-9355
Hours: Mon–Thurs 7:30am–11pm,
  Fri 7:30am–1am, Sat
  9:30am–1am, Sun 9:30am–11pm

EAST END COMMUNITY THRIFT
5123 Penn Avenue
Pittsburgh, Pennsylvania
Phone (412) 361-6010
Hours: Tues–Fri 10–4, Sat 12–4

COUNCIL THRIFT SHOP
822 Fifth Avenue
Pittsburgh, Pennsylvania
Phone: (412) 471-5606
Hours: Mon–Fri 9–:430, Sat 9–3:30

You'll find shelves and racks of inexpensive wares to rummage through at **East End Community Thrift**, farther down Penn Avenue. The prices are great, with most garments selling for 50 cents to $3. East End also stocks heaps of linens and shelves of household objects, including dishes, baskets, luggage, and random sporting equipment. This store is for shoppers who love to hunt and find. The staff is very friendly, and the store offers $1-off coupons (for your next visit) at the checkout. Proceeds from the sales go to the Thomas Merton Center next door.

Council Thrift Shop offers two large floors of thrifting adventure. Upstairs, don't miss "A Step Above," where you can find designer and vintage furniture, linens, housewares, and jewelry. Council Thrift offers an expansive selection with a wide variety of fashions, including some designer labels and hard-to-find brands for fancy apparel. There's also a big section for footwear and ladies' accessories. All the goods are of the "gently worn" variety, mostly quality items in good shape. The shop often features 50 percent off specials on various items, which change frequently. Council Thrift is run by the Pittsburgh Section of the National Council of Jewish Women and has been serving the area for over twenty years, plenty of time to become a much-loved favorite.

On the last Saturday of every month, the **Goodwill** on East Ohio Street offers an "end of the month sale," selling all donated clothing at 50 percent off! On other days, the prices are still great on clothes for men, women, and children. Coats are sold at around $10, and women's blouses go for $4. Get lucky with an abundance of $1 specials! A small area of the shop is devoted to dishes, luggage, and household items. No dressing room is available, but there is a quiet corner with a mirror where you can try on possible purchases. The shop is not huge, but look closely through the racks, as you may stumble across vintage gear mixed in with the corduroy and denim.

GOODWILL
509 East Ohio Street
Pittsburgh, Pennsylvania
Phone: (412) 322-5666
Hours: Mon–Sat 10–6, Sun 10–3

JERRY'S RECORDS
2136 Murray Avenue
Pittsburgh, Pennsylvania
Phone: (412) 421-4533
Hours: Wed–Fri 10–8, Sat 10–6, Sun 12–5

Experience vinyl mania at **Jerry's Records** in Squirrel Hill! This place, recommended to us as a local favorite for music, carries an almost overwhelming selection of vinyl. Located in a large space upstairs from the New Dumpling House on Murray Avenue, Jerry's buys and sells all genres of used records. Looking for some nightlife in Pittsburgh? Check out the extensive flier bulletin along the stairway for upcoming rock shows and other events in town. Jerry's offers an unbeatable selection of recordings from all eras and has something for almost every taste, from classical to alternative, pop, and indie rock favorites. You'll also find a plethora of disco, mood music, spoken word, quirky soundtracks, and other kitschy records. Most albums go for under $10 a pop, although rare imports might be priced a bit higher on the budget scale. Record collectors *should not miss* this treasure trove of old plastic.

A few blocks up from Jerry's Records is **Threepenny Books**, the small bookseller with the bright red door. This appealing little shop carries loads of used books in every category. Expect to see rare and hard-to-find books lurking on the shelves. The owner is an avid collector and aspires to (someday) carry every book in print for the shop. Among the selection find a mixture of favorites and the more obscure, including fiction, nonfiction, art books, children's stories, and a super biography section. College students may even find a few textbooks for their course list. The tall bookcases are packed with hardcovers and paperbacks in equal numbers, but magazines and comics are missing from the lot. Thrifty Threepenny Books buys and trades your old books, then resells them to the community at a mere 25 cents to a few dollars each! Also, if you're in the market for a vintage typewriter, the owner keeps four or five in stock in the back room.

THREEPENNY BOOKS
1827 Murray Avenue
Pittsburgh, Pennsylvania
Phone: (412) 422-5420
Hours: Mon–Fri 2–10, Sat 12–11,
Sun 1–6

RED WHITE & BLUE THRIFT STORE
890 Saw Mill Run Boulevard
Pittsburgh, Pennsylvania
Phone: (412) 381-1060
Hours: Mon–Sat 9–6

It's a thrift bonanza at **Red White & Blue Thrift Store**, locally loved and honored as one of the Best Offbeat Finds of City Search in 2001. Look for the giant sign along Saw Mill Run Boulevard where it intersects with Bausman Street. This hot spot for one-of-a-kind deals overflows with people on the weekends, as does the parking lot out front. Enter the vast warehouse and spot bric-a-brac shelves lining the store, full of curios and other exciting junk. Find it *all* here, including paperbacks, magazines, and shelves of videotapes. A plethora of pots, pans, utensils, and appliances will help you outfit your kitchen. Hoards of men's and women's clothing are clearly marked with large signs, along with a sizable children's department of clothes, plastic toys, and dolls. You'll find oodles of costume jewelry and pretty baubles for next to nothing, along with plenty of footwear options and a jumble of frilly finery. Small furniture items such as nightstands and lamps are readily available as well as a good selection of electronics, phones, clocks, and old typewriters. Red White & Blue is a mean thrift machine, the kind of place that warrants weekly visits. Try schmoozing with the friendly employees to get the scoop on new shipment arrivals.

For more options in the furniture department, follow Bausman Street through McKinley Park to **Charlie's Used Furniture** on Brownsville Road. Charlie's is a pleasant, down-to-earth antique shop selling an interesting mixture of furniture, curios, and decorative bits and pieces, both high style and kitsch. Add a few relics to your glass bottle collection. Large and small hardwood tables, retro dressers, and desks can be found here, along with intricate mirrors, sophisticated paintings, and lovely wall hangings. Try your luck with prices the old-fashioned way: haggle mercilessly.

> **CHARLIE'S USED FURNITURE**
> 143 Brownsville Road
> Pittsburgh, Pennsylvania
> Phone: (412) 481-0550
> Hours: Unavailable
>
> **RED WHITE & BLUE THRIFT STORE**
> 427 Hoffman Boulevard
> Pittsburgh, Pennsylvania
> Phone: (412) 469-9107
> Hours: Mon–Sat 9–6

The final act in Pittsburgh is another unbeatable **Red White & Blue Thrift Store**, located near the renowned Kennywood Park. Situated in a strip mall a short distance from Kennywood Boulevard (turn in at the McDonald's), this Red White & Blue is a superstore of thrift! Snag a shopping cart for this expedition and fill it with almost any item imaginable. You'll uncover heaps of clothing, piles of shoes, an eye-catching assortment of lamps, and more. The store is spacious, neat, and carefully organized, but even so it could take hours to burrow through everything. Prices are extremely reasonable here as well. You may find it difficult to leave this shop empty-handed. Come to think of it, why would you want to anyway?

The thrifting fun may be over for now, but we've saved the most adventurous pit stop for last. Throw all of your purchases in the trunk and head over to **Kennywood Park,** a mystifying wonderland of amusement rides. Kennywood is a national historic landmark, founded in 1898, and has been continually building new additions over the last century, making it one of the most eclectic fun parks in the country. Check out the original carousel pavilion as well as classic rides like the 1920s era "Jack Rabbit" coaster, "Noah's Ark," and a miniature train ride from the 1940s. Scream your lungs out on the "Thunderbolt" and the steel-looping "Phantom's Revenge," two of the many coasters for which Kennywood is well known. On warmer days, spread your picnic on outdoor tables under pretty foliage or scoot down the river to Sandcastle, Kennywood's sister water park.

> **KENNYWOOD PARK**
> 4800 Kennywood Boulevard
> West Mifflin, Pennsylvania
> Phone: (412) 461-0500
> Hours: Change seasonally

Admission prices vary, so consider how long you want to visit before purchasing a ticket. All-day passes are available, as are evening tickets, sold after 6 p.m.

ROUTE #3

Washington, D.C., to Charleston, West Virginia

Top of the Line Quality
Consignment Shoppe,
Winchester, Virginia

Windmill Restaurant,
Parkersburg, West Virginia

Rock Hill Thrift Shop, Sterling, Virginia

On Route #3, your trusty guidebook steers you in a westerly direction, making stops throughout thrifty suburban Virginia. Motoring through Leesburg and Winchester and on into more rural West Virginia, make a few pit stops in towns both tiny and large. Take an optional escapade north to Morgantown for some additional bargain blowouts or head directly to the Charleston area, where you can make out like a bandit without emptying your wallet.

Route #3 Driving Time: (stops not included) 9 hours

Hit the jackpot with super vintage deals in Winchester at **Top of the Line Quality Consignment Shoppe**. Record aficionados won't want to miss two faves for used and collectible vinyl: **Solar Mountain Records** in Keyser and **High Street Antiques and Collectibles** in Morgantown, a surprise superstar. In Fairmont, drop a few coins at the **Penny Pincher** and sift through a barn full of goodies at **Monongah Auction**. Enjoy root beer floats at the **Blossom Deli and Soda Fountain Café** in Charleston. Other hot spots include **Bill's Flea Market,** the trusty **Goodwill,** and the ever-elusive **Inge's Used Furniture and Antiques**.

HERNDON, VIRGINIA

The dirt-cheap excitement of this road trip begins when you motor westward on Route 7 into suburban Virginia. Investigate Herndon for a couple of thrifty stops amid the traffic-y roads and commercial shopping plazas. First head over to the **Bargain Loft** located around the back of the Reston-Herndon Business Park Plaza at the intersection of Spring Street and Victory Drive. Rustle around in the open, airy space. Signs posted around the store will guide you to bedroom furniture, books, and some useful electronics. A steep staircase along the back wall leads you to the lofted second floor, where you can find low-price kitchen items like Tupperware, pots and pans, and dishes as well as some small appliances, several baby items, and fabric remnants. Spot higher-end nicknacks and collectibles, including plates and glasses dotting the shelves downstairs. A great many toys and piles of linens are also available, but clothing and vinyl are sadly missing. The pricing here tends to be erratic, from 25 cents into the hundreds of dollars, but you might find something like a utilitarian dresser for around $40. At holiday times the volunteer staff is busy decorating the shop, especially for Christmas, when the main floor becomes a not-to-be-missed winter wonderland.

BARGAIN LOFT
Herndon-Reston Business Park Plaza
336 Victory Drive
Herndon, Virginia
Phone: (703) 437-0600
Hours: Tues–Sat 10–2

SALVATION ARMY
2421 A6 Centerville Road
Herndon, Virginia
Phone: (703) 713-6691
Hours: Mon–Sat 10–7

Another worthwhile stop in Herndon is our old friend, the **Salvation Army**, tucked away in an enormous shopping center the size of a small village. Plunge into the never-ending racks of clothing and the wide selection of plush furniture toward the back. Scan shelves of shoes and household items for staples or the odd find. A side nook in this colossal thrift store is lined with books and some discarded records. The thrift trend hasn't entirely caught up with the price tags at this Salvation

Army, so you'll see lots of merchandise for under $10. However, the prices on the dusty furniture could use a dirt-cheap overhaul.

STERLING, VIRGINIA

Continue on Route 7 to Sterling, Virginia, for an eclectic array of thrift and consignment shops. Furniture seems to be in short supply in this town, but you'll find a bit of everything else.

A few doors down from the Hula Chinese Restaurant drop in at the **Rock Hill Thrift Shop**, a peculiar, quiet store that has a good selection of this and that. This long, skinny shop arranges its clothing in booth-like displays with prices listed above each rack. Men's, women's, and children's clothing make up the bulk of the merchandise, along with some accessories like shoes, handbags, and cheap-o jewelry. If you're on the prowl for the basics, this place is a good start. Also, check out the well-organized craft section of neatly la-beled bins for buttons, zippers, dress patterns, and appliqués. While you're at it, pick up a couple of pots and pans, a snazzy purse, or a funny patch.

ROCK HILL THRIFT SHOP
Rock Hill Shopping Plaza
46000 Old Ox Road, Suite 107
Sterling, Virginia
Phone: (703) 834-6221
Hours: Mon–Sat 10–6

GOOD SAMARITAN THRIFT SHOP
Cedar Lake Shopping Plaza
46900 Cedar Lake Plaza #140
Sterling, Virginia
Phone: Unavailable
Hours: Mon–Sat 10–8, Sun 1–6

A small weirdo shop in Sterling is the **Good Samaritan Thrift Shop**, lo-cated in the Cedar Lake Shopping Plaza just off Route 7 on Cedar Drive. There's something a bit off about Good Samaritan. It could be the piles of stuff heaped all around, the flickering fluorescent lighting, or possibly the shopping plaza location. Step into this narrow overfull store to check out the crowded racks of clothes and unsteady piles of household linens. Head to the back for a haphazard array of electronics, tapes, and household stuff. Pick up a ce-ramic mug or a television at reasonable rates. Some of the price tags are invisible, so don't look too hard.

Hop from one shopping plaza to the next along Route 7. Hit the Village Center plaza and head to **Clock Tower Thrift Shop** under, you guessed it, the clock tower. This large shop provides the essential goods with average prices anywhere from $1 to $15. Find conservative two-piece suits for men, casual dresses for women, and play clothes for the kids. The housewares section offers wineglasses, jars, souvenir plates, and napkin holders. A huge wall of books for both children and adults is organized by subject. Flip through stacks of mood music (45s are a bargain at three for $1) and snag a Jane Fonda exercise video. While waiting at the register try on some fanciful jewelry. Pack all of your thrifty finds in a handsome suitcase to take home.

Your best bets at the **Good Shepherd Thrift Store** would be to find a pair of Jordache jeans, old Samsonite luggage, or a cassette tape from one of your favorite 1980s artists. On the weekends, this huge one-floor shop is bustling with people. Beware of the dizzying effect of the spinning racks of winter coats and woolen sweaters. Pick up some hip clothes for lying around the house. The store features a remarkably vast collection of audiocassette tapes, including many one-hit wonder "cassingles." Videotapes, LPs, and 45s, are also in abundance. Scan the walls of books for romance titles and biology textbooks. You'll find Good Shepherd in the Regal Shopping Plaza under the archway with the bold red sign.

CLOCK TOWER THRIFT SHOP
Village Center on 7 Shopping Plaza
Route 7
Sterling, Virginia
Phone: (703) 406-2640
Hours: Mon–Fri 10–8, Sat 10–6,
   Sun 10–5

GOOD SHEPHERD THRIFT STORE
Regal Shopping Plaza
47100 Community Plaza, #175
20921 Davenport Drive
Sterling, Virginia
Phone: (703) 444-5956
Hours: Mon–Sat 11–6

LEESBURG, VIRGINIA

Historic Leesburg is a vibrant community buzzing with activity. The old-fashioned downtown has lots of little shops with many upscale an-

Good Shepherd Thrift Store, Sterling, Virginia

tiques venues, galleries, and tasteful restaurants. Farther out, the grass is greener in the sprawling rural sectors. In town, the atmosphere is a little preppy but not too pristine for some thrifting. Don't miss our favorite bakery, Mom's Apple Pie, for a slice of home.

Pick up some quality finds at the **Resourceful Woman Thrift Shop** on Loudoun Street, a cute, clean shop that caters to a diverse clientele. Grab some fancier housewares like glass candlesticks, platters, and decorative items for your living room. A highlight of the store is its exciting record collection. Find your favorite popular musicians for 50 cents apiece. Typical sleeves include David Bowie, Fleetwood Mac, and the Rolling Stones, along with assorted folk and classical. In the book area, self-help, religion, and fiction titles are in large supply. The clothing selection is a little bland, but for under $10 pick up a few necessities. On your way out, be sure to check the free basket of little soaps and shampoos at the register.

> **RESOURCEFUL WOMAN THRIFT SHOP**
> 11 Loudoun Street Southwest
> Leesburg, Virginia
> Phone: (703) 771-8173
> Hours: Tues–Sat 10–5

Check out the popular Tuscarora Mill at Market Station for a bevy of trendy restaurants and shops. Across the way find some down-home eats at the **Mighty Midget Kitchen**. This pint-size outdoor restaurant serves up barbecue specialties, pulled pork, sandwiches, hot dogs, and burgers (veggie, too). The tiny kitchen, an adorable mini silver-top diner, created from an airplane fuselage, is surrounded by a raised porch adorned with tiki torches and umbrella tables. From your perch enjoy "the now famous Leesburg fries," along with other oddities like 'gator meat and kielbasa. Spiff up your sandwich at the condiment cart with a gourmet selection of spreads like chutney, hot and sweet peppers, and "Famous B's BBQ Sauces." The big neon sign over the Mighty Midget Kitchen will lure you over to find out what it's all about.

MIGHTY MIDGET KITCHEN
202 Harrison Street Southeast
Leesburg, Virginia
Phone: (703) 669-1200,
   (703) 777-6406
Hours: Tues–Thurs 11–7, Fri–Sat
   11–8, Sun 12–6

MOM'S APPLE PIE
220 Loudoun Street
Leesburg, Virginia
Phone: (703) 771-8590
Hours: Mon–Fri 7:30–6:30, Sat 8–6,
   Sun 8–5

For some unbeatable desserts visit **Mom's Apple Pie**, a little bakery that sits at the fork of Loudoun and East Market streets. The sign outside advertises, "Bakery, Coffee, and Incredible Pie," and it's true! What you'll find here are delicious assorted pies, fresh-baked breads, iced cakes, enormous frosted sugar cookies, and chocolate-covered brownies. The mini pies are perfect for sampling all the wonderful flavors: strawberry rhubarb, peach, blackberry crumb, and pecan. Just like the pies, the prices are hard to resist—devour a tart for under a buck or a cookie for a dollar or two. Grab a spoon and a mini pie and be good to go. It's hard not to fall in love with the sweetness of Mom's Apple Pie.

Hop onto Route 7 Business, (aka East Market Street) for the more commercial side of Leesburg and hit up a couple of nifty shops while you're at it. For a relaxing shopping experience, stop by **Twice As Nice** in the Tollhouse Center shopping plaza. This large, clean store offers only women's clothing that is well kept and mostly conservative in style. In addition, you'll see a few racks of quality vintage clothing near the front. Try on a pretty 1950s-style frock or an outdated chiffon, puff-sleeve dress for less than $15. Look for clothing, books, and items for the home, including lamps, silverware, and assorted tabletop items with a tiny hint of country flair. The shop is operated by the Ladies' Board, which donates most of the proceeds to the Loudoun Hospital Center.

From East Market Street, turn into the lot at the Good Year Auto Center to find **Blossom and Bloom Shop**. Drive to the far end of the lot, then turn right and head down the driveway to the back basement entrance of a red brick church. Blossom and Bloom is hidden away, but persevere to find a large shop with several rooms full of secondhand odds and ends. Admire the better-quality boutique clothes on a rack near the front. Across from the dressing room, peek into a tiny room of luxurious clothing—glittery beaded shirts, sequin dresses, and elegant fur coats priced up to $25 or so. The less fancy bargains are even better in the enormous back room, which carries apparel for the whole family. Everyday clothes are generally priced at $2 to $3. Grab some good loot from the housewares area, where glasses and mugs go for only 10 cents each. Books, records, cassette tapes, and videos are also selling cheap.

TWICE IS NICE
Tollhouse Center Shopping Plaza
305 East Market Street (Route 7 Business)
Leesburg, Virginia
Phone: (703) 771-0208
Hours: Mon–Sat 10–4

BLOSSOM & BLOOM SHOP
Route 7 Business
316C East Market Street
Leesburg, Virginia
Phone: (703) 777-3286
Hours: Tues–Fri 10–4, Sat 10–1

WHITE ELEPHANT
1045 Edwards Perry Road Northeast
Leesburg, Virginia
Phone: (703) 771-2060
Hours: Mon–Sat 10–5, Sun 12–5

One more quality-but-conservative shop wraps up the secondhand tour of Leesburg. **White Elephant** is a consignment boutique that carries clean-cut clothing styles for all ages. Most of the merchandise is seasonal, and you won't find any retro duds. Oddly, the store has a long list of items that it won't accept, like ski wear (but we love ski wear!), so you'll find a pretty sanitized selection here. Ladies can find some pretty earrings, while kiddies can have their pick from the large toy selection. Score some practically new wicker chairs or make off with a full set of drinking glasses.

PURCELLVILLE, VIRGINIA

The locals, we are told, pronounce the name of this town "Pursey-ville," as opposed to the foreigners (presumably you), who might be so silly as to say "Pur-sell-ville"—good to know if you don't want back talk from the locals. When in Purcellville, do as the Purcellvillians do.

Purcellvillians do their thrift shopping at the **Salvation Army**, located down the center alleyway of a strip mall on Main Street, across from the New Beginning Youth Center. The medium-size store is long and skinny, but it carries its share of kitchen chairs, bud vases, and old coffee mugs. In fact, this store has more furniture, toys, housewares, and accessories than clothing, which is unusual for a Salvation Army store. Prices are generally good, so delve into the happy jumble of wares to find potential treasures.

SALVATION ARMY
725 East Main Street (Route 7 Business)
Purcellville, Virginia
Phone: (540) 338-7993
Hours: Mon–Sat 10–5

Pay attention to the half-price deals that are posted, or you might miss out at the register.

If fancier antiques are more your style, swing by 21st Street in Purcellville's town center, where you'll come across a row of more upscale antique shops. A number of attractive spots offer up well-made furniture, collectible figurines, and little bits of nostalgia. Though these shops are out of the dirt-cheap price range, 21st Street is quite bewitching and makes for a ideal afternoon outing of window-shopping.

BERRYVILLE, VIRGINIA

Move on to the pleasant business district of Berryville, a laid-back town with an old-fashioned sensibility. Main Street (Route 7 Business) is busy with foot traffic and lined with many cute shops. Drop in at the **Once Again Shop** for some high-quality women's consignments. Many of the styles they carry are professional and fashionable, though maybe not very fun for hipster types. The store front windows, lined with pretty flower boxes, display feminine casual and business coordinates. Inside find an array of shoes, jewelry, and accessories such as handbags, hats, and scarves. The shop is right across the street from Daily Grind Coffee and the Berryville Newsstand.

Bon Matin Bakery down the street is a must stop for a leisurely breakfast or a tantalizing afternoon pastry. Treat your sweet tooth to a variety of delicious layered cakes, eclairs, luscious fruit tarts, strawberry shortcake, and mousses in heavenly flavors. On Sundays, stop in for a French-inspired brunch menu of crepes, omelettes, French toast, and veggie quiches. The menu also lists soups, salads, and hearty sandwiches. Pick up a loaf of freshly baked bread and perk up with a cappuccino for the road.

Another worthwhile stop is the **Berryville Old Book Shop**. This cozy little store is crowded with tall bookcases of used reading material, most of it in excellent condition. Choose from numerous nonfiction titles, many priced for just a few dollars. From history, to children's tales, to classics and recent fiction, both grown-ups and kids can find some-

---

ONCE AGAIN SHOP
10 West Main Street (Route 7 Business)
Berryville, Virginia
Phone: (540) 955-3925
Hours: Mon–Tues 10–5, Fri 10–5, Sat 10–4

BON MATIN BAKERY
1 East Main Street (Route 7 Business)
Berryville, Virginia
Phone: (540) 955-1544
Hours: Tues–Fri 8–3, Sat–Sun 9–2

BERRYVILLE OLD BOOK SHOP
17 Main Street (Route 7 Business)
Berryville, Virginia
Phone: (540) 955-7070
Hours: Thurs–Sat 12–5

thing here. The bookshop also has a children's reading room in the back to keep the kiddies occupied. Relax in the comfortable atmosphere while you peruse the shelves, stocked from floor to ceiling with enjoyable reading.

WINCHESTER, VIRGINIA

The thrift fairy seems to have made a special stopover in Winchester, Virginia. Don't pass up the unexpected good deals at the secondhand shops in this town. At the **Goodwill** on Millwood Avenue, weed through color-coordinated racks of garments for an abundance of skirts, hoodies, blouses, and swimsuits, with most items tagged at $5 or under. Pick up a one-of-a-kind lime green leisure suit, which you can try on in the privacy of the dressing room. Ladies can choose from an assortment of fancy ball gowns and footwear. The housewares shelves are crammed with lots of mugs and kitchenware as well as cheap and interesting objects, most priced under $4. Near the front, find offbeat paintings (poodle portrait on black velvet, $5) and a variety of videotapes. Pick out a trashy paperback romance or a dog-eared copy of *Sweet Valley High* from the shelves along the wall.

> **GOODWILL**
> 443 Millwood Avenue
> Winchester, Virginia
> Phone: (540) 723-6864
> Hours: Mon–Sat 9–9, Sun 12–5
>
> **TOP OF THE LINE QUALITY CONSIGNMENT SHOPPE**
> 2021 South Loudoun Street
> Winchester, Virginia
> Phone: (540) 535-0080
> Hours: Mon 10–5, Tues–Fri 10–6, Sat 10–5

If vintage clothes are your weakness, don't skip the super-fantastic **Top of the Line Quality Consignment Shoppe**, tucked away in a small shopping plaza. Though not gigantic, this women's wear boutique sells quantities of fabulous retro duds in the front half of the store. The collection graduates to more contemporary day and business wear toward the back. As you tour the shop, witness a stunning parade of incredible gowns, shirts, quilted jackets, and silky robes. Acquire a tweedy wool suit or try on glamorous and sparkly evening wear, psychedelic patterned casuals, beaded cardigans, and funky patent leather dress-up shoes. The collection of handbags runs the full spectrum, from hippie suede to a beaded evening clutch. Choose from many sophisticated styles from the 1940s through the 1960s. At the counter, the glass cases are a treasure trove of colorful rhinestone pins, earrings, and bangles. Don't forget about the up-to-date styles in the back, which are also worth a peek. The price tags are appropriate to the quality of the merchandise—though many items are not dirt cheap, you can find some excellent deals in the $10 to $20 range. The goods here are worth every penny.

On Weems Street, explore the clean and spacious **Salvation Army**. With the number of possibilities available in this roomy thrift outlet, finding a good score requires a bit of patience. Test out fluffy padded couches in the furniture section and take home a plaid upholstered easy chair or velour loveseat. The shelves hold stacks of colorful dishes, lamps, and kitchen appliances. The clothing inventory includes options for men, women, and children, and most of the prices are under $5. Men's suits and formal clothing are the exception, starting at $10, though there are some worthwhile discoveries. Circle the round multitier shoe rack for a newish pair of kickers.

SALVATION ARMY
404 Weems Lane
Winchester, Virginia
Phone: (540) 722-2749
Hours: Mon–Sat 9–6

PAST & PRESENT
725 Loudoun Street
Winchester, Virginia
Phone: (540) 722-4800
Hours: Mon 10–7, Tues–Thurs
10–5, Fri 10–7, Sat–Sun 10–6

Round out your Winchester expedition with a couple of indoor flea markets. Look in on **Past & Present**, a huge multiroom antiques mall carrying a hodgepodge of collectibles, furniture, and the oddball new item. There's a whirlwind of price ranges at this place, but many of the most fascinating things are reasonably priced between $10 and $20. Find just about anything here, from bird motif drinking glasses, to a set of retro ashtrays, to collectible dolls and strange statuettes. Get yourself

Past & Present, Winchester, Virginia

an armload of 45s for a quarter each, some elegant jewelry, serving trays, or a ceramic planter. The layout of the store has a twinkling magic about it, or maybe that's just the allure of exploring this windfall of beautifully displayed curiosities.

Last but not least, drop by the enormous **Valley Avenue Flea Market and Consignment** shop, where sparkling glassware and china lines the shelves of the large, rounded store front windows. Furniture and assorted odds and ends on the lawn outside will beckon you in from the road, making this stop difficult to pass up. Browse through several rooms on the main floor for a plethora of dish sets; glassware in all shapes, sizes, and colors; quirky figurines; and other small curios. Discover a couple of vintage clothing racks, a shoe display, and a pile of blue jeans. Head upstairs to inspect long rows of wooden chairs

> **VALLEY AVENUE FLEA MARKET AND CONSIGNMENT**
> 1000 Valley Avenue
> Winchester, Virginia
> Phone: (540) 772-6768
> Hours: Mon–Sat 10–6, Sun 10–5

and other secondhand furniture. Just remember to remain calm in the face of clutter.

CAPON BRIDGE, WEST VIRGINIA

Leaving Winchester, hop onto Route 50. After a half-hour drive, crossing into West Virginia, make a quick stop in the little country town of Capon Bridge and poke around **Red Rooster Antiques**. Be prepared to pull over in a flash after the bridge as you enter the town. This little two-room shop carries a mishmash of discarded treasures and random yard sale-type items. Stumble upon old bottles, vintage ladies' hats, pretty bowls, dolls, old vinyl, and household accessories. At Red Rooster you might find a metal mold of a sheep to cast your next masterpiece, a porcelain dog statuette, or some country western music, all scattered willy-nilly around the store. The random assortment includes a number of items for under $10.

RED ROOSTER ANTIQUES
Route 50
Capon Bridge, West Virginia
Phone: (304) 856-3261
Hours: Thurs–Sun 10–4,
   Sat 10–2:30

INDOOR YARD SALE
Route 50
Burlington, West Virginia
Phone: (304) 788-2197
Hours: Tues–Sat 12–5ish
   (or whenever they feel like it)

BURLINGTON, WEST VIRGINIA

Farther west along Route 50, try your luck at **Indoor Yard Sale** in Burlington, a shop that lives up to its name. From the road you'll be pulled magnetically toward the vinyl-covered chairs, old toys, suitcases, or vacuum cleaners that are strewn across the yard. Three rooms of someone else's junk are full of kitchen appliances, headless dolls, videotapes, worn handbags, clothing, and mismatched dishware. Look for old Atari video games, an electronic keyboard, or a Rainbow Brite doll. You really can never tell what you're going to find at the Indoor Yard

Sale, but you can bet that it'll be cheap. Pick up a 75-cent slogan mug, a $1 leather change purse, or a $3 movie on VHS. Look over the variety of alarm clocks and table lamps and sift through a bowl of cheesy plastic earrings from the 1980s. The bargains are overflowing here, with prices ranging from 50 cents to $5 at most. This quirky and quiet shop is a little on the dingy side, so pick through clothing, linens, and curtains at your own risk.

KEYSER, WEST VIRGINIA

In the small quiet city of Keyser, thrifters can score on used books, records, and clothes at three area shops. Vinyl enthusiasts will love **Solar Mountain Records** for kitsch collectible albums, rock, blues, reggae, and much, much more. Scan the flashy vintage cover art that lines the shop walls for a taste of what you'll find flipping through the bins. Music is well organized by genre and artist. Hunt to find everything from classic rock to children's albums. If you have trouble finding anything, don't be afraid to ask Bart, the knowledgeable owner, who will be happy to point you toward hidden crates underneath the tables or offer some good recommendations. The store also carries a wide selection of 45s, some cassette tapes, and rows of CDs, including modern and indie rock. Spend up to $10 or so on most of these hot commodities, with many albums in the 50-cent to $2 range.

SOLAR MOUNTAIN RECORDS
21 Armstrong Street
Keyser, West Virginia
Phone: (304) 788-1055
Hours: Tues–Thurs 11–7,
  Fri–Sat 10-5

KINSMAN BOOK-A-RAMA
121 North Main Street
Keyser, West Virginia
Phone: (304) 788-5550
Hours: Mon–Fri 10–4

If you're looking for some summer reading, cheap in both plot and price, drop in at **Kinsman Book-A-Rama,** a cute little used book shop on North Main Street. Raid the book collection, mostly paperbacks with a few hardcovers, for adult fiction and nonfiction and some nostalgic young adult material. Don't miss the rack of grade school reading near the door, including Beverly Cleary favorites and other preteen heartthrob novelties. Scan the selection for trashy romance novels, star biographies, and just a few classic epics, which are yours for the taking at $1 or $2 apiece. While you're at it, pick up a holiday or religious greeting card as well.

Round out your secondhand experience in Keyser at the **Goodwill** on Route 220. This large store offers a good selection of slightly conservative clothing styles for men, women, and children. Find some used toys, bowls, mugs, and nicknacks, plus a few small appliances to boot. Check out the shoe rack for some still-fashionable sneakers or score a pretty slip for around $3. Other prices here are a tad-bit higher than you might expect.

> **GOODWILL**
> Route 220 South
> Keyser, West Virginia
> Phone: (304) 788-2068
> Hours: Mon–Sat 9–9, Sun 12–5

While this isn't our favorite Goodwill, you should keep your eyes peeled for the random score, like a retro orange television, displayed on top of the clothing racks.

CLARKSBURG, WEST VIRGINIA

After thrifting to your heart's content in Keyser, there's a lengthy two- to three-hour drive along Route 50 to Clarksburg, West Virginia, with very little to stop and see along the way. Once you've arrived, you'll find a number of good thrifting stops to investigate. We've also laid out an optional side trip, heading north along Interstate 79 with stops in Fairmont and Morgantown, which are both less than forty-five minutes from Clarksburg. We highly recommend both towns for dirt-cheap goodies and fun. Thrift listings for the Fairmont and Morgantown side trip will appear in the text after Clarksburg. If you're (foolishly) planning to skip these, proceed to page 106 for towns west of Clarksburg along Route 50.

Clarksburg, West Virginia, is not a typical tourist destination. You may only live three states away, but people will know right away that "y'aren't from around here." Just click your heels three times and repeat: "There's no place like a thrift store."

Minutes outside of Clarksburg proper along Route 50, stop off in Bridgeport for the **Goodwill**. This super-size branch carries clothes for everyone at $2 to $10. Plenty of vintage clothing is sprinkled throughout the racks, especially polyester and double knits from the 1960s and '70s. Fortunately, there are dressing rooms equipped with mirrors to try everything on. For music enthusiasts, this store's small selection may not satisfy, but good alternative purchases include quality used furniture or sporting equipment. Check out the variety of bedroom furniture styles and find a low-rider banana seat bicycle for cheap. We love Goodwill for its dependability and convenient hours.

GOODWILL
1172 West Main Street (Route 50)
Bridgeport, West Virginia
Phone: (304) 842-3288
Hours: Mon–Sat 9–9, Sun 11–5

HUMANE SOCIETY THRIFT SHOP
220 Milford Street
Clarksburg, West Virginia
Phone: (304) 624-5040
Hours: Mon–Fri 11–4

COMING AGAIN
Rosebud Shopping Plaza
509 Rosebud Plaza
Clarksburg, West Virginia
Phone: (304) 622-5655
Hours: Tues–Sat 9–5

On Milford Street in Clarksburg, visit the **Humane Society Thrift Shop** for a bonanza of $1 scores. This crowded little shop is lined with clothing racks, with boxes of shirts and sweaters found underneath. You can find $1 garments at every turn, from polyester prints to suit jackets and trousers. Shoes appear on a large rack in the center of the store. Options are available for the whole family. Find beaded necklaces, bangles, and oddball accessories, too. A "miscellaneous" table is spread with random fare, like an orange ceramic ashtray for the coffee table or a novel cassette tape from 1979. The cheery ladies at the Humane Society Thrift Shop will welcome you warmly in this homey dirt-cheap boutique.

The **Coming Again** thrift store, located in the Rosebud Shopping Plaza next to Family Dollar, is a nice surprise in Clarksburg. For donations, Coming Again will accept any merchandise that it doesn't have to feed, so the selection is a variety of sensible goods and interesting relics. Proceeds go to the needy of the local community. On the racks, women's wear makes up the bulk of the clothing options, but you'll see apparel for men and children, too. In the summer months, bathing suits are well stocked, as are casual separates to outfit you from head to toe. A slew of household items are also available, including linens and dishware. The book area is small but worth a once-over for cheap-o finds. Although the store is impressive in size, it's sometimes low on furniture and retro gear (with some exceptions from the 1980s). Prices at Coming Again are certainly nothing to complain about, with $2 to $15 tags for most items.

TUNA & ROSEMARY'S HOUSE OF STYLE
341 Monticello Avenue
Clarksburg, Virginia
Phone: (304) 622-3424
Hours: Mon–Fri 11–6, Sat 12–4

GOODWILL
Middletown Mall
2500 Fairmont Avenue
Fairmont, West Virginia
Phone: (304) 363-3155
Hours: Mon–Sat 9–9, Sun 11–5

On Monticello Avenue, **Tuna & Rosemary's House of Style** offers a little of this and a little of that. Teeny curios on shelves line the display window. Inside, find an eclectic assortment of quirky furniture and brightly colored glassware, plus clothing, jewelry, and a few small appliances. Squeeze through this crowded shop. Spend just a few dollars to get yourself some stylish trinkets and accessories.

Before leaving Clarksburg, you might want to swing by the bevy of antique shops on West Pike Street. Pick up some quality furniture and "use-for-parts" items here.

FAIRMONT, WEST VIRGINIA

If you decide to take the side trip north to Fairmont and Morgantown, jet up Interstate 79. The town of Fairmont has a few good thrifting stops to offer. In the Middletown Mall, located just off Route 250, check out the roomy department store-style **Goodwill**. This Goodwill has lots to offer in the way of clothing. The first of two giant rooms is crammed full of apparel and shoes for men, women, and children. The goods are going cheap, with most garments tagged for less than $5. You'll also find an impressive stash of well-kept vintage clothing from the 1950s and '60s, along with a few costume pieces (like a handmade Victorian-style jacket), tagged at $2 to $10. There are mirrors all over the store, providing lots of space to try on these stylish ensembles. In the second room are aisles of household goods such as furniture, straw baskets, and decorative pieces. Heaps of striped sheets, flowery curtains, and other linens are offered at super prices, with lots of patterns and styles from the 1970s. Detergent, gardening gloves, and other new goods may also be found here at a discount.

The Penny Pincher Thrift Store is another large shop, although not as densely packed as other area thrifts. Though a little dusty and dingy, Penny Pincher is still worth a quick stop. Don't bother with the grimy, overpriced furniture at the entrance—better deals are to be had in the back. Almost all clothing items are marked at $1.50 or less, with the exception of ball gowns and men's suits, which cost around $10 to $15. A motley selection of miscellaneous plastic housewares, books and old magazines are also cheaply priced. Nothin' fancy here, but take a whirl around the shop to see what you can find.

> **THE PENNY PINCHER THRIFT STORE**
> 113 Fairmont Avenue
> Fairmont, West Virginia
> Phone: (304) 363-6045
> Hours: Mon–Fri 9–4, Sat 9–1
>
> **BEANS & BOOKS COFFEE SHOP**
> 211 Fairmont Avenue
> Fairmont, West Virginia
> Phone: (304) 366-7090
> Hours: Mon–Sat 7am–10pm

Take a break from all that penny pinching at **Beans & Books Coffee Shop** just up the road. The café occupies the ground floor of an old house. On warm afternoons, grab a seat at one of the tables in the front yard and enjoy an iced cappuccino or flavored chai outdoors. Snacks inside include muffins, biscotti, and jars of yummy cookies. Full bookcases line the café, and plenty of newspapers, magazines, and other reading material are scattered around. Beans & Books is open late and frequently hosts live music and open mic nights. Give props to the young owner, who lives upstairs, for opening this loveable pit stop.

From Fairmont, take Route 19 South for a ten- or fifteen-minute drive. **Monongah Auction** is an exceptional treasure trove that is not to be missed. The large barn-style building is jammed with antiques and curios filling every corner. Monongah Auction stocks a mishmash of vintage dishes, crockery, planters, and fig-urines, mainly artifacts from the 1920s to the 1960s. Snag colorful Pyrex, Bakelite, or porcelain rarities. Many collectible items crowd the tables and floors. Find large and small items of furniture in varying condition—some shopworn fixer-uppers and other pieces in beautiful shape. Hunt along the shelves for collectible glasses, rummage through a bowl of buttons, and add some charming finds to your salt and pepper shaker collection. Prices are reasonable, with many individual items marked at $3 to $10. There's only a small amount of costume jewelry and not much apparel, but the eclectic mix of mer-chandise is sure to please.

MONONGAH AUCTION
U.S. Route 19
Monongah, West Virginia
Phone: (304) 534-5416
Hours: Tues–Sat 10–6, Sun 12–5

GOODWILL
Mountaineer Mall
5000 Greenbag Road
Morgantown, West Virginia
Phone: (304) 296-7900
Hours: Mon–Sat 9–9, Sun 11–5

MORGANTOWN, WEST VIRGINIA

There's more secondhand shopping and eating ahead in Morgantown, West Virginia. This lively college town has a calming, picturesque at-mosphere and plenty of secondhand stores to suit your fancy. Think his-toric, collegiate, and hilly, think hippie chicks and football jocks.

Begin your Morgantown adventure at the **Goodwill,** located next to the Wal-Mart in the Mountaineer Mall. This Goodwill is massive and clean, full of an endless sea of clothing racks, a wall of books, and an enormous shoe collection. Music collectors will find some cassette tapes but, sadly, no vinyl. Keep your eyes peeled for storewide half-price deals, although the prices are really good all the time, with plenty of under-$10 finds. This Goodwill could keep you busy hunting for hours, so get out some comfortable shoes or pick up a new-to-you pair! If you're in the market for some brand-new household goods, get some rugs, pillows, and Windex at below-average cost.

Make your way to the hipper part of town, where you'll find tons of goodies at **High Street Antiques and Collectibles**. Don't be fooled by the pricey-looking window displays, as there are plenty of affordable finds inside. Tour the shop's inventory of glassware, dollhouse furniture, rhinestone finery, vintage clothing, and a few pieces of antique furniture. Near the front, a case full of striking vintage pins are dirt cheap at $3 apiece. The clothing selection is minimal, but impressive, especially for vintage ladies' hats and shoes. Get lucky with a pair of two-tone purple patent leather shoes for under $10. A book closet contains a few shelves holding collectible titles, very old yearbooks, and some fiction. Pick up a book on proper etiquette for just a few dollars.

Besides all of these gems of yesteryear, one of the best reasons to shop at High Street Antiques and Collectibles is its amazing vinyl collection! At the back of the shop, a music area offers many organized stacks of records. But the real surprise is the secret basement trove of thousands of LPs and 45s, in almost every genre imaginable. Ask the staff to show you downstairs, where you'll stumble across scads of old rarities and quirky picks. Any serious record collector will want to spend some quality time with the almost overwhelming selection. This two-year-old store is fast becoming a local favorite.

At the bottom of the hill along University Avenue you'll find a great pit stop at **Mountain People's Kitchen**. This low-key natural foods restau-

---

HIGH STREET ANTIQUES AND COLLECTIBLES
206 High Street
Morgantown, West Virginia
Phone: (304) 292-6180
Hours: Tues–Sat 10–6

MOUNTAIN PEOPLE'S KITCHEN
1400 University Avenue
Morgantown, West Virginia
Phone: (304) 291-6131
Hours: Mon–Tues 8–6, Wed–Thurs 8–8, Fri 8–6, Sun 10–2

rant is just what the doctor ordered for vegetarians and vegans and other hungry travelers. The menu offers many tasty salads and sandwiches for lunch, including interesting tofu and tempeh dishes. For breakfast try the fluffy multigrain pancakes or a tofu scrambler. Mountain People's Kitchen is also open for an early dinner six days a week. The restaurant is cute, the staff is friendly, and the coffee will get you going in no time. As a nice addition, next door is a cooperative natural foods grocery where you can pick up bulk items, fresh produce, and snacks. If you forgot your Tom's of Maine toothpaste or Burt's Bees lip balm, this is your chance to restock.

For a mix of antiques and junk visit **University Estate Outlet.** The shop's merchandise is divided into two areas. The main room houses mostly antique furniture like old wooden dressers, nightstands, kitchen tables, and reading lamps, with many pieces dating from the 1940s through the 1970s. The furniture can be a bit steep in price, but there are plenty of budget items in the other half of the store. The dustier, garage sale-style room has shelves of nicknacks and housewares and a few records or old dolls. It's the kind of place to find that forgotten hamburger-shaped catsup dispenser, a Hank Williams album, or a tiny flocked figurine. Most of the good deals here come in small packages.

UNIVERSITY ESTATE OUTLET
1216 University Avenue
Morgantown, West Virginia
Phone: (304) 290-4873
Hours: Tues–Sat 10–4

SALVATION ARMY
1264 University Avenue
Morgantown, West Virginia
Phone: (304) 296-3525
Hours: Mon–Sat 9–5

Stock up on oddities at the **Salvation Army** on University Avenue. This large open store has a good selection of bric-a-brac, with cute salt 'n' pepper shakers, mugs, and colorful plates in the mix. Snag a hilarious 1970s mushroom wall clock. Clothes are in abundance, but in our opinion the selection is less than fantastic, with a few exceptions. Most apparel is reasonably priced at $2 to $8. In the back, look for furniture, books, and records. This Salvation Army merits frequent visits to sift through its rotating stock.

The final stop in Morgantown is a little off the beaten path. From Route 19/7, slightly north of the town center, look for the small sign pointing toward **BEF Collectibles Riverfront Antique and Flea Market**. The little shop is clean and chock-full of goodies. Check out the overwhelming array of rare and collectible glassware, in varying shapes and colors, from fancy glass sets to pitchers, vases, and bowls. Discover old dolls and toys, fancy planters, and collectible ceramic dishware. The store also carries a small selection of vintage ladies' clothing from the Victorian era to the 1950s as well as scarves and fashionable accoutrements. You might find an antique vanity set complete with mirror, brush, and powder jars or a vintage beaded makeup bag for under $20. If you stop by, be sure to say hello to Ziggy, the lovable dog, who may be caught roaming about the shop.

> **BEF COLLECTIBLES RIVERFRONT ANTIQUE AND FLEA MARKET**
> 3529 University Avenue
> Morgantown, West Virginia
> Phone: (304) 599-4301
> Hours: Mon–Sun 9–5
>
> **BARGAIN CELLAR**
> 207 West Myles Avenue
> Pennsboro, West Virginia
> Phone: (304) 659-2237
> Hours: Mon–Fri 9–4, and 1st Sat of the month 9–1

PENNSBORO, WEST VIRGINIA

Pennsboro is a tiny sleepy town just north of Route 50. On the main drag of West Myles Street, you'll find the **Bargain Cellar** thrift shop next door to the Union gas station. The inside of this old brick building is a little grimy, but there is plenty of room to stretch your legs and investigate. The store's super-cheap prices and offbeat selection overshadow its dusty nature. Dresses are only $2, and a bin of folded tops goes for 75 cents each. Some vintage clothing is hidden among the piles and racks. Get lucky with a kitschy 1980s T-shirt or a 1970s appliqué dress. A bathroom equipped with a long mirror is available for trying things on. Dig through messy heaps of lingerie and linens or scan the shelves for dishes and bric-a-brac. For heftier items, check out the home furnishings and appliances to nab an upholstered couch or a kitchen stove. We loved the Bargain Cellar for its thrift appeal and old-school vibe.

ELLENBORO, WEST VIRGINIA

Another slight detour off the highway is Ellenboro. Along Route 16, look out for the "Thrift Store" sign at the roadside. **Community Resources Inc. Thrift Store** is located inside the large white building at the top of the steep hill. One small room carries clothing for the whole family, reasonably priced at around $2. You'll find just the basics, with a good selection of denim. Another room is devoted to housewares and accessories. Pick up a lonely egg cup or a pair of sunglasses for 50 cents. When you're ready to purchase your items, ring the bell at the register for assistance. The little shop is quiet, so don't be surprised if you're the only customer there.

COMMUNITY RESOURCES INC. THRIFT STORE
Route 16
Ellenboro, West Virginia
Phone: (304) 869-3871
Hours: Mon–Fri 8–4

BARGAIN CORNER
3425 Murdoch Avenue
Parkersburg, West Virginia
Phone: (304) 422-3476
Hours: Mon–Sat 10–8, Sun 12–6

PARKERSBURG, WEST VIRGINIA

From Ellenboro, hop back onto Route 50 for a short drive into Parkersburg, a fair-size city that offers plenty of dirt-cheap shopping adventures and a couple of pit stops to boot. The tour begins around the outskirts of town.

The **Bargain Corner** in Parkersburg is a curious place with a lot of local character. Cruise the aisles for new, used, and reconditioned items. The store carries a hodgepodge of goods like computer monitors, stereo components, and furniture as well as videotapes, dishware, and fashion accessories. Pick up a gently used handbag or mug or a discontinued pair of barrettes, still new in the package. Most of the used furniture is nicely priced at $50 or less, and small items are very cheap, from 50 cents to $3. The Bargain Corner may need a good housecleaning, but that's part of its charm.

If you missed out on clothes at the Bargain Corner, try your luck at **Noah's Arc Thrift Shop**, just a hop, skip, and a jump away. This cute, medium-size shop is well organized with areas for shoes, men's, women's, and children's clothing and nicknacks. There's nothing too fancy about Noah's Arc, but it's a good place to pick up a casual ensemble or maybe an odd-shaped candle. So dig through your wallet for spare change and scrounge up $2 or $3 for some secondhand sweaters or vests.

NOAH'S ARC THRIFT SHOP
628 West Virginia Avenue
Parkersburg, West Virginia
Phone: (304) 422-2591
Hours: Mon–Sat 10–6

WINDMILL RESTAURANT
801 Ann Street
Parkersburg, West Virginia
Phone: (304) 442-2900
Hours: Mon–Thurs 10:30–7,
Fri 10:30–8

7TH STREET SECOND HAND STORE
823 7th Street
Parkersburg, West Virginia
Phone: (304) 442-8755
Hours: Mon–Wed 9–3, Fri 9–3,
Thurs 9–11am

Hungry yet? Drop by the unique-looking **Windmill Restaurant** located on Ann Street. The building, with a miniature windmill perched on top, is easily spotted at the big curve in the road, where 8th Avenue and Ann Street intersect. The interior décor of the restaurant isn't as exciting, but the menu does offer up some classic roadside American food. For dinner or lunch choose from sandwich, salad, and burger combinations, plus an assortment of pies and other treats for dessert. With all of the thrift stores ahead in Parkersburg, it's a good thing that a meal at Windmill Restaurant only costs around $5.

Serious antique furniture collectors should visit the **7th Street Second Hand Store**. The shop is big and long, with stacks of home furnishings creating aisles full of incredible dressers, nightstands, and chairs from the 1930s to the 1970s. To take anything home, you're going to have to fork over some cash, as furniture prices start at around $80. If your budget won't allow a spending spree, the shop also offers some smaller, less expensive items. Search for collectible dolls and Barbies, glassware, and a great selection of old 45s. Records go for $2 apiece, a little more than thrift store prices, but worth the extra dollar.

On 5th Street, look for the "Sats on Fifth" sign, code name for the local **Salvation Army** thrift store. This branch is a bit cheaper than some of its sister stores. Most clothing is under $3, except for fancy disco dresses that can cost up to $15. Shoes are only $1.50, and records are 50 cents each. The store is spacious but not particularly clean. Still, find plenty of good stuff here. For furniture, check out couches, chairs, and lamps. Pots and pans and dishware can also be found for cheap. Make a getaway with an electric organ, a gospel LP, or a pair of snow boots. At the register, ring the bell for the salesclerk if no one's in sight.

> **SALVATION ARMY: SATS ON FIFTH**
> 570 5th Street
> Parkersburg, West Virginia
> Phone: (304) 485-3654
> Hours: Mon–Sat 9–5
>
> **TOO SMALL SHOP**
> 2100 Camden Avenue
> Parkersburg, West Virginia
> Phone: (304) 485-1500
> Hours: Mon–Thurs 10–5, Fri 10–7,
>   Sat 10–4
>
> **BLENNERHASSETT HOTEL**
> Fourth and Market Street
> Parkersburg, West Virginia
> Phone: (304) 422-3131

Next, try the **Too Small Shop**, a consignment store for women and children. This little boutique, situated in the shopping strip next to a nail salon, carries mostly clothing, but also has a few areas for costume jewelry, toys, and decorations. Seek out T-shirts, name-brand jeans, seasonal dresses, and slacks in up-to-date styles. Pricing is a little erratic, but clothing items are generally between $3 and $15. The Too Small Shop is a great place to find stickers and inexpensive gifts, especially for the kiddies.

While in town, check out the historic **Blennerhassett Hotel**, located in downtown Parkersburg. This elegant, and reportedly haunted, hotel has recently been revamped to its original 1930s splendor. Rooms are offered in luxurious suites, some with two floors! If money is no concern, splurge on this cushy, five-star accommodation. If you're dirt cheap, just drop in for an evening cocktail in the swanky first-floor lounge, furnished with opulent deco leather chairs and curtain-draped walls.

CHARLESTON, WEST VIRGINIA

From Parkersburg, motor down Interstate 77 south toward Charleston, West Virginia, where you can drop in on a few thrift stores, consignment boutiques, junk shops, and a soda fountain. As a bonus, we've also included listings for the nearby towns of Nitro and Saint Albans as part of the Charleston area, where you can expect to pick up even more oddities at indoor antiques malls and other quirky spots.

For a city this size, Charleston doesn't have many attractions. We're told that it's a good place to raise your kids. There are a couple of museums, a mall, and a cute downtown area, but, of course, our main reason to visit Charleston is its wide selection of secondhand shops.

First, head to downtown's shopping district and stop by the **Consignment Company**. Look for the colored sale tags and seasonal specials at this boutique for women and girls. Find contemporary styles of good-condition clothing in this spanking clean environment. Scan the racks of tennis wear, blouses, two-piece ensembles, and slacks. Shoes, belts, and cases of jewelry appear at the front as well as a great collection of silk scarves in polka-dot, floral, and psychedelic patterns. Get yourself some fanciful undergarments like a ruffled lavender slip. Vintage clothing and retro styles aren't so popular here.

Just a few doors down on Quarrier Street, flash back fifty years at the **Blossom Deli & Soda Fountain Café.** This restaurant very well may

CONSIGNMENT COMPANY
926 Quarrier Street
Charleston, West Virginia
Phone: (304) 343-0551
Hours: Tues–Fri 10–5, Sat 11–3

BLOSSOM DELI AND SODA FOUNTAIN CAFÉ
904 Quarrier Street
Charleston, West Virginia
Phone: (304) 345-2233
Hours: Mon 8–3, Tues–Thurs 8am–9pm, Fri 8am–10-pm, Sat 10–10

be the best example of a 1950s soda fountain ever! The place beams with chrome and mirrors, accented with bright red-and-blue vinyl seats. It's especially fun to sit at the extremely long counter and order a tall ice cream soda. The root beer floats are out of this world!

You can order ice cream for breakfast, lunch, and dinner. Or try the Blossom Reuben, Crabcake Delight, or Chicken and Artichoke Salad. Vanilla, chocolate, and strawberry are the only ice cream flavors available, but the staff can serve you up sundaes, cones, shakes, sodas, and floats any way you like them. Get the royal treatment with a decadent hot fudge cake à la mode.

Find some nifty threads for only $5 at the **Salvation Army** on Wyoming Street, a marvelous place to pick up some new-to-you clothing. Suits and coats are marked at around $8, and furniture prices start at $15. The record selection isn't huge, but you're sure to find some classical LPs or Ferrante & Teicher mood music. The book and toy areas are more sizable. We didn't see much astounding furniture, but you might be able to pick up a sturdy dresser or desk for your den. This mildly chaotic shop is home to many quirky, hidden prizes.

SALVATION ARMY
207 Wyoming Street
Charleston, West Virginia
Phone: (304) 344-5531
Hours: Mon–Wed, Fri 9:30–5:50,
Thurs 9:30–7:50, Sat 10–4:50

GOODWILL
209 Virginia Street West
Charleston, West Virginia
Phone: (304) 346-0811
Hours: Mon–Sat 9–6, Sun 12–5

If you're looking for an even bigger spread, visit the enormous **Goodwill** on Virginia Street. For furniture and clothing, this place has it all. Choose from many unique dresses from the 1950s and blouses from the 1980s. Clothing is organized on racks by garment type and color, with prices marked at $2 to $8. There is plenty of glittery evening and prom wear to try on and enough fitting rooms so that you won't have to wait in line. Furniture here is incredible for a thrift store, but can be very pricey at $200 and up. Exquisite antique wood pieces are creatively displayed. Take home a beautiful carved wood bedroom set from the 1930s. Useful household items can be found here as well, and don't leave before exploring the sizable book area.

Pay a visit to **Bill's Flea Market**, an itty-bitty junk shop on Washington Street. The store is just one small room, a little dank and musty, the way a junk shop should be. Among the piles and shelves, find a random stash of videos, records, dishes, romance novels, stuffed animals, and bike tires. Dig deep to find hilarious decals from the 1970s or some useful handyman tools. If the shopkeeper isn't around for pricing, you may have to dig deep for him as well.

The very last stop in Charleston is **Inge's Used Furniture & Antiques**. When we visited, the store had only been open for a few weeks, but it was already stocked full of fascinating things, nonetheless. Squeeze into the small and crowded shop, where you'll find furniture, including beds, couches, chairs, and more. In the back room, search through a mishmash of clothing items, decorative bottles, figurines, and a few dishes. Grab some table linens, a chiffon scarf, or a crafty wall hanging. Furniture prices are erratic, from $25 to $250, but smaller items are very reasonable at $10 or less. Store hours are hard to pin down, but drop by if you're in town. Inge stocks some great things in her little shop.

> **BILL'S FLEA MARKET**
> 1457 West Washington Street
> Charleston, West Virginia
> Phone: (304) 344-4337
> Hours: Mon–Sat 1–6
>
> **INGE'S USED FURNITURE AND ANTIQUES**
> 1213 West Washington Street
> Charleston, West Virginia
> Phone: Unavailable
> Hours: By chance
>
> **NITRO ANTIQUE MALL**
> 110 21st Street
> Nitro, West Virginia
> Phone: (304) 755-5002
> Hours: Mon–Sat 10–6, Sun 11–5

NITRO, WEST VIRGINIA

A few indoor antiques malls in Nitro are worthy of a visit as you wind up your trip. Both of these stores are located on a small main street devoted to antique-y type shops. **Nitro Antique Mall** is the smaller of the two. Stately looking furniture is displayed in the front window, and inside you'll find several rooms of dealer booths. Collectible figurines, dolls, tabletop decorations, and jewelry from the last century are the main fare. Pick up candy bars and soft drinks at a little country café area in the front room.

The **Somewhere In Time Antique Mall** is the more impressive shop on the block, located in a huge warehouse building that houses an endless sea of booths. Everything is beautifully displayed. You can find unusual sets of dishes, jadeite and Fire King, fancy silverware, and other, more peculiar collectible items. For furniture, the selection includes desk lamps, vintage kitchen tables, matching chairs, and higher-quality pieces. Head toward the back area for some crazy and chaotic fun. This side of the store is cluttered with tons of dolls and costume jewelry, board games, toys, and some vintage clothing. Sort through the selection of funky pins and necklaces, old plastic powder boxes, TV memorabilia, and baby dolls. Many of the finer antiques at Somewhere In Time can be up there in price, but there are certainly deals to be had from $3 to $10. Take your time to look carefully through the masses and masses of stuff.

> **SOMEWHERE IN TIME ANTIQUE MALL**
> 307 21st Street
> Nitro, West Virginia
> Phone: (304) 755-0734
> Hours: Mon–Wed 10–6, Thurs 10–8, Fri–Sat 10–6, Sun 10–5
>
> **TAMMY'S CONSIGNMENT SHOP**
> 1822 Kanawha Terrace
> St. Albans, West Virginia
> Phone: (304) 722-1005
> Hours: Tues–Thurs 1–6, Fri–Sat 10–4

SAINT ALBANS, WEST VIRGINIA

On the thriftier side, Saint Albans has a few good options. It might take a little navigating to get to **Tammy's Consignment Shop** on Kanawha Terrace, so pull out that trusty map and don't be afraid to ask around. The store carries newer clothing, toys, books, and household items. Clothing is conveniently organized, with half of the store for adults and the other half for children. Accessories are in abundance with a stellar selection of purses, belts, and shoes. Find a pair of vintage Wrangler cowboy boots or other fine leather fabrications. Pick up some pretty perfume bottles for a dollar or a cute ceramic ashtray for 50 cents. Garments are affordably priced between $3 and $12, and shoes only go up to $6. Tammy's Consignment Shop is a great place to find an unusual gift or a nice addition to your wardrobe.

The quirkiest stop in Saint Albans is the **Variety Store,** a haven for used furniture. Browse the spacious room and score on good-condition sewing machines, old mirrors, and lamps in varying shapes and sizes.

VARIETY STORE
707 6th Avenue
St. Albans, West Virginia
Phone: (304) 727-5271
Hours: Mon–Fri 10–2 and 3–5,
   Sat 10–12

SALVATION ARMY
400 B Street
St. Albans, West Virginia
Phone: (304) 727-0923
Hours: Mon–Fri 10–6, Sat 10–5

Larger furniture pieces include patterned couches, easy chairs, and wooden writing desks. The collection of novelty mugs near the register is sure to yield a special find. Beat the summer heat with a big fan and find stacks of books and other prizes scattered throughout the shop. Prices are mostly reasonable, so you'll leave without breaking the bank.

For the final act in Saint Albans, take some time for a visit to the always-reliable **Salvation Army** thrift store. It's imperative to note how inexpensive this branch is, with most clothing under $2 and bric-a-brac for less than a dollar. Though tiny in size, the store carries a little bit of everything, with the exception of large furniture. Clothing, including shoes and accessories is available for men, women, and kids. The back of the shop is crammed with all kinds of kitchenware, junk, puzzles, toys, and miscellaneous curiosities. Neat cases of baubles and bangles appear at the front. "Ring the bell once" at the register when you're ready to make a purchase.

ROUTE #4

Washington, D.C., to Winston-Salem, North Carolina

Save & Serve Thrift Shop,
Manassas, Virginia

Dinosaur Land,
White Post, Virginia

Goodwill,
Manassas, Virginia

Route #4 motors south to southwest, twisting and turning through Virginia before crossing the border into North Carolina. Starting out from D.C., the most direct path is to take the Beltway to Interstate 66 and head west. For much of the trip, our path follows Route 11, which alternately meets up with and then separates from Interstate 81. After Wytheville, you can opt for a meandering journey to a few small-town secondhand shops, eventually arriving at Winston-Salem, our final destination.

Route #4 Driving Time: (stops not included) 9 hours

Make your way out of town, steering the thriftmobile in a southwesterly direction. In Fairfax, drop in on the **Second Hand Rose** thrift emporium and snag some new threads while you're at it. In Harrisonburg, grab some cheap goodies at the **Gift & Thrift** before enjoying lunch at our beloved **Little Grill Collective**. Farther down the highway, visit **Zelma's** haunted vintage shop in Staunton, along with the creatively named **Thrift Shop,** before raiding both floors at **Schoolhouse Used Furniture**. Ooh and aah over the amazing anthodites in an Indiana Jones-style tour of the **Skyline Caverns** and enjoy a picnic at wacky **Dinosaur Land**. In the tiny town of Pulaski, don't pass up the trinkets and curios from **Nana's Nook** and **Upstairs Downstairs** before landing in Winston-Salem, home of several enormous **Goodwills**.

VIENNA, VIRGINIA

Your voyage begins by heading west on Interstate 66 toward Vienna. Exit the highway for an eclectic mix of weird new things as well as some intriguing old ones at the aptly named **Some Things Old, Some Things New**. There's a definite cutesy flavor to this little shop with the bright pink door, located next door to a barbershop. Inside the peaked-roof cottage, it's an oddball mix: a rack of secondhand clothes, "country"-style pillows, crockery, and a small army of stuffed pink flamingos. You'll find teapots, pretty perfume bottles, jars of old buttons, and vintage Virginia postcards for a quarter each. Though not strictly thrift, it's worth a short trip to stop in and see what's lying around.

> **SOME THINGS OLD, SOME THINGS NEW**
> 111A Park Street North East
> Vienna, Virginia
> Phone: (703) 242-7007
> Hours: Tues–Sat 10–6, Sun 10–2
>
> **PENNYWISE THRIFT SHOP**
> 144 Church Street Northeast
> Vienna, Virginia
> Phone: (703) 938-7062
> Hours: Tues–Wed 10–4, Thurs
> 10–6, Fri 10–2, Sat 11–3
>
> **CONSIGNMENT BOUTIQUE**
> 141A Church Street Northwest
> Vienna, Virginia
> Phone: (703) 281-0759
> Hours: Mon–Fri 10–6, Sat 10–5

Also in Vienna, stop in for a visit at the **Pennywise Thrift Shop**. Clamber up onto the large wooden porch, where you can find the odd piece of furniture, along with a few bins of free books and other miscellaneous giveaway items. Pennywise is a cheery shop, a good place to find weirdo threads and an interesting mix of household items, from colored glass to china plates. Stuffed animals, games, and toys inhabit the upper shelves over racks of clothes for men, women, and children.

Only a few blocks away on Church Street, Vienna's **Consignment Boutique** is hidden away at the back of a small cluster of shops. You'll find all the clothes here (women's only) in tip-top shape: clean, undamaged, and almost like new. The housewares are also high quality. Check out the neat presentation of tea sets, picture frames, tableware, and woven wall hangings. There are lots of jewelry options in the glass case near the register, with plenty of attractive, well-priced pendants, bracelets, and earrings. In style, most of the garments lean toward the conservative, with a grown-up suburban woman vibe permeating the selection. Prices on everyday articles of clothing range from $5 to $20, and footwear is priced around $15. The welcoming and helpful staff can point you toward the small dress-up section if formal wear is on your shopping list. The few small pieces of furniture in the shop are all antiques, with price tags a bit higher on the budget scale.

FAIRFAX, VIRGINIA

Next stop is Fairfax, Virginia, where you'll do better on clothes and home items than anything else. Navigate your way to Lee Highway for the **Thrift Shop to Benefit the Inova Fair Oaks Hospital**, located in the Fairfax Circle Center shopping plaza. Here you can find records, tapes, books, and magazines for $1 and a little collection of 50-cent snow globes—while they last! Peek into the small housewares area and find shelves of frosty sherbet bowls, casserole dishes, glassware, and tons of woven baskets. There is very little furniture at this shop, but you might pick up a bedside table lamp or some paper or cloth lampshades. Heading over to the clothing area, you'll find a small dress-up rack of silky blouses and 1970s-style dresses for the ladies. Several well-ordered shelves make up a tidy little shoe department in the rear. Keep your eyes peeled for possible sales, such as the red dot sale, offering 50 percent discounts on dotted items.

> **THRIFT SHOP TO BENEFIT INOVA FAIR OAKS HOSPITAL**
> Fairfax Circle Center
> 9667 Lee Highway
> Fairfax, Virginia
> Phone: (703) 273-3519
> Hours: Mon–Sat 10–5

Quality Consignments Plus carries mainly clothing for men and ladies, including a good selection of fancy outfits and wedding attire. Serious investigators may encounter a few designer labels, such as a Cynthia Rowley dress, amid the crowded racks. Super deals on sequined tops, men's suits, and bridal gowns can easily be found. A step up from thrift, Quality Consignments Plus is a good place for those in search of stylish scarves, belts, and other almost-new accessories. There's also a moderate selection of items to gussy up your dwelling—decorator pillows, wall hangings, clocks, and framed art prints. The shop can be a bit difficult to find, since it's tucked away in a mini strip mall on Old Pickett Road (not to be confused with Pickett Road). Don't hesitate to call the shop for directions if you are having trouble finding your way.

If thrifting on a bigger scale is your game (as it is ours), you'll probably dig **Yesterday's Rose**, which we recommend, with three dirt-cheap stars, above other area thrifts. The store's massive size makes for a more diverse and eccentric offering than that of the smaller shops. There are tons of shirts, pants, suits, and dresses to sort though, and the prices can't be beat. Nicknacks, dolls, toys, and curios can be had for a song, as can fancier goods like a set of frosty dessert dishes, a pair of ornate ceramic lamps, or a fine, white china tea set. There's even a small but interesting selection of furniture—dressers, a display cabinet, wooden end tables, a vintage couch. A large book corner will keep the bookworms happy for hours. Yesterday's Rose equals today's jackpot, so cram your finds into a shopping cart and make out like a bandit.

> **QUALITY CONSIGNMENTS PLUS**
> 3220 Old Pickett Road
> Fairfax, Virginia
> Phone: (703) 591-8384
> Hours: Mon–Sat 10–6, Sun 1–5
>
> **YESTERDAY'S ROSE**
> Main Street Center Shopping Plaza
> 9960 Main Street
> Fairfax, Virginia
> Phone: (703) 385-9517
> Hours: Mon–Wed 10–6, Thurs
>   10–7, Fri-Sat, 10–6, Sun 12–5

Plato's Closet, in Greenbriar Town Center Shopping Plaza, is a chain resale shop specializing in clothes for teens. Young, young-at-heart, and more petite thrifters will find super-trendy duds and accessories here. The aisles are full of many popular brand names such as Gap, J Crew, Echo, Guess, Wet Seal, and others. Along with the booty brands, you'll find super-cheap prices that are hard to argue with. Hip shirts can be had for as little as $3, and there are lots of great shoes, boots, and sneakers for $6 to $15, remarkable because of the shortage of modern footwear styles at other thrifts. Plato's Closet is a fairly large shop, offering mostly active wear and everyday clothes for young ladies, with a smaller selection for the guys. Jackets are typically priced at around $25, jeans from $12 to $18, with plenty of shorts, skirts, and khakis rounding out the selection. Be prepared—fellow shoppers will be singing along to the sugary pop music on the radio—loudly, too. "Oh-ma-god, I like, *love* this song."

CENTREVILLE, VIRGINIA

Continue on Lee Highway to nearby Centreville for a few good second-hand outlets. **Antiques & Things** is a sprawling, cluttered mass of stuff: old, new, and new-but-made-to-look-old. This is a particularly great spot for outdoor wicker furniture, wrought iron tables and chairs, old birdbaths, and miscellaneous garden objects, which are spread out across the front lawn. The dark, creaky interior of the store is filled to the brim. Vases, ceramic planters, and salt and pepper shakers crowd the shelves, and you might find small tables, wooden headboards, and decorative wall shelves scattered around. Mixed in with all these goodies are the odd "country decorator" goods: candleholders, figurines, wall plaques, miniature chairs, and petite upholstered divans. Rummage around in a basket of odd postcards near the register. Antiques & Things is a quirky assortment of items small and large, with prices ranging from very inexpensive to slightly overpriced.

PLATO'S CLOSET
Greenbriar Town Center
    Shopping Plaza
13033 Lee Jackson Memorial
    Highway (Route 50)
Fairfax, Virginia
Phone: (703) 378-7009
Hours: Mon–Sat 10–8, Sun 1–5

ANTIQUES AND THINGS
13617 Lee Highway
Centreville, Virginia
Phone: (703) 503-9337
Hours: Mon–Sun 10–5

The soothing mauve interior and the low-level Muzak may lull you into a dreamy state at **Clocktower Thrift Shop** (just off of Centrewood Drive in the Centreville Square II shopping plaza). In the middle of all this consumer madness, find Clocktower, an especially good source for home items. You can almost fully outfit your kitchen here, with smaller appliances like blenders and coffeemakers or the usual pots, pans, and tableware. You'll find lots of kitchen gadgets and doodads. There's a large selection of other household items as well, notably a large cache of glassware, picture frames, decorative baskets, and brass objets d'art. In both the men's and women's clothing departments, prices are a tad higher than dirt cheap, with dresses going for $10 to $15, ladies' blouses for $5, and formal wear pricing out at around $20. Accessories and handbags are in the more reasonable range of $2 to $5. Styles are mostly conservative, with some happy exceptions. Try on your finds in a spacious, department store-style dressing room. You can find books and records at Clocktower as well, but the real hot spot for music and books is just a few steps away in the same shopping plaza.

CLOCKTOWER THRIFT SHOP
Centreville Square II
6031 Centreville Crest Lane
Centreville, Virginia
Phone: (703) 803-3337
Hours: Mon–Fri 10–8, Sat 10–6,
Sun 12–5

MCKAY USED BOOKS AND CDS
Centreville Square II
6011 Centreville Crest Lane
Centreville, Virginia
Phone: (703) 830-4048
Hours: Mon–Sat 9–10, Sun 10–8

McKay Used Books and CDs is an enormous, busy outlet for recycled CDs, VHS videos, DVDs, audio books, and hardback and softcover books, books, books! Almost every topic imaginable has a home here, from classic and modern poetry to Internet business practice and world history. A plentiful cookbook section caters to a variety of tastes and cuisines. A gigantic side room is stacked floor to ceiling with trashy paperback romance, historical thrillers, fantasy, horror, even time travel. Many of the paperbacks are under $1, with others priced up to a whopping $3. There's even a decent section for art books. In addition to books, McKay's carries a moderate selection of used CDs, priced from

$4 to $8—take your pick of soundtracks, hip-hop, pop music, and some indie rock. The merchandise is meticulously organized, and the huge staff is happy to help you ferret out anything that you might be seeking.

MANASSAS, VIRGINIA

It practically takes a treasure map to find the **Save & Serve Thrift Shop,** hidden away in a funny little shopping center near the intersection of Balls Ford Road and Route 66 in Manassas. (See the special directions under the store listing.) Persevere, and you'll find a quirky secret spot for thrifty finds. Another bigger-than-first glance shop, Save & Serve is made up of a string of interconnecting rooms, none of which you'll want to miss. Grab a shopping cart and navigate the small spaces between crowded circular racks of apparel in the front of the store. Here you'll find plenty of strange and unusual clothing options, with many items priced very cheaply at around $3. The back warehouse room is full of furniture, along with shelves of smaller nicknacks. Find kitchen table sets, dressers, and a large linens bin, plus shelves of candleholders, mugs, goblets and baskets. Don't miss the small nook of books, tapes, and records (45s go for a quarter each) or the many bins of kiddie clothes. Save & Serve is a good spot for oddball finds, like a plastic faux-crystal cake plate for $2. Few things are tagged at the store, so check out the prices posted at the counter or ask the staff for potentially cheaper deals.

> **SAVE & SERVE THRIFT SHOP**
> 7234 Nathan Court
> Manassas, Virginia
> Phone: (703) 330-8777
> Hours: Mon 10–5, Tues 9–9, Wed
>   10–5, Thurs 9–9, Fri–Sat 10–5,
>   Sun 1–5
>
> *Special directions:* From Balls Ford Road, turn onto New Market Court, passing the U-Haul rental, and turn left at the end of the lane. Make the next left again into the strip of stores and you'll see the Save & Serve farther down the row, on your right.

The **Goodwill** on busy Sudley Road can be described using two of our favorite words for thrift stores (or anything else, really)—*big* and *cheap*. Most of the clothing articles are priced from $4 to $10, with a few exceptions in outerwear (up to $15). The fashions are mostly from the 1970s and '80s, plus modern inexpensive casual styles, with a few outrageous items mixed in. Men's slacks are generally priced at around $5, and suit jackets can be had for under $10. Get ready for a night on the town with some new fancy duds or spend some time browsing through the items for house and home. You'll find several shelves of dish sets, mismatched glasses, and some mysterious objects. There's a massive selection of table lamps, along with electronic goods like televisions, toaster ovens, and old computer equipment. Relax on a plush couch for $70 or a cushy chair for $40. Poke around in the art department, where you might find an art school experiment gone awry or a framed photo of the NASA space shuttle for just a few bucks.

GOODWILL
8014 Sudley Road (Route 234)
Manassas, Virginia
Phone: (703) 551-3200
Hours: Mon–Sat 11–7, Sun 12–6

RAINBOW THRIFT STORE
9902 Liberia Avenue
Manassas, Virginia
Phone: (703) 393-2314
Hours: Mon–Fri 10–6, Sat 10–5

Head east to Liberia Avenue for the **Rainbow Thrift Store**. This shop is of the smaller variety, but is equally as cheap and has a comfy mellow atmosphere. Come here for funny slogan mugs for just a quarter each. The records are also inexpensive at 50 cents each—you'll find these in various stacks throughout the shop. Spend some time investigating the cute little wooden-shelved book nook. Pick up a 1970s dinette set, velvet couch, or curio cabinet from the small offering of home furnishings. Most of these items are practically new and a bit pricier than the rest of the merchandise. In general, there's just a bit of this and that, but there are some quality items to be found. Be prepared for Jesus music on the radio.

In Old Town, the small historic district in Manassas, drop in for good clean fun at the **Prince William Auxiliary Thrift Shop**. The lamps and housewares near the front are offered at first-rate prices—china cups and saucers, bowls, and serving platters are almost all tagged at $1 or less. Women's clothes are plentiful, with a smaller offering for men and children. Some interesting costume jewelry is stashed at the front counter, and flashy and fashionable scarves are only $1 each. Depending on the day's selection, you may be able to snag one or two pieces of furniture, such as a small table or wooden cabinet. Everything is well priced, and the hodgepodge includes a few oddball finds.

Pop in for a cup of tea and a sweet tidbit just a few short blocks away at the **Victorian Tea Room and Bakery**. Black, Oolong, Darjeeling, herbal, and fruit teas, served hot or iced, make up the largest tea selection for miles around. But the real specialties are "the dainties"—scrumptious coconut meringue pie, tuxedo cake, and lemon bars dusted with powdered sugar. A huge assortment of shortbreads, cookies, crumbcakes, and other delicacies are freshly baked on the premises.

PRINCE WILLIAM AUXILIARY THRIFT SHOP
9215 Center Street (Old Town)
Manassas, Virginia
Phone: (703) 361-4344
Hours: Mon–Fri 10–4, Sat 10–2

VICTORIAN TEA ROOM AND BAKERY
9413 Battle Street (Old Town)
Manassas, Virginia
Phone: (703) 393-8327
Hours: Mon–Fri 6–5, Sat 10–5

SHIRLEY'S CONSIGNMENT
9792 Center Street
Manassas, Virginia
Phone: (703) 369-3609
Hours: Mon–Fri 10–4, Thurs 10–6, Sat 9:30–3

Leah maintains that she will remember the pineapple blackberry upside-down cake for the rest of her days. A menu of tea sandwiches (under $6) is also available at lunchtime. Relax awhile in these unpretentious surroundings.

When you've had your fill of deliciously fattening and delectable snacks, drive over to **Shirley's Consignment**, located much farther out along Center Street in a brick building with bright pink trim. The merchandise at Shirley's consists mainly of clothes, all in excellent condition and selling at consignment store prices. Many of the fashions are women's suits and formal wear ($20–$40) geared toward the mature woman with a sense of style. There are also a few nice examples of vintage clothing. You'll find a small selection of housewares as well, many of them antiques and collectibles (mushroom cookie jar set, silver tea service). The jewelry selection is also quality here—turquoise, silver, and rhinestones sparkle in the cases. You won't find the best bargains in town, but you'll still pay less than full price, and the merchandise is classy.

FRONT ROYAL, VIRGINIA

Past the town of Manassas, the road begins to open up. The miles between each town increase as you drive onward, and the general vibe becomes less traffic-snarled and more laid-back. Leaving Manassas, there are two options for getting to Front Royal, Virginia, about forty-five miles down the road. On a sunny, lazy day, thrift adventurers may want to meander their way along Route 55, which offers a relaxing, tree-and-field-lined drive, away from the stoplights and SUVs of city life. A better option for type-A personalities is to take Route 66, a faster-moving highway running roughly parallel to Route 55.

The little town of Front Royal is known as "the gateway to the Shenandoah Valley." Consider staying the night at the old-school Pioneer Motel, an inexpensive roadside stopover. Drop in on two thrift stores in Front Royal, the Salvation Army and A Second Chance. With area attractions like the deep, dark Skyline Caverns and the kitschy and quirky Dinosaur Land located nearby, there's plenty to keep you busy. Explore a corner of Shenandoah National Park, including Skyline Drive, the famous scenic motor route.

Front Royal's **Salvation Army** is smaller than most and probably not as clean as it could be. Nevertheless, the little lofted shop has some random good finds and great prices all around. The shop is sunny and open, with old hats hanging about. Some of the furniture is a little shoddy, but then again, you might stumble across a downright hand-

> **SALVATION ARMY**
> 296 South Street
> Front Royal, Virginia
> Phone: (540) 636-8872
> Hours: Mon–Sat 9–5

some set of green vinyl and chrome barstools. The selection of clothing on the top floor is not so great, but stop by to check out the rest of the merchandise—from a tea set to recycled Christmas decorations to a green glass vase to wooden and ceramic table lamps, you'll find an unpredictable assortment.

A Second Chance is located amid a cluster of pricier antiques and collectibles shops in the little historic district of Front Royal. A Second Chance is decidedly better for clothing than the Salvation Army. Many items are around $3, except dresses, which can go from $8 to $15. Even fancier stuff may be priced as high as $25. In addition, you'll find at least a few half-price racks with even better deals. Wedding dresses will cost a bundle. The fashions here range from flannels to vintage-y finds and plenty of steals from the 1970s. Belts, scarves, hair accessories, and beaded necklaces can be easily found. There's also a large toy and kiddie clothes section (think tight T-shirts for a buck!). Check out the crates of old dress patterns and shelves of goblets and cup and saucer sets.

Explore the dark, graveled paths of **Skyline Caverns**, located on Route 340, just south of town. There are lots of caves in this region, but Skyline Caverns is home to the amazing fuzzy anthodite, a snowflake-like mineral formation. Lovingly referred to as "the Orchid of the Mineral Kingdom," the anthodite can be found in only a few places around the world. Skyline Caverns also boasts the super-cool reflecting pool at Fairyland Lake and a kind of religious experience in Cathedral Hall. (You'll just have to take the tour to find out what we mean.) In the gift shop, pick up some magic growing rocks, Viewmaster reels, shot glasses, snow globes, and (Chriss's favorite!) squished pennies. Skyline Caverns is open for guided tours every day of the year, even on Christmas, so you

> **A SECOND CHANCE**
> 317 East Main Street
> Front Royal, Virginia
> Phone: (540) 636-7020
> Hours: Mon–Sat 10–5
>
> **SKYLINE CAVERNS**
> On Route 340, just south of
>   Front Royal
> Phone: (540) 635-4545
> Hours: Mon–Sun hourly tours
>   9–6:30
> Web site: www.skylinecaverns.com

have no excuse. Print out discount coupons from the Web site before you leave home.

Photo opportunities abound at **Dinosaur Land**, an oddball dinosaur-replica theme park about ten minutes north of Front Royal. Bring a picnic lunch to eat in the shadow of more than thirty medium- and large-scale fiberglass creatures. The dinos line a path that winds from one end of the shady, tree-lined park to another. Have your photo taken next to saltoposughus, yaleosaurus, or a seventy-foot octopus. Witness the "Epic Battle between Tyranosaurus and Titanosaurus." It's hard to know if Dinosaur Land is completely geeky, completely awesome, or both. It just doesn't matter.

Back in Front Royal, not far from the Skyline Caverns, look for the sunshiny yellow sign out in front of the **Pioneer Motel.** For around $40 you can have a clean, cheery room at an old-school motel with an outdoor pool, brightly painted doors, and white wrought iron porch railings. Pioneer isn't a four-star resort, but it is inexpensive and has that road trip flavor that we love so much. And the owners are the coolest.

> **DINOSAUR LAND**
> 3848 Stonewall Jackson Highway
> (Route 340 / Route 522)
> White Post, Virginia
> Phone: (540) 869-2222
> Hours: Vary seasonally, call ahead
> Web site: www.dinosaurland.com
>
> *Special directions:* From Front Royal, take Route 522/ Route 340 north for about 7 miles. Dinosaur Land is on the left, near the intersection of Route 77. It really is pretty hard to miss.
>
> **PIONEER MOTEL**
> 541 South Royal Avenue
> Front Royal, Virginia
> Phone: (540) 635-4784

STRASBURG, VIRGINIA

Between Front Royal and the next few stops in Strasburg, you'll have a quiet half-hour drive along Route 66. Both of the listings in Strasburg are antiques and collectibles stores—while not the cheapest along the route, they offer some specialty items that you may want to investigate.

While the furniture is pretty pricey at the **Great Strasburg Antique Emporium**, there are many affordable finds in other departments, from high-quality vintage clothing to collectible 45s and LPs. Sort through a bunch of vintage button sets, priced from $1 to $4. Throughout the store, you can find cases and cases of dazzling jewelry, from rhinestone finery to pricier gems. The place is huge, with several large rooms as well as a back area full of furniture: carved wooden bed frames, Victorian vanities, armoires, and painted folding screens. Stop in for a relaxing browse or a snack at the Daily Grind Coffee Shop, past all the fancy furnishings at the far end of the warehouse.

> **GREAT STRASBURG ANTIQUE EMPORIUM**
> 160 North Massanutten Street
> Strasburg, Virginia
> Phone: (540) 465-3711
> Hours: Mon–Thurs 10–5,
>   Fri–Sat 10–7
>
> **STRASBURG FLEA MARKET**
> 160 North Massanutten Street
> Strasburg, Virginia
> Phone: (540) 465-3550
> Hours: Sun–Thurs 10–5,
>   Fri–Sat 10–7

Next door, the **Strasburg Flea Market** may yield a more fruitful search for bargains. Another large and rambling shop, here you'll discover cluttered booths and plenty of random retro finds. Snag a wall clock shaped like a pear, an owl lamp, a plastic bird in a plastic birdcage, and other wacky finds of this nature. Check out several small collections of cheap baubles and shiny jewelry. Sort through the used records for Jimi Hendrix and Pink Floyd albums, priced from $8 to $15. Lots of quirky goods can be taken home for $10 or less.

TOM'S BROOK, VIRGINIA

From Strasburg, hop onto Route 11, heading south and running parallel to nearby Interstate 81. On its way into Harrisonburg, Route 11 runs directly through the centers of a string of small towns, with good thrift stops in Tom's Brook, Woodstock, Mount Jackson, and New Market. Along the way, the remarkable landscape of the Shenandoah Valley offers plenty of great opportunities for hiking, camping, and otherwise bumming around.

Drop in to **Bargain Place**, located right on Route 40 in the tiny town of Tom's Brook. You have to call ahead to see if Bargain Place is open—or just use your eyes. If the doors are wide open, then the store is open. If they're not, then it's not. The stained glass window above the door says, "Granny's," but this is a lie, it really is the Bargain Place, a small junk shop full of random curios, drill bits, old tires, and stereo components. Here you might find a few old-fashioned handbags or some miscellaneous home furnishings, like kitchen chairs for $5 each. Pick up a flowery photo album for only $2 or an electric keyboard for $16. There's no telling what you might encounter while exploring this garage sale-style shop.

WOODSTOCK, VIRGINIA

Stop off for a mini cluster of dirt-cheap shops located along Route 11 in Woodstock. Pick up some oddball household goods at **Shenandoah County Thrift Store**. Flowerpots, glass jars, and candy dishes are spread across tabletops and shelves at the front. Up a small set of stairs toward the back find racks of clothing, a bit raggedy, but very cheap. If polyester printed tops or below-the-knee dresses are your deal, you've come to the correct place. Prices are very low, with most clothes selling for $4 and the nicer stuff selling for around $8. Shelves of toys, puzzles, and board games are well stocked and offer a number of curious finds. There's also a small amount of furniture. While not always the highest quality, you can find most pieces priced at $50 or less, with a few good steals available. Pick up some show tunes and classical music on vinyl as well as some eight tracks and used cassette tapes.

BARGAIN PLACE AKA GRANNY'S
3380 North Main (Street Route 11)
Tom's Brook, Virginia
Phone: (540) 436-8118
Hours: Sometime in the
morning–5:30

**SHENANDOAH COUNTY
THRIFT STORE**
659 North Main Street (Route 11)
Woodstock, Virginia
Phone: (540) 459-2939
Hours: Tues–Sat 10–5

Walk around the side of the building to check out **R & S Bargain Barn**, located in the basement of Shenandoah County Thrift. Although the shop hours here are more limited, you should stop in to find furniture and even more nicknacks. Explore the basement rooms full of miscellaneous odds and ends, as the ceiling creaks under the footsteps of the people thrifting upstairs. The Bargain Barn offers lots of $1 finds in the form of ashtrays, plates, strange vases, and weird framed artwork.

Valley Treasures, a clean, air-conditioned, indoor mini market is right across the road. Inside you'll find many small booths full of antiques and collectibles, with some great finds at more-than-thrift but less-than-boutique prices. Snap up a frosted orange pitcher and glasses set for only $20 or take home a rhinestone-rimmed glass ashtray in the shape of a poodle for $7. There are plenty of good kitchen collectibles here, including Smurfs or Flintstones drinking glasses, stacks of dishware, and plenty of vintage mixing bowls. Old books, fabrics, fashionable handbags, and weirdo postcards are also in the mix. A few booths carry country decorator items, and there are some tag sale-style sections as well. Find plenty of reasonably priced and interesting stuff here.

Two other spots in Woodstock are The Clothes Closet and Hot Spot,

> **R & S BARGAIN BARN**
> 659 North Main Street (Route 11)
> Woodstock, Virginia
> Phone: (540) 459-8558
> Hours: Tues–Thurs 10–2,
>   Fri–Sun 10–4
>
> **VALLEY TREASURES**
> 660 North Main Street (Route 11)
> Woodstock, Virginia
> Phone: (540) 459-2334
> Hours: Mon–Thurs 10–6, Fri–Sat
>   10–8, Sun 12–6
>
> **THE CLOTHES CLOSET**
> 159 South Commerce Street
> Woodstock, Virginia
> Phone: (540) 459-2306
> Hours: Wed 10–4:30, Sat 10–4:30

across the street from each other. **The Clothes Closet** is a small, linoleum-floor, fluorescent-lit shop, mainly offering casual clothes for women. Try on lots of 1980s–'90s styles here. Flip through racks of slips, pajamas, shorts, and skirts. Leatherette bags and canvas belts are also on the menu. Check out the housewares shelves for an assortment of very random items, like a white rotary phone, lamp fixtures, TV trays, baskets, puzzles, and funny coffee mugs. Most items are priced under $3, with only a few exceptions.

Across the road, there's a small permanent flea market attached to the **Hot Spot**, a peculiar sort of tanning salon/gift shop. You can sort through rickety furniture, secondhand records and books, dishes and mugs, and an assortment of other random stuff. Find lots of cheap baby clothes, too. Hot Spot also offers $1 toy grab bags. If you see anything you want, walk past several long aisles of ceramic wolf and warrior figurines to the cash register and just ask about the price.

MOUNT JACKSON, VIRGINIA

Mount Jackson's **Search Thrift Shop** is a dirt-cheap superstar along this road trip. The charmingly disheveled store was opened years ago by a local woman, and all the proceeds are donated to Mt. Jackson's group home for the mentally disabled. The shelves and aisles here are crammed full of offbeat bargains. Check out the display of brightly colored plastic bangles and other costume jewelry near the front. Clothing prices are cheap, cheap, cheap—sports coats for $3, dresses for $2, and winter coats for $5 to $10. Paperback books are only 10 cents each, or pay a dollar to bring home a bagful! Nab some 1980s music cassettes for 50 cents apiece. The shop also has a nice selection of items for the home, such as glasses, cups, plates, and bowls in all colors and varieties. Grab some used kitchen utensils and get cooking with small appliances and casserole dishes. Furniture accessories like table lamps are priced at $15 or less. Search for old typewriters and sewing machines, too. The luckiest shoppers will experience the famous "all you can fit into a bag for $1" sale at the end of every month.

> **HOT SPOT**
> 160 South Commerce Street
> Woodstock, Virginia
> Phone: Unavailable
> Hours: By chance
>
> **SEARCH THRIFT SHOP**
> 5742 North Main Street
> Mount Jackson, Virginia
> Phone: (540) 477-2808
> Hours: Thurs–Fri 9–4, Sat 9–2

Vintage enthusiasts will want to head down the block to the Old Theatre Building, which houses **Even More Stuff**. Here, find fancy clothes, accessories, and objects with a feminine flair, like a pair of pink ballerina tutus in the front window. Check out scads of great glassware, delicate vases, makeup trays, and boudoir items. Ladies can try on fancy scarves and vintage handbags. Men will want to investigate tweedy suit jackets, patterned shirts, and Hawaiian print casuals for $4 to $13. Uncover a pair of striped woolen leg warmers for only $5. You can also search the place for brightly colored kitchen objects, from cake plates to serving bowls. Browse a few shelves of old books, too. Even More Stuff is slightly more expensive than a thrift shop, but not at all unreasonable given the quality goods.

NEW MARKET, VIRGINIA

On Route 11 in New Market, **Valley Pike Antique Mall** is worth a few minutes of your time. Skim through its collections of old coins, vintage magazine ads, stacks of china, and old tins. Select a few colorful glass marbles from a giant bin. With luck, you might also pick up glass candy dishes or small china sets. There are a number of large pieces of quality furniture as well as linens, handmade quilts, and chenille bedspreads. The prices are average, but with a little patience you can probably score a deal or two here.

EVEN MORE STUFF
Old Theatre Building-North Main Street (Route 11)
Mount Jackson, Virginia
Phone: (540) 477-9606
Hours: Sat–Sun 10–5, or by chance or appointment

VALLEY PIKE ANTIQUE MALL
9440 South Congress Street (Route 11)
New Market, Virginia
Phone: (540) 740-2866
Hours: Mon 10–6, Wed–Sat 10–6, Sun 11–6

PAPER TREASURES
9595 South Congress Street (Route 11)
New Market, Virginia 22844
Phone: (540) 740-3135
Hours: Mon–Sun 10–6
Web site: www.papertreasures books.com

Bookworms and brainiacs are really in luck. **Paper Treasures** carries tons of used and rare books and all sorts of paper collectibles. The labyrinthine store stocks tremendous quantities of books, rare and common, some for reading, some for collecting. Shelves, bins, and bookcases are all carefully arranged and organized. Beyond the massive selection of volumes on every topic, the store is jam-packed with vintage vinyl and old magazines, plus bins and bins of comic books. Check out the postcards, collectible prints, and oversize old-school movie posters, too. The huge selection here can really suck you in! Give yourself some time to scan this enormous library of paper items.

HARRISONBURG, VIRGINIA

Harrisonburg offers a bountiful string of thrifty stopovers, many of which are closed on Sundays. You might want to pick up a small city map for scooting around. Spend some time and visit them all, but whatever you do, don't miss the best roadside food on the whole route, the Little Grill Collective!

Crafty types are in thrifty heaven at the stellar **Gift & Thrift Shop.** Notable for its fruitful sewing section, the G&T is home to bags of buttons or findings for a just a quarter, along with small bundles of fabric remnants, zippers, yarn, thread, patterns and how-to craft manuals. Ladies' clothes are arranged by color on the circular racks, with jeans tagged at $3 and dresses going for up to $6. Men will find a full range of belts, ties, and jammies, along with suits (around $15) and sportswear. In the back search through the small appliances, kitchen items, random office supplies, and decorative wreaths and baskets. Housewares of glass and china are usually less than $1 apiece. Find bargains all around and in a sunny shop with a down-home atmosphere to boot!

> **GIFT & THRIFT SHOP**
> 227 North Main Street
> Harrisonburg, Virginia
> Phone: (540) 433-8844
> Hours: Mon–Sat 9:30–5
>
> **LITTLE GRILL COLLECTIVE**
> 621 North Main Street
> Harrisonburg, Virginia
> Phone: (540) 434-3594
> Hours: Mon–Thurs 7am–2:30pm
>   and 5pm–9pm, Fri 7am–2:30pm
>   and 5pm–10pm, Sat 7am–10pm,
>   Sun 9am–2pm

Our favorite pit stop along this route was dinner (and then breakfast again the next morning!) at the **Little Grill Collective**. Don't miss it.

This colorful, worker-owned grill cooks up lots of delicious vegetarian and a few vegan meals, all at really great prices. While waiting for your Potato Boat breakfast, a Little Grill specialty, sift through the napkin drawings, love notes, photos, and postcards in the Miss Piggy Lunch Box (on the shelf in the back corner booth), an archeological record of the people who ate here before you! The atmosphere is completely laid-back, the food is great, and the staff is really friendly, too.

Granny Longlegs, a branch of the Mercy House Thrift Shop, carries mostly ladies' clothes in conservative styles, with most priced between $6 and $10. A formal wear room in the back holds racks of dresses for around $30 as well as matching evening bags and satiny shoes. Beyond clothing, there are a few small shelves of both fiction and nonfiction books in excellent shape, along with some plain-jane glasses, potpourri dishes, and other housewares. Check the sign at the front door—there is 50 percent off something every day that the shop is open.

> **GRANNY LONGLEGS**
> **(MERCY HOUSE THRIFT SHOP)**
> 16 South Main Street
> Harrisonburg, Virginia
> Phone: (540) 433-4097
> Hours: Mon–Sat 9–5
>
> **NEW TO ME CONSIGNMENTS**
> 635A West Market Street
> Harrisonburg, Virginia
> Phone: (540) 432-5551
> Hours: Mon–Sat 9–5
>
> **MERCY HOUSE THRIFT SHOP**
> 1005 South High Street
> Harrisonburg, Virginia
> Phone: (540) 433-3272
> Hours: Mon–Fri 9–5:30, Sat 9–5

A similar selection awaits at **New To Me Consignments**. Clothing racks are squished full of apparel, priced mostly at $10 or less. Formal wear, including wedding gowns, is the only exception, priced much higher. New to Me carries men's and children's clothes as well. A colored tag system offers even deeper discounts, from 10 to 40 percent off, depending on how long the item has been in stock. There are lots of purses, a nice collection of inexpensive jewelry and baubles, and a few bookshelves. Friendly salespeople keep the store homey and inviting.

The main location of **Mercy House Thrift Shop** is a lot bigger than the Granny Longlegs boutique, but it's a bit more dingy. One entire side of the large store is devoted to furniture. You'll find a few keepers, like a 1930s dresser with mirror for $100, mixed in with some not-so-attractive pieces. Sporting goods, exercise equipment, and larger appliances can be found here, too. Investigate the large spread of home items for drinking glasses and other kitchen goodies.

On the other side of the shop, find clothing for the whole family. Any vintage items tend to be located in the formal wear section and are steeply priced at $25 to $50. Everything else is dirt cheap, with many racks of $2 shirts and $3 dresses. Score with the "three for $1" bargains on belts and ties and snatch a quality handbag from overflowing piles on the shelves. A small area for table linens, pillowcases, and neatly folded bed sheets connects the two main rooms.

A clean, sunny, upscale consignment experience is what you'll find at **Second Time Around**. Tons of almost-new clothes for women, juniors, and toddlers line the racks of this busy shop. Find a matching silk ensemble, barely used jeans, or a pair of fashionable sandals. The selection is seasonal, and most of the clothes are recent fashions. This is not the place to look for 1970s polyester. Say hello to Jo-Jo, the resident parrot, whose perch is right next to the front door.

SECOND TIME AROUND
1153 South High Street
Harrisonburg, Virginia
Phone: (540) 564-2773
Hours: Mon–Fri 10–6, Sat 10–5

SALVATION ARMY
245 East Washington Street
Harrisonburg, Virginia
Phone: (540) 433-8770
Hours: Mon–Wed 9–5, Thurs 9–7,
   Fri–Sat 9–5

Before you leave Harrisonburg, stop by the **Salvation Army** on East Washington Street, which seems to have the best furniture deals around town. Pick up an orange velour easy chair or a low-slung olive-color couch for $60 or less. Antique dressers may go for around $150. The store is spacious, with plenty of room for a large children's clothing and toy area. In the housewares area, pick up cookie jars, old dishes, gravy boats, and juice pitchers, priced from 25 cents to $3. Flip through numerous racks of clothing for both women and men, full of commonplace thrifty fare with a few quirky finds mixed in. Ignore the framed quilt samplers and duck art, but don't miss the little craft area, where you can snag some unusual how-to books and dress patterns.

STAUNTON, VIRGINIA

Continue in a southwesterly direction along meandering Route 11 or jet down Interstate 81 to Staunton. Old lampposts on brick sidewalks set the tone for the quirky character of Staunton's downtown area. The streets are a pesky set of one-ways, so find a parking space and don't bother trying to negotiate them. The first four listings are within easy walking distance of each other.

Start at **Zelma's** on East Beverly Street, a little shop that sells vintage and antique clothing and accessories. Find bright flowery dresses and retro swimwear for $12 and plaid or tweed leisure suits for $10 to $15. Rummage though a super selection of ladies' dresses in pinstripes, swirls, and patterns. Try on one of the old-fashioned hats, which go for $6. The wigs and costumes in the back room are rented out for Halloween and special occasions. Cute flower pins and other jewelry scores can be found at the front counter. Also, take a peek at the vinyl collection ($1 to $3) of old favorites like the Kinks and the Osmonds. Zelma's is haunted by a ghost with an affinity for Doris Day, so most likely you'll hear her on the record player.

ZELMA'S
114 East Beverley Street
Staunton, Virginia
Phone: (540) 885-3966
Hours: Mon–Thurs 10–5,
 Sat–Sun 10–5:30

SCHOOLHOUSE USED FURNITURE
126 West Beverley Street
Staunton, Virginia
Phone: (540) 213-1673
Hours: Mon–Fri 10–6, Sat 10–5

Next, check out **Schoolhouse Used Furniture**, where you can find all kinds of home furnishings from various eras, from writing desks to vanities, dining tables, and nightstands. But the real deals are found upstairs on the second floor, where furniture is stacked at every angle. Many of these items are in need of repair or at least a little bit of love. Also find paintings, lamps, dishes, and housewares. The basement holds even more fixer-upper furniture deals. Scan the small $2 book area, which includes titles in poetry, fiction, science, and history. Prices here are negotiable, so don't hesitate to ask if an item catches your eye.

Warehouse Antiques started out as a hardware store over a hundred years ago, but now the shelves and counters are covered with an interesting and random accumulation of antiques and collectible merchandise. Carefully make your way through the narrow, overfull aisles, where you can pick up anything from rusty saws and old baseball bats to ornate cash registers and ancient oil lamps. There are a few examples of vintage clothes, old-fashioned irons, crockery, and garden planters. Prices vary—there are some great deals and some pricey pieces, but take some time to get lost in the impressive jumble of this oddball shop.

WAREHOUSE ANTIQUES
26 West Beverley Street
Staunton, Virginia
Phone: (540) 885-0891
Hours: By chance or appointment

THE THRIFT SHOP
18 South New Street
Staunton. Virginia
Phone: (540) 886-1110
Hours: Mon–Fri 10–4, Sat 10–1

HABITAT FOR HUMANITY
  RESALE SHOP
321 North Main Street
Lexington, Virginia
Phone: (540) 464-4663
Hours: Tues 10–4, Thurs 10–4,
  Sat 9–1

The Thrift Shop is dirt cheap. The store is very low key and quiet, and though the space is large, it's not as packed full as other shops we've visited. Still, the prices are right. Check out the clothes for men, women, and children and the small housewares selection. Shoes and handbags can also be found here, but again, the selection is not huge. May the force be with you.

LEXINGTON, VIRGINIA

Next stop, Lexington. The **Habitat for Humanity Resale Shop** carries a little bit of everything. Linens and gauzy curtains are neatly piled onto shelves, and there are several stacks of vinyl at 10 for $1, board games, and paperback books for 30 cents apiece. How-to manuals, yarns, and sewing supplies make up a craft section that's worth looking into. Find furniture in the basement, with plenty of tables, comfy chairs, and couches going for only $70 or so. This very neat and tidy little shop is notable for excellent prices on almost everything.

Find the **Stonewall Jackson Hospital Auxiliary Thrift Shop** across the street from the large neon sign for the Southern Inn Restaurant. Enter on the side of the red brick building. Inside, you'll encounter plenty of bargains on secondhand clothing and household accessories. Grab some stacks and sets of dishes, china, and glasses, or satisfy your nicknack addiction with small figurines and curio cabinet objects. Though they don't carry any furniture to speak of, drop by for the deals on household goods and apparel.

> **STONEWALL JACKSON HOSPITAL AUXILIARY THRIFT SHOP**
> 30 South Main Street
> Lexington, Virginia
> Phone: (540) 463-9840
> Hours: Mon–Fri 10–4:30, Sat 10–1

Stonewall Jackson Hospital Auxiliary Thrift Store, Lexington, Virginia

Next, investigate the goodies at Lexington's large, department store-like **Goodwill**. Located off of Route 60, just east of the downtown area, this Goodwill has great deals on clothing, with many offbeat treasures hiding among the color-coordinated racks. Pick up ladies' blouses or fuzzy sweaters for $2.75, full suits for $6, and shoes for the low, low price of $2.25. The store has some electronic gear, a few lamps, and an area for dishes, platters, and coffee mugs. Pick from a huge rack of $1 belts for one to wear out of the shop.

GOODWILL
8 Woodcote Lane
Lexington, Virginia
Phone: (540) 464-1117
Hours: Mon–Sat 8–9, Sun 12–8

GOODWILL
Market Square North Shopping Plaza
7210 Williamson Road (Route 11)
Roanoke, Virginia
Phone: (540) 366-4765
Hours: Mon–Sat 8am–9pm,
   Sun 12–8

SALVATION ARMY
5511 Williamson Road (Route 11)
Roanoke, Virginia
Phone: (540) 563-5585
Hours: Mon–Sat 10–5:30

ROANOKE, VIRGINIA

About an hour down the highway (Interstate 81/Route 11), Roanoke offers many tried and true favorites, like Salvation Army and Goodwill stores, as well as some lesser-known, yet sizable thrifts. Roanoke also boasts an awfully cute busy downtown area with a bustling farmers' market and weirdo hot dog eateries.

Route 11 brings you straight into Roanoke amid the shopping plazas on Williamson Road. The **Goodwill** in the Market Square North Shopping Plaza is another dusty shop full of clothes and household stuff. Prices on apparel are good and cheap, with almost every item priced under $5. The housewares shelves in the back stock a clutter of cookie jar lids, mismatched cups and saucers, funky candles, old Tupperware, and other mysterious items. Have your pick of electronics gear, from televisions and blenders to coffeemakers and used irons. The collection of weirdo table lamps is notable. Root around for valuable finds under the flickering fluorescent lights.

Look for the comforting and familiar red and white trim of the **Salvation Army** on Williamson Road. The store is sparkling-clean, spacious, and tidy and is filled with deals on clothes and objects for the home. Browse the carefully arranged shelves of ceramic vases, dishware sets, Christmas ornaments, and iced tea jugs. Though small, the furniture selection offers some real bargains. Find a sturdy wooden end table for $15 or a writing desk for $35. Clothing racks are at the other end of the shop, where you can snoop around for good-as-new shirts, dresses, pants, and shoes. For little tykes, check out the several racks of toddler clothes that fare for a buck or two apiece. Before leaving, snatch some board games and plush toys and cruise the small book area, just for kicks.

NOW & THEN SHOP
3133 Williamson Road
Roanoke, Virginia
Phone: (540) 366-1905
Hours: Tues–Fri 10–4, Sat 10–2

For a wide variety of collectibles and household goodies, spend some time at the **Now & Then Shop**, a favorite in Roanoke. The store carries a mixture of furniture, accessories, household linens, books, and other odds and ends, all attractively grouped into little booth-like sections. Find a basket of silverware or a bowl of plastic fruit. Crafters should investigate the nifty array of satiny ribbons, embroidery hoops, yarns, and old

Now & Then Shop, Roanoke, Virginia

patterned fabrics. Peruse the outdated crafting magazines for hints and tips. The selection of home furnishings is of good quality, although the pricing can be erratic: find an eight-foot dresser with trifold mirror for $230 or an equally nice chest of drawers for $70. For just a few bucks, take home an attractive coverlet or decorative patterned throw. Near the register, find an odd mishmash of baubles, including a few pieces of unusual turquoise jewelry. This appealing shop carries just the right combination of fine items and miscellaneous stuff.

For a small assortment of this and that, visit **Mini World Thrift Shop**. Pick up inexpensive kitchen gadgets like popcorn poppers and blenders or grab a newish lamp for the living room here. A table full of folded linens at the front is stacked with placemats, curtains, and rugs. Choose from just a few home furnishings like a small end table or a glass-top coffee table. Hunt around for weirdo decorator objects like a seashell-encrusted owl, some framed artwork, or a bouquet of fake flowers. There's no telling what you might find for clothing, but dig through a bunch of used handbags and an assortment of flats and high-heeled shoes.

MINI WORLD THRIFT SHOP
2310 Melrose Avenue Northwest
Roanoke, Virginia
Phone: (540) 342-1196
Hours: Thurs–Sat 11:30–5

SANDRA'S CELLAR
Bush-Flora Shoe Building
109 Campbell Avenue Southwest
Roanoke, Virginia
Phone: (540) 342-8123
Hours: By chance or appointment

Sandra's Cellar is a wondrous curio cabinet full of strange and mysterious collectibles and oddball antiques. Find the store in the ground-floor shop front of the Bush-Flora building, not far from the Roanoke City Market. Don't miss the bizzarro window display, featuring a green and red garden gnome, a figurine of a ballerina doing the splits, and a skull with a fake human arm stuck between the jaws. Find old movie posters, vintage dishware, fancy silverware, stunning lamps, and other one-of-a-kind collectibles among the peculiar assortment. Though some items are on the pricey side, the enchanting array of weirdo stuff here will leave you spellbound. Make an appointment before you visit, as the store does not keep regular hours.

Thrifters on the hunt for used books and vinyl should visit the **Salvation Army**. Dive into massive stacks of records for 35 cents each. The collection contains plenty of old country crooners and "devotional" music. You can also thumb through tons and tons of paperback books, priced at only 25 cents apiece. There are just a few small racks of men's and women's clothes, but the goods are going cheap—less than $3 for almost any item. Furnishings are also a bargain. Nab a pair of olive green velour chairs for $35 or a long coffee table for $25. Smaller housewares are scattered here and there around the place. Find useful home appliances, like a stove, washing machine, or a working computer monitor, or dig through a shopping cart overflowing with hockey sticks for just a dollar each. Score with a pair of red, white, and blue roller skates for just a few bucks.

SALVATION ARMY
828 Jamison Avenue at 9th Street
Roanoke, Virginia
Phone: (540) 345-7141
Hours: Mon–Sat 9–4:30

RESCUE MISSION THRIFT STORE
421 4th Street Southeast
Roanoke, Virginia
Phone: (540) 777-7676
Hours: Mon–Sat 9:30–5:30

Sort through a giant bin of leather, pleather, and woven handbags at the **Rescue Mission Thrift Store**. The large shop offers excellent deals on furniture, too—pick up a 1950s-style Formica and chrome kitchen table for $50. The selection includes end tables, office desks, easy chairs, sofas, and vanity sets. China, dishes, plates, and cups are only 50 cents apiece. For clothing, check out men's dress shirts, ladies' skirts, pants, and dresses. Score on a $4 rodeo print skirt. The "Boutique Area" offers some new clothes with the tags still on, but you'll have to look hard to find any interesting purchases there. Better deals and steals can be found in the secondhand stash throughout the rest of the store.

SALEM, VIRGINIA

In nearby Salem there are a number of good places to get some new duds or quirky finds for the home. Investigate the huge **DAV (Disabled**

American Veterans) Thrift Shop for records, apparel, and an oddball collection of household goods. Clothing for men and children is inexpensive, with almost every item marked at less than $6. Old luggage, thermoses, and Tupperware make up the bulk of the housewares. A cabinet full of costume jewelry offers plastic earrings and other cheap-o trinkets, neatly attached to small colored cards. Pick up an old puzzle or sort through bazillions of once-loved dolls, with and without clothes. Take home a velvet Mona Lisa painting from the small gallery of thrifty artwork.

DAV (DISABLED AMERICAN VETERANS) THRIFT SHOP
2381 Roanoke Boulevard
Salem, Virginia
Phone: (540) 345-0560
Hours: Mon–Sat 9–5

GOODWILL
1493 East Main Street
Salem, Virginia
Phone: (540) 986-1319
Hours: Mon–Sat 8–9, Sun 12–8

J & L THRIFT SHOP
East Calhoun and South Broad Street
Salem, Virginia
Phone: Unavailable
Hours: Fri–Sat 9:30–5

Revamp your wardrobe in a single visit to the **Goodwill** on Main Street. Find dirt-cheap bargains on two-piece suits for $6, sleepwear for $3, and dresses for $4. The sea of clothing racks is filled with steals on turtlenecks, dressy shirts, and cardigans. A moderate selection of taffeta bridesmaid dresses and other formal wear is reasonably priced at $25 to $35. Find winter coats for $5.50, including a number of leather, suede, and fur-trimmed options. There is also a huge selection of belts and ties for a dollar apiece. Beyond clothing, find great price tags in the houseware aisles, with most items priced at less than $2.

J & L Thrift Shop is probably the quirkiest stop in Salem. Housed in a tiny building, an ex-wedding chapel, as we were told, the shop sells mainly household miscellany, in addition to a small selection of furniture. Pick up a pair of brown leatherette barstools for just $20 or a toy trunk for around $15. Cruise the shelves for pots and pans, a few books, small appliances, and kitchen implements, all priced at next to nothing. You could encounter just about any variety of doodad or gizmo here. Pick up a dog-eared paperback copy of *Elvis, What Happened? Three of*

His Closest Companions Tell a Shocking, Bizarre Story at the bargain blowout price of 50 cents.

Around the corner, raid **Vickie's Closet** for vintage and modern clothing for ladies and children. Try on one of the flowery vintage hats, priced at $5 to $30. Racks of dresses from the 1950s through the 1970s are generally marked from $25 to $40. Find a gown with beaded trim or an evening jacket with rhinestone buckles. Investigate the colored price tags for better deals and discounts. The store also carries the odd serving dish, wineglass set, and the like. Check out all corners of the little shop for good deals on contemporary clothing, children's play clothes, and costume jewelry as well.

> **VICKIE'S CLOSET**
> 4 East Main Street
> Salem, Virginia
> Phone: (540) 375-9010
> Hours: Tues–Sat 10–5
>
> **GOODWILL**
> 255 Peppers Ferry Road Northeast
>   (Route 114)
> Christiansburg, Virginia
> Phone: (540) 381-1544
> Hours: Mon–Sat 8–9, Sun 12–8

CHRISTIANSBURG, VIRGINIA

Continue in a southeasterly direction toward Christiansburg for the **Goodwill**. The aisles are full of woolen, striped sweaters, and even a few handmade cardigans. Find a puff-sleeve, polka-dot dress for just $2.50 or a fall jacket priced at $3.50. Don't miss the colorful soccer team T-shirts in the children's section—another clothes bonanza, courtesy of Goodwill! In addition to the overflowing racks, the shop offers computer monitors, printers, and lots of build-it-yourself components at great prices. Look through a small assortment of neatly stacked vinyl before you go.

PULASKI, VIRGINIA

The itty-bitty town of Pulaski offers a number of offbeat stops for thrifty and collectible merchandise. On shady Main Street, keep your eyes peeled for the purple painted shop front of the **Upstairs Downstairs Boutique**. On the main floor, find attractively displayed vintage fabrics, fringed Victorian lampshades, antique needlepoint and table linens, and fancy chandeliers. For the best stuff, head up the scarf- and shoe-lined stairwell to the second floor, where you can flip through racks of 1940s dresses, silk pajamas, and beaded cardigans for ladies. Try on a few fancy hats or feathery boas. Many items here are priced between $5 and $25. Downstairs, glance over the jewelry, where you can also find a few surprising bargains.

UPSTAIRS DOWNSTAIRS BOUTIQUE
27 West Main Street
Pulaski, Virginia
Phone: (540) 980-4809
Hours: Mon–Tues 10–5, Wed 10–1,
    Thurs–Sat 10–5, Sun 2–4

VINTAGE INVESTMENTS
80 West Main Street
Pulaski, Virginia
Phone: (540) 994-5848
Hours: Thurs–Fri 10–6, Sat 10–5

NANA'S NOOK
76 West Main Street
Pulaski, Virginia
Phone: Unavailable
Hours: Tues 1–5, Wed–Fri 10–5,
    Sat 10–1

Vintage Investments is another Main Street shop in Pulaski. Billed as "an old-fashioned junk shop," this place offers moderate deals on furniture and collectible antiques. Although the collection is a bit sparse, you can get yourself some nice furniture, such as old wooden chairs and rockers, and a few dressers and larger pieces. Find old *Life* magazines, collectible coins, and oddities like a "sip 'n' smoke" set, a ceramic ashtray and coffee cup combo.

Nana's Nook is the place to go for well-priced carnival glass and old Raggedy Ann dolls. The sign out front actually reads Main Street Flower Shop, but what you'll really find inside is a mixture of antiques and junk. Unearth an Avon perfume bottle shaped like a cupcake or a curious ceramic planter. There are a few pieces of furniture, like wooden dressers and tables, scattered throughout the shop, along with throw rugs and a few pieces of old paintings and artwork. Hunt down dresser bottles, jewelry boxes, and candy dishes, some at great bargains. Haggle for an even better deal.

The Blessing Station is the only true thrift shop in town. The store is located inside the old NAPA/Nipper's Machine Parts building on East Main Street, near the intersection with Route 99. The Blessing Station is not for the faint of heart. Sort through the messy jumble of housewares and clothing inside to find plastic measuring spoons, a crocheted tissue box cover, and baby strollers, along with sweaters, shirts, and dresses for less than $5. You won't find any fancy merchandise here at all, but delve into the stash and you just may find a salvageable goody or two. Super-cheap closeout items can be found up front for 25 cents to $3. Get thrifty with the store's everyday clothing special: cram everything that you can fit into a brown paper bag for just $5.

WYTHEVILLE, VIRGINIA

Continue your adventures down Interstate 81 and stop by the very clean and organized **Goodwill** in Wytheville. Find lots and lots of clothes here as well as more shoes than you can shake a stick at. Prices at this store are thrifty, and a little bit of investigation will probably turn up some offbeat apparel or fashionable basics. Thumb through titles in the large book corner for deals on hard- and softcover fiction. A small collection of jewelry and accessories near the front is full of steals as well.

THE BLESSING STATION
319 East Main Street
Pulaski, Virginia
Phone: (540) 980-5700
Hours: Mon–Sat 9–5

GOODWILL
1155 North Fourth Street
Wytheville, Virginia
Phone: (276) 228-8200
Hours: Mon–Sat 8–9, Sun 12–8

DIXIELAND FLEA MARKET
1035 North Fourth Street
Wytheville, Virginia
Phone: (276) 228-3555
Hours: Mon–Tues 10–5, Thurs–Sat 10–5, Sun 1–6

The **Dixieland Flea Market** is yet another adventure in secondhand shopping. The Flea Market is situated a bit off the road, so look out for the sign. Encounter lawn and garden furniture from many eras on the concrete front porch. Inside, objects are strewn on tables and shelves in roughly booth-like groupings. Find masses of junk and possible hidden treasures as well. Snag a hand-blown glass pitcher, a small grouping of owl figurines, an old saw, or some stereo equipment. Several small rooms toward the front carry bona fide collectibles, while the rest is an odd assortment of things that someone somewhere might someday collect.

SPARTA, NORTH CAROLINA

Heading south, you'll finally cross over the state line into North Carolina. If you've made it this far already, you're on your way to becoming a thrift expert. The school of secondhand shopping isn't over yet, as there are plenty more thrift scores in North Carolina—maybe even some of our favorites.

You can take Route 21 south to investigate a few hometown thrifts in Sparta, Roaring Gap, and Elkin. The little road weaves and winds through the mountains, offering some lovely scenic views and a few good secondhand shops, but not much beyond that.

If you'd rather take the fast track to Mount Airy, motor down Route 77 to Interstate 81 South. After about thirty miles, hop onto 89 East and proceed directly to Mount Airy.

Crafters should make it a point to drop in on Sparta's **Alleghany Cares Thrift Store** for dress patterns, colorful yarns, ribbons, macramé manuals, and other how-to books. Score with a bag full of yellow crocheted flowers for only 75 cents. Peek through several bins of slips and camisoles and try on some neat-o costume jewelry from the glass cases surrounding the counter. The clothing selection is very inexpensive, and lucky thrifters will find a few retro items mixed in. Pick up a new-to-you couch for only $35. Find coffee mugs, mismatched plates, and brightly colored Tupperware, all tagged at under $1 at this rural dirt-cheap depot.

> **ALLEGHANY CARES THRIFT STORE**
> 25 Womble Street
> Sparta, North Carolina
> Phone: (336) 372-5959
> Hours: Fri 10–7, Sat 10–3

On Main Street in Sparta, pick up a few good reads at **Books 'N Friends**. Snag six paperbacks for a dollar here. Everything else is dirt cheap as well—it would be hard to find anything here for more than $5. Get hard- and softcover books on health, cooking, history, and religion. Check out the biography section or find a secondhand book of poems, which never wear out. Though the shop is not huge, you're sure to find plenty of interest. The place is run by the Friends of the Library, who donate all proceeds to the Alleghany County Library.

ROARING GAP, NORTH CAROLINA

Make a quick stop at the **Alleghany Memorial Hospital Thrift Shop**, which shares a building with the Roaring Gap Post Office along Route 21. This is a great little shop for men's, women's, and children's clothing—ladies' slacks and skirts are tagged at $4. Bag a homemade red woolen poncho or a shiny blue raincoat for next to nothing. Hunt through the racks for a woolen men's sweater or a pink paisley dress. Find cheap-o paperbacks for just a quarter each. Though the shop is not enormous, time spent hunting through the accumulation of stuff can yield more than a few oddball items on the cheap.

BOOKS 'N FRIENDS
35 North Main Street
Sparta, North Carolina
Phone: (336) 372-5155
Hours: Wed–Sat 10–5

ALLEGHANY MEMORIAL HOSPITAL THRIFT SHOP
11372 U.S. Highway 21
Roaring Gap, North Carolina
Phone: (336) 363-3194
Hours: Summer hours Wed–Sat 9–1

HOSPITAL AUXILIARY THRIFT SHOP
103 West Main Street
Elkin, North Carolina
Phone: (336) 835-7909
Hours: Mon–Tues 9:30–5, Wed 9:30–2, Thurs–Fri 9:30–5, Sat 9:30–2

ELKIN, NORTH CAROLINA

Just off Route 21 on West Main Street in Elkin, you'll find the neat and orderly **Hospital Auxiliary Thrift Shop**. The shop tends to carry clothing items seasonally but always has some inexpensive household goods in stock. In the summer, pick up men's patterned swim trunks and ladies' swim apparel for just a few bucks each. Short-sleeve shirts, T-shirts, and other warm-weather styles are also cheap. Find an interesting selection of used books and old magazines, with occasional special ten-for-$1 deals. Inexpensive glassware, ceramic vases, and other household goods line the top shelves over racks of clothing. The "Best Quality" section offers special deals on higher-quality finds.

MOUNT AIRY, NORTH CAROLINA

Mount Airy is the hometown of Andy Griffith, hence the town's nickname of Mayberry. If you're really into the show, you'll be happy to find funny Aunt Bee and Andy souvenirs in practically every shop in town. If you hated that show, it could get a little annoying. There's always the drive-in movie theater to take your mind off things.

Stop by the small **Crossroad Thrift Shop** first to find books, books, and more books lining the window ledges and the book nook in back. Hardback titles go for only 50 cents, and paperbacks can be had for a quarter. Also find basic clothing for men and women here, with almost every item selling at $2 or less. Clothes for the kiddies are 50 cents each. The shop also offers a few sturdy pieces of furniture and just a few nicknacks and curio-type items. The store isn't open on weekends, but luckily there are a number of other interesting stops in the area.

CROSSROAD THRIFT SHOP
150 Franklin Street
Mount Airy, North Carolina
Phone: (336) 786-7240
Hours: Mon–Fri 10–2

SALVATION ARMY
446 West Pine Street
Mount Airy, North Carolina
Phone: (336) 786-9253
Hours: Mon–Fri 9–4, Sat 10–3

The Mount Airy **Salvation Army** is housed in a square-ish-shaped brick building on Pine Street. Browse the racks for suits, dresses, skirts, denim, and even formal wear. Most garments are priced at around $5. Sift through a rack full of leather, pleather, and canvas belts. Furniture and toys are in the back. Grab some plushy stuffed animals or pick up a well-priced sofa or loveseat here. Test out one of the many bikes, preferably not in the aisles, unless you want to make a real scene.

If nicknacks, figurines, and decorative house objects are what you're seeking, pull over for **Loretta's Antiques & Junk**. Spruce up your living room wall with a three-foot mushroom, frog, and butterfly assemblage, a real conversation starter. You could also take home a macramé art project, some cast iron pans, mixing bowls, or old teakettles from Loretta's collection. All smaller items are reasonably priced. The furniture selection includes plenty of quality finds, although the prices on these are higher. Spend $250 to $300 for an oak dresser with a beveled edge mirror. Vanity sets, curio cabinets, rocking chairs, and other home furnishings are also available. All the same, score with plenty of quirky discoveries from this funky shop.

LORETTA'S ANTIQUES & JUNK
1107 West Pine Street
Mount Airy, North Carolina
Phone: (336) 719-6800
Hours: Mon–Sat 9–5

MAYBERRY FLEA MARKET
1275 U.S. Highway 52
Mount Airy, North Carolina
Phone: (336) 789-0920
Hours: Fri 9am–12pm, Sat–Sun
7am–3pm

Mayberry Flea Market is a huge hodgepodge of old stuff, new stuff, junk, secondhand clothes, and sometimes a few little treasures mixed in. Experience chaos here on summer weekends, with people selling televisions, antique beads, fresh tomatoes, socks, and clocks made out of slices of wood under the awnings out front. Someone even tried to give us a free puppy when we visited. The adventure continues inside. Look for our favorite booth, full of little toys, miniature collectibles, and tiny oddities. Snack on an elf cup and saucer, $1 toys, funny plastic jewelry, and bizarre small objects. Snack on a snow cone or some cotton candy from the truck parked out front.

A great local attraction is the **Bright Leaf Drive-In Movie Theatre.** This classic slice of Americana has been open since the mid-1950s. Stop off at the concession stand, then park the thriftmobile for the after-dark screening. The drive-in is open all year round, and you can call ahead to find out what's playing.

WINSTON-SALEM, NORTH CAROLINA

Winston-Salem is the final thrifting destination along Route #4. Here you should check out several enormous Goodwills and a couple of other surprises as well. Pull out your trusty map to get around the city—it's probably bigger than you think.

First navigate your way to Patterson Avenue. The really big selection at the **Salvation Army** means that there's something for everybody here. The store is warehouse-size, so give yourself a little time to dig through it all. Delve into the huge housewares collection, found covering the shelves lining the left-hand side of the shop. Plenty of electronics items are lined up in rows, with many turned on so you can see that they work. Cruise the many clothing racks for tons of items priced at $3 or less or try on a suit or heavy winter coat for around $6. Unearth a few vintage finds, too. In the furniture section, test out the springs on a living room couch or easy chairs. Snag a varnished kitchen table or a nightstand for next to nothing.

> **BRIGHT LEAF DRIVE-IN MOVIE THEATRE**
> Andy Griffith Parkway
> (Highway 52 North)
> Mount Airy, North Carolina
> Phone: (336) 786-5494
> Hours: Open year round, Wed-Sun;
> call for movie times.
>
> **SALVATION ARMY**
> 4239 Patterson Avenue
> Winston-Salem, North Carolina
> Phone: (336) 723-9552
> Hours: Mon–Sat 9–6

Find clean and conservative clothing at **Yours Truly Consignment** in the Old Town Shopping Center. Locate lots of denim sundresses and sleeveless shirts. Flip through a large formal and bridal wear section, offering tons of beaded gowns and sequined numbers. Nifty casual ensembles are displayed on mannequins throughout the store. Also find scads of shoes and other accessories, such as fancy handbags and belts. Check the colored tags for discounts of up to 75 percent.

Make lots of thrifty discoveries at one of several local **Goodwills**. The University Parkway branch is colossal, offering clothes, home furnishings, books, and more. Breeze through racks of colorful corduroys, jeans, and khakis, all tagged at around $4. Shirts and tops are around the same price, with plenty to choose from. Pick up a soft sweater or an almost-new hooded sweatshirt. The small assortment of furniture is also very reasonably priced—pick up a velour easy chair, a cushy couch, or a mirrored coffee table for $20 to $45. Browse around in the book area, where titles are arranged according to subject matter. Spend hours digging around in this oversize treasure chest of secondhand goods.

> **YOURS TRULY CONSIGNMENT**
> Old Town Shopping Center
> 3800 Reynolds Road
> Winston-Salem, North Carolina
> Phone: (336) 924-6865
> Hours: Mon-Thurs 10–6,
> Fri-Sat 10–5
>
> **GOODWILL**
> 2701 University Parkway
> Winston-Salem, North Carolina
> Phone: (336) 725-1203
> Hours: Mon–Sat 8–8, Sun 1–7
>
> **TONY'S USED MERCHANDISE**
> 3442 Patterson Avenue
> Winston-Salem, North Carolina
> Phone: (336) 725-9996
> Hours: Mon–Fri 9–5:30, Sat 9–3

Look out for the lawn mower collection under tattered orange-and-white streamers at **Tony's Used Merchandise**. This little junk and stuff shop stocks an eccentric mix of vacuum cleaners, stereos, and televisions, plus much more. Check out the oddball collection of artistic masterpieces on the back walls. Find a few pieces of used-but-not-quite-antique home furnishings like a set of kitchen chairs or a bed frame. Browse though a random mix of old fabrics, cookie jars, ashtrays, and nicknacks. There are a few shelves of books to glance through, too. Lucky shoppers will come away with unique finds at dirt-cheap prices.

The Waughtown Street **Goodwill** has clothes, clothes, and more clothes to look at and try on. Jeans go for $4.25, and you can find fur coats and wraps for only $15. Find a red polyester dress with an anchor appliqué on the front for just a few dollars. Men can pick up business suits for only $10. The electronics corner carries curling irons and old telephones, among other random finds. Only $8 will buy you a fancy lamp for the living room. Take home a hat stand or a loveseat from the home furnishings area or score with a Yamaha electronic keyboard.

GOODWILL
514 Waughtown Street
Winston-Salem, North Carolina
Phone: (336) 777-0619
Hours: Mon–Sat 8–7, Sun 1–6

GOODWILL
208 Jonestown Road
Winston-Salem, North Carolina
Phone: (336) 768-9778
Hours: Mon–Sat 8–8, Sun 1–6

And last but not least on our road trip of thrifty good times, drop into one more area **Goodwill**. The Jonestown Road branch is a little bigger than the one on Waughtown Road. Find more electronics like old typewriters, coffeemakers, phones, and alarm clocks. Peek into the linen area for curtains and bedspreads. The shop offers lots of videotapes, some used CDs, and a few crates of records, including some offbeat finds like Olivia Newton John and the *Goldfinger* soundtrack for just a few dollars. Uncover some good books along the shelves for only $1.50. Mugs and glasses from the housewares shelves are usually $1 each. In the clothing department, find slips and lingerie for $2 and plenty of footwear options for $3 to $4. Drop by the formal wear racks for rustling evening gowns and something to wear to your next ball. Make a final sad attempt to squeeze it all into the trunk and count up all the pennies you saved on the ride home.

ROUTE #5:

Washington, D.C., to Raleigh-Durham, North Carolina

ACTS Thrift Store,
Dumfries, Virginia

Life Line Outreach Thrift Store
Henderson, North Carolina

Little Dodge City Antiques,
Ashland, Virginia

Route #5 heads due south through the heart of Virginia and into the northern parts of North Carolina. Following an almost straight path along Highway 1, breeze through the thrifty towns of Fredericksburg and Richmond, cross the border into North Carolina, and hit the Raleigh-Durham area for more secondhand odds and ends. Drop into lots of small-town thrifts along the way as the route deviates onto smaller roads.

Route #5 Driving Time: (stops not included) 8 hours

Steer the thriftmobile south and visit **Thrift Shopper's** collection of curios in Stafford before heading to the mecca of Fredericksburg for collectibles and stuff. The **Corner Thrift Shop, Second Time Around**, and the **Thrift Shop of Hospice Support Care** are only a few of the bargain centers you'll discover. In Ashland, you can root around in a roadside motel-turned-antiques-center at **Little Dodge City** or drop in for a delicious bite at **Homemades By Suzanne**. Your prayers have been answered in Richmond, home of **Luxor, Halcyon**, and **Pleiades**, the holy trinity of vintage apparel boutiques. The last stop on the route is the Raleigh-Durham area, where you can thrift the afternoon away at **Thrift World** and pick up just about **Everything But Grannies Panties**.

SPRINGFIELD, VIRGINIA

The thrift adventure begins a few minutes outside the Beltway in suburban Springfield. Pick up some quality used items at **Treasure Trove III**, which you'll find in the enormous Springfield Plaza. For men and women, clothing is a wee bit on the conservative side with many proper slacks, tops, and dresses. For accessories, scavenge for paisley scarves, a pair of oxfords, or some clip on earrings. The housewares department has no shortage of colorful retro bowls and plates, including small sets for $6 to $10, but those are about the only good vintage items that you'll find here. Coffeemakers, paperback books, and wooden furniture can be found near the back of the store, along with many lamps, chandeliers, and light fixtures for $5 to $10. Snag a silver candelabra while you're there.

TREASURE TROVE III
6416 Springfield Plaza
Springfield, Virginia
Phone: (703) 569-7751
Hours: Mon–Fri 10–8, Sat 10–6,
    Sun 11–4; in summer Sat 10–5

ACTS THRIFT STORE
14414 Jefferson Davis Highway
    (Route 1)
Woodbridge, Virginia
Phone: (703) 490-9697
Hours: Mon–Thurs 10–4:30,
    Fri–Sat 10–7

Many tags can be found at under $10, and many half-price deals are floating about the shop.

WOODBRIDGE, VIRGINIA

As you continue your journey along Route 1, you'll find more shopping plaza thrift stores in Woodbridge. Don't breeze through this town without stopping for two enormous secondhand dealerships. The first one on the list is the **ACTS Thrift Store**. Cruise through two large rooms with clothes, furniture, and bric-a-brac. You'll see one room with mostly threads for guys and gals alike. Find stylish denim or silky blouses or make for the impressive rack of wedding attire. The display counter up front contains baubles and bangles, fancy purses, and other boutique-quality accessories. In the second room spot plenty of sturdy couches, kitchen tables, and shelving options as well as many dishes, linens, and decorations for the home. ACTS Thrift Store is a super spot for clothes as well as for the random find.

Featherstone Square Antique Mall, Woodbridge, Virginia

The **Featherstone Square Antique Mall** is a gigantic warehouse with a gazillion dealer booths of large and small antiques and collectibles. Though not all the treasures here are dirt cheap, there are still many good deals kicking around if you look carefully. Pick up high-end antique tables and chairs, dusty books and collectible magazines, memorable dolls and figurines, ladies apparel, and tons of interesting dishware. Find a 1960s pearlized mug set or Victorian silk jacket for under $20. This mammoth antiques mall is a great place to find eclectic gifts and goodies, even for those on a budget.

DUMFRIES, VIRGINIA

Stay on Jefferson Davis Highway all the way into Dumfries for a second **ACTS Thrift Store**, located at the split in the road. This store has a different look from the Woodbridge branch, but the appeal is still the same—dirt cheap! Wheel a shopping cart through the various departments of the store to find special "off seasonal" clothing racks. Also browse through the usual fare of pants, tops, and formal attire, commonly priced at $6 or less. Test out an array of patterned couches and give the selection of wood cabinets and dressers a once over. Check the daily sales board for half-price and $1 sales. Find everyday steals in the large bin of records, offering tons of rock and lounge tunes.

ACTS THRIFT STORE
3670 Jefferson Davis Highway
   (Route 1)
Dumfries, Virginia
Phone: (703) 221-3298
Hours: Mon–Thurs 10–4:30,
   Fri–Sat 10–7

MILLERS THRIFT
18805 Fuller Heights Road
Triangle, Virginia
Phone: (703) 445-8481
Hours: Mon–Fri 10–6:30,
   Sat 10:30–6

THRIFT SHOPPER
3349 Jefferson Davis Highway
   (Route 1)
Stafford, Virginia
Phone: (540) 657-8166
Hours: Tues 11–5, Thurs–Sun 11–5

TRIANGLE, VIRGINIA

At **Millers Thrift** in Triangle, snoop through a small assortment of chrome percolators, old toasters, bright mixing bowls, and retro kitchen gear. Some better vintage items may be found at higher-than-average thrift prices; however, there are lots of options here—snag a 1960s macramé-style necklace or a bracelet with turquoise-color beads for just a few dollars. Also, check out a few larger home items like lamps, old trophies, and candy dishes.

STAFFORD, VIRGINIA

It's back on Route 1 again for a few quick stops in Stafford. Visit **Thrift Shopper**, a cluttered little store with a super collection of housewares, vintage clothing, and accessories. Shelves are piled high with an assortment of mismatched bowls, plates, glasses, and serving dishes. Find funky salt 'n' pepper shakers and old Avon bottles, along with some other random bric-a-brac. In the back, squeeze your way into the clothing rack and pull out a green chiffon gown or a pretty 1950s embroidered cardigan. Test out (outside) an elegant vintage umbrella with a Bakelite handle for only $3 or accessories like beaded handbags and handkerchiefs. At the counter, check out a rotating case with shimmering jewels. Thrift Shopper is overloaded with kitsch items that can be snatched up for under $5. Even the more expensive goods are still very reasonable, making this a favorite stop.

The **Goodwill Store** is just a couple of miles down the road. This big shop has a lot in the way of clothes, especially styles from the 1980s. The clothing is neatly organized, with prices clearly posted above the racks. Outfit every member of the family here with apparel going for less than $5 per item. Pick up some useful housewares, toys

> **GOODWILL STORE**
> 2840 Jefferson Davis Highway
>   (Route 1)
> Stafford, Virginia
> Phone: (540) 659-5939
> Hours: Mon–Sat 10–6, Sun 1–5
>
> **SECOND TIME AROUND
> THRIFT SHOP**
> 1183 Warrenton Road (Route 17)
> Fredericksburg, Virginia
> Phone: (540) 286-1962
> Hours: Tues–Fri 8–4, Sat 9–5,
>   Sun 9–3

for the kids, or an armload of books. Sort through stacks of old picture frames or take home one of many drinking glass sets for just a few dollars.

FREDERICKSBURG, VIRGINIA

Continue south along Route 1 and get ready for hours of thrift and antiques shopping in the small town of Fredericksburg. The center is a walkable historic district full of small shops, restaurants, and antiques malls.

Start out on the outskirts. As you approach the city, take a detour onto Route 17 for next-door neighbors Second Time Around Thrift Shop and PaTootie's. **Second Time Around** sorts its merchandise into a series of small rooms. There is a room for toys, one for kitchenware, and a main room crowded with curios, nicknacks, and all kinds of useful, colorful stuff. The shop sells pretty ceramic and glass dishes, stuffed animals, and games as well as a few cheap LPs and 45s. Score some offbeat finds on vinyl, like an Avon "Happy Birthday" record. Rifle through old biscuit tins, owl clocks, barrettes, vintage stationery, and salt 'n' pepper shakers. Shell out between $2 and $8 for most items and some buried 75-cent dirt-cheap deals.

Walk all the way through Second Time Around to get to **PaTootie's** antiques and collectibles. This homey, old-fashioned spot offers nicer collectibles than the thrift next door, but still has some cheap-o finds to uncover. Find fur collars, kitsch Avon collectibles, little figurines, and antique accessories for the home. Fine furnishings like a 1930s vanity may cost over $200, but smaller items can be found for $3 to $10. Most of the antiques here date from the Victorian era up to the 1960s. Get lucky and find a pink metal wastepaper basket with hand-painted flowers for $13 or a green straw sewing basket for around $15.

PATOOTIE'S
1183 Warrenton Road (Route 17)
Fredericksburg, Virginia
Phone: (540) 752-9688
Hours: Tues–Sat 10–4

FREDERICKSBURG SEVENTH DAY ADVENTIST COMMUNITY SERVICES THRIFT SHOP
717 Sophia Street
Fredericksburg, Virginia
Phone: (540) 373-5794
Hours: Mon–Thurs 10–5, Fri 10–2, Sun 12–5

Follow Route 3 into the historic district of Fredericksburg and steer toward Sophia Street for the **Fredericksburg Seventh Day Adventist Community Services Thrift Shop**. Huge orange letters on the front spell out T-H-R-I-F-T S-H-O-P. That's right, thrift shop. Inside you'll find multiple racks of clothing for men and women faring for under $5 each. Spot winter coats, tailored shirts, pajamas, and a rack of men's ties. Miscellaneous items might include some old glass bottles or a handmade ceramic bowl for only $4. The back room has lots of interesting dishes, lamps, and textured wall hangings. You might see a small end table or chair, but you'll have to go elsewhere for a large selection of furniture.

The **Antique Court of Shoppes** has such large quantities of merchandise that it had to open two shops on the same block. At the 914 address, explore the two-floor mayhem. Scan the displays for a punch bowl set or some shot glass souvenirs. Score on a hilarious beaver-shaped ashtray or an old stand-up lamp. There is also a booth full of old vinyl, with tons of mood music and classic rock options. Head upstairs for sale items. There you can find an old trunk, a few racks of vintage clothing (in poor condition), or a basket of $1 necklaces, among other things. More household accessories, like plaster statuettes, wall mirrors, and wooden benches, are scattered throughout. At this location pick up plenty of deals for under $20. Steer clear of the "crafty" Caroline Square Court of Shops that is inexplicably attached.

Jewelry, jewelry, jewelry! Find lots of it at the **Antique Court of Shoppes** at 1001 Caroline Street. This massive floor-through is a collector's paradise. In large display cases all over the shop, find a feather tiara, big glass gem rings and necklaces, rhinestone finery, and many one-of-a-kind jewelry pieces dating from the 1940s through the 1960s. You can find a bit of everything else here as well, like Barbies and action figures, a couple of booths of ladies' hats and dresses, plus tons of vintage housewares and linens. You can easily spend a whole day here browsing through the aisles.

ANTIQUE COURT OF SHOPPES
1001 Caroline Street
914-916 Caroline Street
Fredericksburg, Virginia
Phone: (540) 371-0685
Hours: Mon–Sat 10–5, Sun 12–5

UPSTAIRS DOWNSTAIRS ANTIQUES
922 Caroline Street
Fredericksburg, Virginia
Phone: (540) 373-0370
Hours: Mon–Tues 10–4, Thurs–Fri 10–4, Sat 10–5, Sun 12–5

If you have some extra time, visit a few more antiques malls in this historic area, like **Upstairs Downstairs Antiques**. There is no upstairs, and there's no downstairs. It's just a name. Get over it. This place isn't short on treasures, either. Along with sparkling jewelry and colorful drinking glasses, you can pick up an old set of Hardy Boys or Nancy Drew books. Find an array of collectible lunch boxes and a booth of vintage clothing. Kitchen accessories and utensils are well stocked. You can look for deals here, but will you find them? Dig deeply for the answer.

At the **Fredericksburg Antique Mall** on William Street, you'll find two floors of great stuff with many affordable price tags. Pick up a rainbow of Pyrex bowls, tasteful artwork, or a crocheted handbag. You'll also see attractive displays of vintage clothing and jewelry from Victorian times to the 1960s. In the back, look through the impressive selection of vintage textiles and lovely old linens. Find quilt pieces, embroidered napkins, and handkerchiefs at reasonable rates. Furniture prices run high, with many tagged between $95 and $275, but there are some very stylish pieces to dream about.

FREDERICKSBURG ANTIQUE MALL
211 William Street
Fredericksburg, Virginia
Phone: (540) 372-6894
Hours: Mon–Sat 10–5, Sun 12–5

CORNER THRIFT SHOP
2619 Princess Anne Street
Fredericksburg, Virginia
Phone: (540) 371-6738
Hours: Tues–Sun 9:30–4:30 unless
  weather conditions are really bad

Enough of antiques malls. Next, head to **Corner Thrift Shop** and thrift out. A row of furniture on the sidewalk outside will magnetically attract serious thrifters. Inside the shop on a summer day, it's stifling hot and a little dusty. There aren't any clothes here, but you can rummage through the piles of random stuff for mind-blowing finds. Hunt for coffee mugs with funny slogans, oddball kitchenware, holiday decorations, and odd nicknacks. Score with old photo or film equipment, still in the box. Upstairs, there's more room to stretch your legs and scavenge the collection of hit-or-miss castoffs. Record collectors shouldn't overlook the hefty stash of vinyl that's kept on the second floor. The prices here are good and thrifty. Chit chat with the colorful characters who hang around the shop before you go.

Corner Thrift Shop, Fredericksburg, Virginia

Head to Route 1 Business, aka Lafayette Boulevard, for the **Salvation Army Thrift Store**. The shop is clean and orderly, open and airy. Here you'll find a bit of everything—clothing, books, records, housewares, and furniture. Find floral print couches and basic wooden dressers for only $20 to $50. The prices here can't be beat. Score on some slogan T-shirts or other clothes for just a few measly dollars. There aren't too many extraordinary finds here, but you never know what may appear in the aisles.

SALVATION ARMY THRIFT STORE
4000 Lafayette Boulevard
(Route 1 Business)
Fredericksburg, Virginia
Phone: (540) 891-2242
Hours: Mon–Sat 9–4:45

To end the lengthy thrift tour of Fredericksburg, drop in on the **Thrift Shop of Hospice Support Care,** an incredible shop with many surprises up its sleeve. In the main room, check out a large wall of 50-cent earrings, many 25-cent mugs, and a huge cache of $1 to $3 housewares. Take home an unusual set of yellow and orange translucent glass plates. Head down the narrow passageway in the back for several smaller rooms of goodies. Browse through tons of interesting books and records, a room of Tupperware and other plastic storage devices, and an electronics room. The stellar craft room holds bins of dress patterns, trimmings, zippers, and yarns as well as old-school needlepoint and sewing books. The nice employees at HSC will make you feel right at home.

**THRIFT SHOP OF HOSPICE
  SUPPORT CARE**
3994 Lafayette Boulevard
  (Route 1 Business)
Fredericksburg, Virginia
Phone: (540) 361-7071
Hours: Mon–Fri 10–5, Sat 10–4

SOFT ENDS ANTIQUE & FLEA
On Washington Highway (Route 1)
Ashland, Virginia
Phone: (804) 798-6811
Hours: Thurs–Sat 10–5, Sun 1–5

ASHLAND, VIRGINIA

Stay hot on the thrifting trail with a short drive along Route 1 to Ashland. All of the shops are conveniently located directly on this road, otherwise known as Washington Highway.

Keep your eyes peeled for a white building on the side of the road, about two miles north of the intersection with Route 54. The name of **Soft Ends Antique & Flea** accurately describes the split personality of this shop. It really *is* half antiques and half flea. Here, you could find an incredible 1950s kitchen table set with shiny chrome trim and patterned seats. Unearth vintage Avon bottles, glass lamps, metal teapots, and kitchen appliances like electric mixers and blenders. The messier back area is the "flea market" part of the store, where you can rummage for coffee cups, linens, shower curtains, and a collection of sewing supplies. Score on an old reel-to-reel tape player or some vintage hatboxes. Add some 1960s dishes to your collection or spend a few dollars on an art deco tie tack.

Restock your closet with lucky finds from the **Goodwill** in Ashland. Look for polyester patterned dresses, ruffled secretary-style shirts, and some eclectic knits. There are also lots of options for fancy footwear, rubber-banded together in cubbyholes. Pick up low-key fashions and conservative styles as well, with many priced at $5 and under. There is also some discounted new clothing for women and teens mixed in. In the back of the store, scan rows of neatly organized dishware and electronics. Investigate the wall of books and records. Cassette tapes can be found at the register on your way out.

Don't miss quirky Little Dodge City, a deserted motel transformed into a row of antiques shops. First drop in on **Antiques of Tomorrow**, which has taken over the former motel lobby and an additional room. In the converted office space, pick up some collectible salt 'n' pepper shakers, shot glasses, and fanciful curios that line the front wall. Head to the register for pretty vintage pins and necklaces of the faux gem variety. Ornate lamps and intricate glass bowls may be found in the back. Flip through the box of 45 rpm records or snatch up a kitschy Orphan Annie mug before heading across the driveway to the furniture room. This little space is crowded with more lamps, tall wooden dressers, tables, rocking chairs, and statuettes. There are some nice pieces in here, but for furniture, the prices are higher than dirt cheap.

Next pay a visit to **Sister's Vintage**, an itty-bitty shop in the motel room next door. This darling boutique is filled with a variety of pretty things

GOODWILL
Washington Highway (Route 1)
  at Dow Gil Road
Ashland, Virginia
Phone: (804) 798-3871
Hours: Mon–Sat 9–8, Sun 12–6

ANTIQUES OF TOMORROW
Little Dodge City Antiques
12067 Washington Highway
  (Route 1)
Ashland, Virginia
Phone: (804) 752-4871
Hours: Mon–Sat 9–6, Sun 3–6
  in good weather

SISTER'S VINTAGE
Little Dodge City Antiques
12083 Washington Highway
  (Route 1)
Ashland, Virginia
Phone: (804) 264-1336
Hours: Mon 3–6, Thurs–Fri 3–6,
  Sun 2–5

in small quantities. There are a few dresses hanging on the wall, fancy purses, and a few stacks of vintage linens. Nab an embroidered pillow, a new-to-you tablecloth, or a June Cleaver apron. Lucky shoppers could uncover a pair of 1970s-era, hand-painted red wooden mules. Snag a few trinkets or decorative bottles, printed curtains, or a jewelry box from this tiny shop.

Find larger quantities of stuff to sort through at **Billy's Collectibles**, a treasure trove of unique things from the past. Venture inside to find a chaotic jumble of baskets, utensils, and license plates hanging from the ceiling. At first the store appears crammed, but the sea of snarled merchandise parts toward the back, where items are more spread out and elegantly displayed, with a hint of country charm. Find an array of plates, collectible glasses, and bowls. Investigate the rotating case of jewelry, old pens, and decals. Doll collectors will have their choice of Barbies, Smurfs, and other kitschy collectibles. Find a booth of vintage hats and a few older garments. Don't forget to check out the great lunch box collection up front and the books and old postcards. Prices vary, and the oak furniture is especially high, but get lucky with several items for under $10.

> **BILLY'S COLLECTIBLES**
> Little Dodge City Antiques
> 12083 Washington Highway
>   (Route 1)
> Ashland, Virginia
> Phone: (804) 798-9414
> Hours: Mon 10–5, Thurs–Sat 10–5,
>   Sun 1–5
>
> **HOMEMADES BY SUZANNE**
> 102 North Railroad Avenue
> Ashland, Virginia
> Phone: (804) 798-8331
> Hours: Mon–Fri 9–2, Sat 9–3

For lunch, cross the tracks to the charming old railroad district of Ashland for lunch at **Homemades By Suzanne**, a great luncheonette. This little café serves up delicious sandwiches, amazing prepared salads, quiches, and assorted bakery treats. Place your order at the counter for a barbecue sandwich, veggie wrap, or some deviled eggs. Meals come with your choice of fresh, southern-style side salads like marinated vegetables or peas with cheese. For dessert, have a slice of lemon meringue or pecan pie and get yourself a cup of coffee to go with it. Enjoy your meal in one of the little wooden booths.

GLEN ALLEN, VIRGINIA

Slightly off the beaten path, look for Route 33 in Glen Allen to find **Dick & Jeanette's Antiques** on Staples Mill Road. Snoop through two buildings, full of enough collectibles to satisfy almost anybody. In the main shop find rows of green and umber glassware and a crazy collection of shot glasses, punch bowls, and pitchers. Pick up offbeat salt 'n' pepper shakers, outdated food choppers, kitchenware, and cooking utensils. Get turned on to Avon bottles, Snoopy memorabilia, and western belt buckles. Fashionable ladies will flock to the floral chokers and rhinestone and beaded jewels. Outside, in the big furniture

> **DICK & JEANETTE'S ANTIQUES**
> 10770 Staples Mill Road (Route 33)
> Glen Allen, Virginia
> Phone: (804) 672-6138
> Hours:Unavailable

Dick & Jeanette's Antiques, Glen Allen, Virginia

shed, find old vanities, dressers, and chairs—even a stray pipe organ. As usual, the smaller items are in the more affordable price range.

RICHMOND, VIRGINIA

Richmond, Virginia, is a dirt-cheap city. Expect lots of incredible thrifting in the stores here as well as a few noteworthy vintage shops to mix it up a bit. Many of the shops are in the cute college area of town.

From Route 1, turn onto Azalea Avenue and look for the Richmond Henrico Turnpike. The first stop in Richmond is the **Arc of Virginia Thrift Store,** across from the Amoco gas station in the Meadowood Square shopping plaza. Arc of Virginia is a great store for clothes. Get threads for the entire family, and for creative dressers there are lots of interesting T-shirts circa 1982. Average prices on clothing run from $3 to $10, and prom dresses can go up to $25. The furniture has a wide price range and can cost up to $100, and the selection is not the best. The record collection contains an impressive mix of artists from Beethoven to Donna Summer. Get lucky and pick up a highly collectible mod lamp from the 1960s or '70s for only $5.

ARC OF VIRGINIA—THRIFT STORE
Meadowood Square Plaza
5116 Richmond Henrico Turnpike
Richmond, Virginia
Phone: (804) 329-8500
Hours: Tues–Fri 10–7, Sat 9–5

SALVATION ARMY STORE
4307 West Broad Street
Richmond, Virginia
Phone: (804) 359-5554
Hours: Mon–Sat 10–6

Vinyl buffs should head south for the **Salvation Army Store,** a two-room cavernous warehouse for thrifty exploration on West Broad Street. In the back room, there's an unbelievable record collection, rows and rows of LPs that would take at least a few hours to flip through. Find most of the vast clothing selection in the main room, including a great lingerie section with neatly hung racks of pajamas and frilly slips. Snag a batwing sequin top or Debbie Gibson-esque outfit from the aisles. Anyone on the hunt for furniture is in luck. There are lots of good-quality upholstered couches and chairs, wooden dressers, and kitchen tables in the $30 to $60 dollar range. Take home an incredible pair of green glass vintage lamps with velvet shades for only $6 each. Inquire about the dollar day sales for even more amazing steals.

The Southside Plaza on East Belt Boulevard is home to a few noteworthy shops. First stop by the **Good Samaritan Ministries** thrift store for polyester, an armload of shoes, and endless aisles of dishware. Look through racks of clothing for all ages or test out some used exercise equipment. Quirky mugs and swarms of little figurines inhabit the shelves. For furniture, find pairs of couches, dining room sets, desks, trunks, and filing cabinets at erratic prices from $40 to $400. Pick up a GE electric wall clock, circa 1972, at the discount price of only $10. Stock up on a few computer parts if you're an electronics genius.

GOOD SAMARITAN MINISTRIES
Southside Plaza
4680 East Belt Boulevard
Richmond, Virginia
Phone: (804) 232-7228
Hours: Mon–Tues 9–5, Wed 9–4,
   Thurs–Sat 9–5

GOODWILL STORE
Southside Plaza
4646 East Belt Boulevard
Richmond, Virginia
Phone: (804) 230-4935
Hours: Mon–Sat 9–8, Sun 11–5

If you are in need of a bowling ball, then head to the **Goodwill Store**, a couple of stores down in the same plaza, for a used one. If bowling isn't your sport, then pick up a set of golf clubs, instead. Besides sporting equipment, this Goodwill store carries most of the usual. The store is huge, and the overwhelming selection of clothes hasn't escaped the colored tag sales. Everything is well organized, and prices are listed above racks unless specially marked. Lamps, thrift-style paintings, and stacks of TVs are readily available, but don't expect to find much furniture. For an odd find, hit the book area for cookbooks and crafts manuals.

Try the area around West Cary and West Main streets for a lively shopping area of cafés and funky boutiques. **Pleiades** on West Main Street is part vintage clothing store, part bridal shop, part costume shop, and part thrift. Get past the spastic dog on the porch and you're in for a golden treat. On the main floor you'll find many pretty vintage dresses and shirts from the 1950s and '60s, mixed in with some handmade reproductions. Also find some newer used jeans and tops in the mixture. Accessorize burlesque style with sequins, tassels, and lace, or be bold and daring with a bustier or slip from the lingerie collection. In the back, part the curtain to explore the bridal room, containing stunning vintage and handmade gowns. Charla, the owner of the shop, also happens to be a fashion designer who creates custom-made wedding attire as well as some of the other handmade garments in the shop.

PLEIADES
1208 West Main Street
Richmond, Virginia
Phone: (804) 355-5462
Hours: Tues–Sat 11–5

FAN TASTIC THRIFT
1914 West Main Street
Richmond, Virginia
Phone: (804) 358-7164
Hours: Mon–Sat 10–6

Upstairs, men can get some retro duds like polyester suits, tuxedo shirts, and shoes. There is also a record room with rows of LPs and shelves full of 45s and comic books. Don't miss the old books in the hallway, and before you leave, take one last look around for a new scarf or silk tie.

The world of **Fan Tastic Thrift** is super-fantastic, so pull up and park your vehicle in its private lot. The bustling warehouse store can fill all of your clothing and houseware needs, and furniture, too, if you're lucky. Grab a toaster oven, electric mixer, coffeemaker, and an iron, perfect for poor college students who need some cheap, but working kitchen appliances. Kids will have big eyes when it comes to the toy department, a huge two-sided row of stuffed animals and action figures. The full racks of clothes reveal many up-to-date fashions and have an especially wide range of tops and pants for teens. For a more dapper look, play dress-up in the aisles with a fur wrap or fur-trimmed coat. Dishware is fantastically cheap at under $1 apiece. Clothes are almost all $10 or less. Test out a couple of fluffy couches in the smallish furniture area. Liberate a new-to-you tricycle from the stash in the back and ride out.

For a vintage bazaar, turn to **Luxor Vintage Clothing** boutique on West Cary Street. This shop has some stupendous fashions on the main floor and an upstairs room with special surprises. Apparel here is of the best quality. Pick out flowing velvets and chiffons from a rack of Aubrey Beardsley-style gowns. Other racks contain various retro looks from the 1950s, '60s, and '70s. Nab a swinging A-line cape, a strapless ballerina dress, or a multitier-ruffled shirt. The shop's selection of glitzy shoes, purses, and scarves will complete any outfit. Encircling the cashier, a glass counter display of multicolored rhinestones and shiny metals is like a jewelry store on its own. Junkier and less costly baubles sit apart in their own treasure box.

Upstairs find a disheveled collection of odds and ends. Spot household items like teapots, dishes, and silver-plated services. A few collectible figurines and dusty books are scattered about the tables and floor. Dip into the huge bin of vintage ladies' hats. The prices at Luxor are city-size, so expect to pay at least $15 for any special finds.

> **LUXOR VINTAGE CLOTHING**
> 3001 West Cary Street
> Richmond, Virginia
> Phone: (804) 359-6780
> Hours: Mon–Thurs 11–6, Fri–Sat
>   11–7, Sun 12–5
>
> **BYGONES VINTAGE CLOTHING**
> 2916 West Cary Street
> Richmond, Virginia
> Phone (804) 353-1919
> Hours: Mon–Sat 10–6, Sun 11–4

If by some chance Luxor didn't fulfill your deepest vintage wear desires, head down the street to **Bygones Vintage Clothing** for a similar experience. The creative window display (mannequin suspended in mid-air) will entice you to peek inside for a look around. Near the front of the shop find fashion books of the "eras," along with complimentary fashion plate stickers. Surf the racks to find delicate dresses from the 1920s, a case of glittering accessories, and a silky collection of bras, tap pants, and peachy slips. Spot costumes galore, from pinafores and Daisy Dukes to go-go minis and fly-collar shirts. Prices span from $8 to $80, with many in the middle range, depending on the quality of the vintage.

Don't dismay, because true bargains are on the way at **Diversity Thrift** a few blocks down the road. Explore three large rooms of clothing, furniture, housewares, and accessories. Sort through contemporary clothing and formal wear for men, women, and children. Dig through the crowded racks for the odd retro piece and expect to pay only $2 to $4 for most. Men's suits cost around $12, and prom wear can be up to $25, but deep discounted tags might reveal 75 percent off steals.

Save a bundle on washing machines, dishwashers, computers, and fax machines. The huge vinyl area has a vast selection of pop and classic rock hits, but some of the records are inexplicably overpriced. For better bargains, get some candles, Tupperware, and ceramic flower pots over in housewares. Comb through carefully for many quirky finds.

The furniture room at Diversity Thrift may be the highlight of the store. Furniture is stacked from wall to wall in a back room, and the selection is brimming with unusual pieces. Find many pianos and pipe organs, old trunks, wardrobes, entertainment centers, dressers, and rugs. An "aroma spa" (don't ask) or a pink 1950s chrome trimmed table could be waiting for you just around the corner.

DIVERSITY THRIFT
1729 West Cary Street
Richmond, Virginia
Phone: (804) 353-8890
Hours: Wed–Sat 10–6

FAMILY THRIFT CENTER
5432 Midlothian Turnpike
Richmond, Virginia
Phone: (804) 231-1737
Hours: Mon–Sat 9–6

Last stop in Richmond is the warehouse-style **Family Thrift Center** on Midlothian Turnpike. On your way in you'll notice a puzzling sign advertising designer brands like DKNY. We have no idea what that's all about. As far as we could tell, Family Thrift is just your basic mega thrift store. It does have a "Boutique Unique" section in the back with cases of jewelry, collectible dolls, and curios (no DKNY here). Revel in $2 dresses and slashed price tags, but try not to get lost in the many aisles of clothing. Mosey into the additional room of electronics, books, and records and try to remain calm about the dishware selection. Pick up a nice set of "TAB" drinking glasses to take home. Save your furniture aspirations for future stops.

CHESTER, VIRGINIA

Head farther south along Route 1 toward Chester. Stop into the **Chester Antique Center**, an immense multidealer mall/theme park for antiques. Find everything from an Egyptian pharaoh statue to a set of Hanna Barbera drinking glasses. There are many booths offering up chairs, vanities, end tables, and desks, but most of the furniture is on the high end in price as well as in style. Vintage clothing, action figures, and retro housewares are the more affordable choices here. Take home a crocheted blanket, a set of china, and a fashionable poodle-shaped pin. Sniff out $10 deals in this surprisingly quiet place.

> **CHESTER ANTIQUE CENTER**
> 11700 Jefferson Davis Highway (Route 1)
> Chester, Virginia
> Phone: (804) 768-7679
> Hours: Mon–Sun 10–6
>
> **GOODWILL STORE**
> 24 Pickwick Avenue
> Colonial Heights, Virginia
> Phone: (804) 520-7122
> Hours: Mon 9–6, Tues 9–8,
> Wed–Thurs 9–6, Fri–Sat 9–8,
> Sun 12–6

COLONIAL HEIGHTS, VIRGINIA

Continue the journey south along Route 1 to Colonial Heights and check out the **Goodwill Store**, our familiar friend. This carpeted shop contains many round racks of clothes with clearly marked signs for garment type and prices. Spend only $7 on a pair of blue jeans or $3 on a pencil skirt. Pull leatherette belts and purses off the rack. Deeper into the store you'll encounter shelves full of brassware and silver platters and clusters of tapes and CDs. Mayhem ensues when spontaneous $1 sales are announced over the loudspeaker—hustle to grab the goods before the end of the fifteen-minute sale. Fifty percent off early bird specials are also a treat (if you get up at the crack of dawn) between 7 a.m. and 10 a.m. on certain days of the month.

Avoid thrift overload in the several rooms of multifaceted junk at the **DAV (Disabled American Veterans) Thrift Store**. For threads find anything from fabric remnants to lacey lingerie. Check out the appliance room for a slew of phones and answering machines, toasters and coffeemakers, hair dryers, curling irons, and dishwashers. Another room has kids' clothes plus living room furniture and TVs. Grab a shopping basket and fill it up with inexpensive trinkets, scarves, and tote bags. Bump into a few well-dressed mannequins hiding in corners around the shop.

DAV (DISABLED AMERICAN VETERANS) THRIFT STORE
2112 Boulevard (Route1/301)
Colonial Heights, Virginia
Phone: (804) 526-8660
Hours: Mon–Sat 9–6

TRADING POST
314 North Sycamore Street
Petersburg, Virginia
Phone: (804) 733-4772
Hours: Mon–Fri 9–5, Sat 9–2

PETERSBURG, VIRGINIA

To the southeast, Petersburg is a city for the brave. Though it used to be a prosperous city, over the last few decades, Petersburg has seen lots of economic difficulties. Watch your step after dark in some neighborhoods. Head to the Old Town area for a few old antiques and junk shops that have withstood the test of time.

Old Town Petersburg may look like a ghost town, but look closely for hidden treasures. **Trading Post** on North Sycamore Street consists of three cavernous rooms filled with used furniture and other good junk jumbled all around. Dusty 1940s dressers, in-cabinet record players, and boot-changing stations are among the many wooden finds. The center room contains a record trove of used favorites, from country music to disco and rap. Search in dark corners for shelves of antiquated books (bring your flashlight). Investigate farther back for random items like a treadmill, oceanic paintings, or a leather horse saddle.

Around the corner pay a special visit to **Second Hand Rose**, the little vintage jewel of Petersburg. Though not huge, the boutique is packed with highly sought-after vintage apparel for women. Spot Victorian high-collared shirts, 1950s cashmere sweaters, wool suits, feathery hats, dainty gloves, and fur-trimmed coats. Drool over the picture-perfect displays of merchandise and try to refrain from buying up everything in sight. As for prices, expect to spend $12 and up (often on the upside) for these fineries, except for the special $2 sales racks.

> **SECOND HAND ROSE**
> 16 West Old Street
> Petersburg, Virginia
> Phone: (804) 733-5050
> Hours: Tues–Sat 10–5
>
> **SALVATION ARMY THRIFT STORE**
> 3229 South Crater Road
> (Route 301)
> Petersburg, Virginia
> Phone: (804) 526-8558
> Hours: Mon–Sat 10–6
>
> **GOODWILL**
> 619 East Atlantic Street (Route 58)
> South Hill, Virginia
> Phone: (434) 447-3565
> Hours: Mon–Sat 8:30–7

On your way out of town, quickly hit the **Salvation Army** on South Crater Road (Route 301) for a tried and true thrift experience. Dirt-cheap prices prevail at $3 to $7 for clothes, with some additional half-price sales. A sizable area of cushy patterned couches, wardrobes, wood bed frames, and mattresses can be found, along with many nicknacks, dishes, and toys, in the back. Take over the aisles with one of the red shopping carts and wheel your purchases (or your friends) around.

SOUTH HILL, VIRGINIA

It's true—good things do come in small packages, which is what's in store for the die-hard thrifter who ventures to the string of small towns past Petersburg. Route 1 now bears to the southwest toward South Hill. First, hit up the local **Goodwill** store. This branch is especially cheap for clothes, with mostly $1 to $3 labeled racks. Pick up some basic articles of lounge or career wear. There's a tiny furniture room in the back, with just a few pieces for sale. The library of hardcover and paperback books, records, and eight-track tapes will yield more special finds.

For a great selection of nonclothing goods, check out the sprawling multiroom **South Hill Value Center**. Get everything you need to outfit your home, along with some surprise lucky catches of the day. Acquire a four-poster bed, a velvet chair with gold tassels, furry toilet seat covers, pots, pans, or salad bowls. The book room is packed with hundreds of titles for adults and kids, and another room has exercise equipment and large appliances. Sort through a bin of played-out Barbies and a few piles of hubcaps. If you start to feel like an out-of-towner here, tell them you're on a dirt-cheap mission from outer space.

> **SOUTH HILL VALUE CENTER**
> 813 North Mecklenburg Avenue
> (Route 1)
> South Hill, Virginia
> Phone: (434) 447-5890
> Hours: Mon–Fri 9–5, Sat 9–3
>
> **DISCOUNT VARIETY CENTER**
> 208 Wilson Street
> South Hill, Virginia
> Phone: (434) 447-8889
> Hours: Mon–Thurs 9:30–5,
> Fri 9–5:30, Sat 9–5

For similar fare on a smaller scale, try the **Discount Variety Center** on Wilson Street. This place is also clothing-free, but there's lots of furniture in the back room with little space to walk. Find a pair of owl-shaped wall relief hangings, a groovy old-school umbrella, and maybe even a working electric guitar. Sort through the melange of old Tupperware and kitchen utensils, computers, coffee tables, beds, and couches. Big items cost anywhere from $15 to $100, depending on quality. Deck out your house for under $5 with nicknacks and accessories. The oddities are easy to spot, even in this cluttered environment. Discount Variety Center does a pretty good job in the bargain department.

Explorations into the back rooms of the **Lake Country Indoor Flea Market** will reveal a few nice surprises. First, snoop through the mix of new and used crafts and curios up front, along with token vintage dishware and jewelry. Then proceed straight to the back room for better fare. Drop by the booth of just vinyl, with bins full of everything from Frank Sinatra to Stevie Wonder hits. Across from the record booth, browse the used book nook. Keep going to find a small setup from Madeline's Corner, benefiting the Southside Center for Violence Prevention. In this area everything is super-cheap, from 10 cents to $1. Stuff clothing in a bag for a buck, grab a 25-cent leather purse, and acquire an earring tree for a dime! Nearby, there's a cutesy little display from a lady with a collection of quirky Avon products ("man with a turban"-shaped comb, 50 cents) and other collectible rarities.

LAKE COUNTRY INDOOR FLEA MARKET
935 West Atlantic Street
South Hill, Virginia
Phone: (434) 447-3993
Hours: Wed–Fri 10–5, Sat 8–5, Sun 11–5

LIFE LINE OUTREACH THRIFT STORE
2014 Raleigh Road
Henderson, North Carolina
Phone: (252) 430-6115
Hours: Mon–Fri 8–5, Sat 7–4:30

HENDERSON, NORTH CAROLINA

Still following Route 1, the thrifting trail now crosses over the state line into North Carolina. **Life Line Outreach Thrift Store** appears at first to be just a dark doorway in a practically windowless, tan cinderblock building. But inside—holy smokes! Find cluttered racks and mounds of clothes, most priced from $1 to $2, with a number of retro finds lurking in the aisles. An ongoing special on clothes allows you to cram whatever you can find into a bag for only $5. Nose through the maze of aisles to find fancy dresses, baubles, handbags, and accessories—all cheap, cheap, cheap! Glance through the shifting stacks of books (watch your step here) and a small collection of weirdo greeting cards. Find rock-bottom price tags on dishes, mugs, belts, scarves, old cameras—you name it. Devote some extra time to investigating this little jewel, maybe our favorite shop on the route. On Fridays and Saturdays, the upstairs is open, too, offering old furniture and plenty of warm coats in addition to the bargains downstairs.

Find more inexpensive clothing options at the **Salvation Army Thrift Shop** on West Montgomery Street. Throw down a few pennies for mostly basic finds from the stockpile of apparel for men and women. The selection is nothing special, but almost everything is tagged at around $3, a great deal for any offbeat treasures that you might encounter. Especially fine bargains are located in the book department, where you can unearth colorful children's storybooks and lots of encyclopedia sets. Take note of any special daily deals, which are posted on the chalkboard behind the counter.

SALVATION ARMY THRIFT SHOP
222 West Montgomery Street
Henderson, North Carolina
Phone: (252) 492-9552
Hours: Mon–Sat 9:30–4:30

GCF DONATION CENTER & STORE
Market of Wake Forest Plaza
12269 Capital Boulevard
Wake Forest, North Carolina
Phone: (919) 570-8292
Hours: Mon–Fri 9–8:30, Sat 9–6,
 Sun 12–6

SECOND HAND ROSE
 THRIFT STORE
708 North Main Street (Route 1A)
Wake Forest, North Carolina
Phone: (919) 562-8687
Hours: Mon–Sat 9:30–5, Sun 12–7

WAKE FOREST, NORTH CAROLINA

GCF (Goodwill Community Foundation) Donation Center and Store is a large thrift, located in a sprawling plaza in Wake Forest. Cruise the racks for a nice selection of low-priced quality apparel. Have your pick of warm woolens and blouses for only $3. Also find better labels, such as Banana Republic, Ralph Lauren, and Express. Don't miss out on some crazy finds in the used record and book stacks. Take home a pretty glass vase or ceramic spoon rest from the housewares area. Larger chain stores have donated slightly imperfect, but never used items to the stash—find a brand-new sleeping bag for $12 or some shelving units, still in the box.

After the bright fluorescent lights of a chain thrift, drop by the **Second Hand Rose Thrift Store**, a privately owned, cheery, ragtag kind of shop. Flip through a huge assortment of bargain belts and funky clothes at great prices—most clothing items are tagged at $2 or $3. Pick up a soft maroon cardigan or a polyester button-up blouse. Everything in the shop has its own appointed area. Drop by the crafts cabinet in the back for drawers full of findings, yarns, and dress patterns or peek through the folded fabric remnants along the shelves. Bundle up with hats, scarves, and other discoveries from the winter room. For housewares, snag some cheery yellow dinner plates or a sparkly candleholder for next to nothing. We think this place is out of sight.

DURHAM, NORTH CAROLINA

From Wake Forest, take either Route 98 or Interstate 540 west to Durham. Drop by a few of our local favorite stops for basic clothing, inexpensive furniture, and glitzy vintage wear in hot spots all over town.

Everything But Grannies Panties is a big, crazy house full of stuff! The name really says it all. Find masses of interesting objects inside and out at this secondhand extravaganza. Comb through tons of $1 records and used videotapes or choose from the huge selection of punch bowl sets for under $20. In the pantry, you can look for pots, pans, microwaves, ironing boards, and casserole dishes. Upstairs, encounter an old bed piled high with cheap decorator pillows. Find a one-of-a-kind writing desk for only $35. Peer into the linen closet for neatly folded sheets and pillowcases for $2 or less. In the bathroom, you'll find the tub overflowing with fabric odds and ends and a nearby shelf stacked with sewing how-to books and knitting manuals. Tables in the backyard are covered with "anything for $3" deals. Pick up furnishings from the front yard and various locations upstairs and down. Everything But Grannies Panties is like a giant, never-ending moving sale. Don't skip this one!

> **EVERYTHING BUT GRANNIES PANTIES**
> 2926 Guess Road
> Durham, North Carolina
> Phone: (919) 471-0996
> Hours: Mon–Fri 10–5:30, Sat 10–5

Find a cluttered commotion at the Latta Road **Salvation Army**. The all-ages clothing selection is cheap, but this store might be better for housewares and home furnishings. Sort through bin after bin of old sewing patterns. Find more used vinyl and take home some cool thrifty art, like a giant painting of a toreador for just $10. Along with kitchen appliances, you could find anything from stereos to stacks of old clocks to typewriters or even a toilet bowl. Get some new light fixtures or lampshades for extra-cheap prices or a desk or floor lamp from the 1960s.

There's tons of merchandise to dig into at this large shop, including plenty of furniture, some of which is priced a bit high along the budget scale. Bang out a few tunes on one of several pianos and electric organs before you go.

SALVATION ARMY
124 Latta Road
Durham, North Carolina
Phone: (919) 477-5457
Hours: Mon–Sat 9–5

GOODWILL INDUSTRIES
5267 North Roxboro Road
Durham, North Carolina
Phone: (919) 479-1141
Hours: Mon–Fri 9–8:30, Sat 9–6,
    Sun 12–6

THRIFT WORLD
2000 Chapel Hill Road
Durham, North Carolina
Phone: (919) 490-1556
Hours: Mon–Fri 9–7, Sat 9–6,
    Sun 11–5

Next, visit the **Goodwill Industries**, located on North Roxboro Road between Latta and Seven Oaks roads. You can't see the building from the street, but if you turn in at the Burger King and drive back, you'll see a red brick building with a GCF sign. Inside, delve into the aisles to find lots of clothes, especially a very large offering for men. The most expensive item on the menu is men's suits, priced at around $10. Poke through the assortment of higher- and lower-quality furniture to find sectional sofas, tables, chairs, and shelving units. Probably the best reason to visit this Goodwill is to hunt for offbeat finds in the racks.

Step into the huge **Thrift World** in the Shoppes at Lakewood Plaza to sift through lots and lots of great clothes for men, women, and children. Pick up a denim skirt for $3 to $5 or some jeans and cords for $4 to $7. Snag a satiny blazer for only $6. Dresses range from $2 to $9, and there's a fantastic variety to choose from. Look over a collection of old magazines like the *New Yorker* and *National Geographic* or plow through the overloaded bookshelves for 50-cent finds. The record area is small, but you could find musical oddities like Shawn Cassidy or Jethro Tull in the bunch. Select from rows and rows of working televisions, priced from $20 to $90. You'll encounter a large collection of chairs: rocking chairs, easy chairs, office chairs, and bar stools. Also look over the other home furnishings, like sofas and end tables, for some really good deals.

Scout out the great stash of retro duds at **The Untidy Museum**, the best clothing vintage shop for miles around. You'll find lots to take home for between $10 and $45. Rifle through the racks to find dress after fabulous dress, like a marvelous lavender tulle cocktail dress, with the bodice covered in tiny flowers. Or snag a turquoise wool fur-collared coat for the winter. Try on the collection of hats—satin ones, fancier ones with sequins, or even a flowery bathing cap. A large men's wear room carries everything from silk PJs to corduroy jackets. Don't forget the bin of $3 ties. Find leather jackets, leather pants, bowler hats, and shoes in all styles. The shop is full from floor to ceiling with amazing finds. Lots of beaded and glimmering jewelry can be found up front, along with pins, earrings, compacts, barrettes, belt buckles, and cuff links. There's also a huge selection of funky handbags, clutches, and wallets. Snag a circus-type leotard, old-fashioned slip, or elegant dressing gown from the amazing stash.

> **THE UNTIDY MUSEUM**
> 1116 Broad Street
> Durham, North Carolina
> Phone: (919) 416-1800
> Hours: Tues–Wed 11–5,
>   Thurs–Sat 11–7
>
> **HABITAT HAND-ME-UPS STORE**
> 3215 Old Chapel Hill Road
> Durham, North Carolina
> Phone: (919) 403-8668
> Hours: Tues-Sat 10-5

Thrifters in search of nice furniture should pay a visit to the **Habitat Hand-Me-Ups Store** for a wide selection of home furnishings. The affluent surrounding neighborhood means that the shop carries some high-quality goods and sometimes gets in nicer vintage furniture, too. Almost everything found in this shop is in excellent condition. Snag a pair of rattan chairs for $25 each or a cozy sectional couch for up to $300. Some of the deals here are great, while others offer questionable savings. Take home some elegant brass light fixtures for $85 or pay closer to $25 for plainer models. Look over the collection of desk and floor lamps to find $10 to $20 bargains. Pick up a sturdy dresser for $40 or a carved wooden desk for $100. Chill out in your living room in front of a secondhand TV from this shop or ride home on a new-to-you bike for just $15. A second room is full of sheets, linens, nifty luggage, old trunks, books, and larger home appliances. Though sometimes a bit more than dirt cheap, this place is pretty darn good on the whole.

For the final stop in Durham, check out the goods at the medium-size **Nearly-New Shoppe**, near Duke Medical Center. You'll probably find the place busy with customers on most days of the week. The store carries a quirky selection of formal and vintage clothes, mixed together on one rack and generally priced between $4 and $10. You can also score on everyday garments from decades past, along with more contemporary styles, all organized by size throughout the racks. Take home a glamorous fur coat for heavy winter wear for $40 or less.

NEARLY-NEW SHOPPE
615 Douglas Street
Durham, North Carolina
Phone: (919) 286-4597
Hours: Mon 10–5, Tues–Thurs 10–2, Fri 10–5, Sat 10–2

There's a small selection of furniture, like a child-size desk or a few chairs, or take home some new lighting options for around $25. Pick up some glassware, mugs, and plates for your kitchen and make additions to your personal library with hard- and softcover books for $1 or less.

RALEIGH, NORTH CAROLINA

Nearby Raleigh is home to a bunch of larger chain thrift stores, which are great for their wide variety and large quantity of junk and precious finds. To get there, hit Interstate 40 and proceed directly to thrift land.

Start out with another **GCF Donation Center & Store** in a shopping plaza near the corner of Six Forks Drive and Strickland Road. While the large clothing selection is just mediocre, the housewares shelves do offer their share of eccentricities. Keep your eyes peeled for a set of orange plastic coasters, a recipe box covered with tiny shells, or a pair of brass candelabra, all at rock-bottom prices. Look carefully through the record bins for 1980s pop and 1960s folk rarities. Pick up a new shoulder bag from a rack near the front or test out some secondhand stereo equipment or small household gadgets in the back.

Take Glenwood Avenue to Davis Circle to find another **Goodwill**, this one offering better choices and a wider variety of clothing styles. The prices are cheap, but oddly specific— skirts are tagged at $3.10, and ties, hats, or shoes are $1.15. Uncover glasses, mugs, pots, and pans in the housewares department, in addition to sets of china with the pieces sold separately for $1.15 each. Or drop a buck or two for some groovy tunes in the small collection of mood music. Explore your options in the small furniture area, where a newish sofa bed will run you around $70 or a loveseat, $25.

GCF DONATION CENTER & STORE
9005 Baileywick Road
Raleigh, North Carolina
Phone: (919) 518-2878
Hours: Mon–Fri 9–8:30, Sat 9–6,
   Sun 12–6

GOODWILL
6808 Davis Circle
Raleigh, North Carolina
Phone: (919) 782-2435
Hours: Mon–Fri 9–8:30, Sat 9–6,
   Sun 12–6

CREATIVE CONSIGNMENTS
905 West Morgan Street
Raleigh, North Carolina
Phone: (919) 833-6635
Hours: Tues 2–7, Wed–Sat 12–7

Next, visit a small, hippie-flavored resale shop called **Creative Consignments**, where you can find plenty of young-at-heart clothing styles. Hit the marvelous vintage rack for an array of funky patterns and frilly fabrics, where you can pick up a 1970s polyester gown for no more than

$15. The remainder of the clothing racks are devoted to consignment slacks, shirts, and accessories in more contemporary styles for men and women. Also choose from a few racks of patchwork love child dresses and home-sewn summer tank tops. Don't pass up the chance to model a funky leather shoulder bag or a brightly colored scarf. Color tag discounts can mean up to 40 percent off whatever retro treasures you might dredge up.

Buy two clothing items and get one for free at **Thrift USA**! Hardcore secondhand shoppers will love digging through the stash of pants, shorts, and skirts, all mixed together on a single rack. Tags are generally in the $2 to $10 range for clothes, which are individually priced. Make for the 48-cent rack for super blowout deals. Revamp your living room with a new $55 couch or replace your bathroom light fixtures with finds from here. Sort through some racks of old books, greeting cards, and magazines. Also investigate the bits of costume jewelry near the register as you wait to purchase your discoveries.

> **THRIFT USA**
> 427 Chapanoke Road
> Raleigh, North Carolina
> Phone: (919) 779-6000
> Hours: Mon 9–6:30, Tues 10–6:30,
>   Wed–Thurs 9–6:30, Fri 9–7,
>   Sat 9–6:30
>
> **SALVATION ARMY**
> 205 Tryon Hills Road
> Raleigh, North Carolina
> Phone: (919) 773-3004
> Hours: Mon–Fri 10–6, Sat 9–6

Next, pull the thriftmobile over at the **Salvation Army** on Tryon Hills Road. Flip through tidy racks of used clothes at decent prices. Men can snag slacks for $5 here or three-piece suits for around $13. Ladies' nice wool suits can be had for $10. Prom hopefuls should look over the large formal wear rack for silken finds. The bookshelves hold plenty of 50-cent finds and, nearby, the small gallery of framed pictures and prints. Score some really great buys on furniture, like a coffee table for $30 or couches as low as $15. Don't skip "Evangeline's Boutique," a small sectioned-off area for nice antique-y items: artsy paintings, sets of china for the table, dolls, figurines, and fancy furniture.

Make a few excellent additions to your closet with finds from the **Tryon Hills Thrift Shop**. With ladies' purses and bags priced at $1 to $5, you're sure to pick up a few fashionable accessories. Though you won't find tons, what vintage and dress-up clothes the store carries are together on a small rack. Other clothing is priced between $2 and $4. Furniture prices are also extremely reasonable. Make off with an almost-new outdoor patio set or a nightstand in excellent condition. Get a few silver picture frames for the mantle or take home an old tin recipe box or a few decorator baskets from the housewares area. Look for special daily colored tag sales for super blowouts.

Step into the clean, bright **American Way Thrift Store** on Crabtree Boulevard to find a good variety of furniture and clothes, clothes, clothes! The cavernous store has many racks of apparel, even a huge section just for kids' clothes. Look here for retro bowling team T-shirts or try on a corduroy jacket for around $6. Furs and fake furs are mixed in with the fancier dress clothes. A couch from the big offering of home furnishings might run you around $40, or pick up kitchen chairs for about $15. Bookworms can delve into scores of interesting titles and old magazines to look for bargains. On the sidewalk out front, pick out a bike to ride home for only $10 to $25. Though many of them will need a little work, you can find cool low-rider styles in lots of colors.

The last stop in Raleigh is practically right across the street. The **Disabled American Veterans Thrift Store** is a hot spot for furniture

TRYON HILLS THRIFT STORE
331 Tryon Road
Raleigh, North Carolina
Phone: (919) 772-3711
Hours: Mon–Sat 9–7

AMERICAN WAY THRIFT STORE
2409 Crabtree Boulevard
Raleigh, North Carolina
Phone: (919) 832-3199
Hours: Mon–Thurs 9–7, Fri 9–8,
    Sat 9–6, Sun 12–6

**DISABLED AMERICAN VETERANS
    THRIFT STORE**
2418 Crabtree Boulevard
Raleigh, North Carolina
Phone: (919) 832-8667
Hours: Mon–Fri 10–7, Sat 9–6

finds and old records. The music area offers many shelves squeezed full of albums. Find everything from 1950s cha-cha-cha to 1980s rock and pop. All records are $3 each, which is pretty high compared to other stores. For clothes, women's wear and polyesters are the main attractions—grab almost anything on the rack for $2 or $3. A giant backroom stocks loads of housewares, from china and drinking glasses to glass lampshades and oodles of light fixtures. Don't miss the out-of-control computer area, with carefully organized bins and shelves of keyboards, motherboards, modems, cables, and sound cards. Assemble a completely thrifted computer for under $50! Also score on old sewing machines, turntables, speakers, and stereo equipment, all at bargain basement prices. Haul all your new finds back to home base and try to figure out where to put it all.

ROUTE #6

Washington, D.C., to the Delaware and Maryland Coasts

Thrift Store USA,
Norfolk, Virginia

DAV Tidewater Thrift Store,
Virginia Beach, Virginia

Estate Treasures,
Chester, Maryland

Route #6 leads you on a coastal adventure around the Chesapeake Bay. Cruising east through Annapolis and across the Chesapeake Bay Bridge, the route zigzags east and south through Maryland, Delaware, and Virginia. The tour wraps up in the Virginia Beach, Norfolk, and Portsmouth area.

Route #6 Driving Time (stops not included): 7 hours

The Annapolis area boasts such thrift wonders as **Compassion Center**, **Regal Rags**, and the **Annapolis Junque Boutique**. Heading over the bridge and into Delaware, you'll find lots of collectible goodies at **Bridgeville Emporium** and **Art's Antique Alley** in Bridgeville, while nearby Seaford offers strange thrifting adventures at the mysterious **Because We Care** and crazy deals at **Seaford's Thrift Store**. Stroll the beaches and boardwalks of Ocean City, then enjoy the coastal scenery on the drive toward Virginia Beach. Crash near the beach at **Angie's Guest Hostel** and wrap it up at area bargain centers like **P-Town Thrift** and **Thrift Store USA**, where a bevy of hidden treasures awaits.

BOWIE, MARYLAND

Your first stop on Route 6 is an educational one—drop in on **Déjà Vu Books** in Bowie. With used hard- and softcover titles at great prices, you're sure to find at least a few good books to relax with. There's a huge cookbook section, tons of self-help, and many classics to choose from. For crafters, there are plenty of instructional books, like a four-color quilting book for only $6, and everything from needlepoint to home decorating. Recent fiction and nonfiction titles are also in good supply. Don't miss the small selection of used CDs and the bins of vinyl, which contain mostly rock music, along with some country, spoken word, and novelty records. Snag some INXS, Billy Idol, the Go-Go's or Brenda Lee. The shelves in the smaller side room are full of sci-fi, humor, and books on tape.

> **DÉJÀ VU BOOKS**
> 13600 Annapolis Road (Route 450)
> Bowie, Maryland
> Phone: (301) 464-2999
> Hours: Tues–Fri 10:30–7:30, Sat
> 10–5, Sun 12–5
>
> **NEW TO YOU, INC.**
> 1916 Forest Drive
> Annapolis, Maryland
> Phone: (410) 263-2211
> Hours: Mon–Tues 10–5:45, Wed
> 10–7:45, Thurs–Sat 10–5:45,
> Sun 12–4:45

ANNAPOLIS, MARYLAND

The Annapolis area offers an impressive number of stores, ranging from the small consignment business to the mega thrift shop. It's a great city to pick up some new duds or creative home furnishings.

The **New To You, Inc.** consignment shop is a great place for ladies' clothes and accessories, but the housewares department is far more interesting. In the clothing section, find slightly conservative threads from labels like Express, Ann Taylor, and Gap. Sweaters run from $8 to $12, and you can find lots of good bags and smaller purses for $10 and under. Compared to a bona fide thrift store, some prices here are unexplainably high, but they are combated by color tag sales of 30 to 50 percent off. The collectibles room is really big, lined with shelves full of a strange medley of wrought iron candlesticks, jam and jelly jars, "crystal" glasses, and odd figurines. Also score on kitschy collectibles like a pair of elf figurines or kitchenware like a McDonald's glass set.

Keep your eyes peeled for the Bay Forest Center shopping plaza, which is home to **Second Look**, a little consignment shop packed full of clothes, accessories, and a few household items. Again, you can find lots of clothes that are modern but a wee bit conservative. Teens can find recent trends in denim and fitted T-shirts. However, the brimming racks also hold the odd vintage piece, plus some more unusual finds. There are jewelry and bangles at the counter, lots of bags and backpacks, and a rack of scarves. The price tags are all very reasonable, and you can pick up most items for less than $12. There are lots of seasonal items, and more colored tags make the prices even better.

The **Lutheran Mission Society's Compassion Center** is petite but bursting at the seams with potential treasures. Besides offering a surprisingly broad range of stuff (all in small quantities), this thrift shop also has the dirt-cheap prices. A little clothing corner offers men's suit jackets, shoes, and belts as well as ladies' dresses, tops, and pants. A big stuff-it-in-a-bag bargain clothing bin contains everything from a collegiate sweatshirt to a 1960s dress. The housewares area carries a mishmash, too, like a set of six pink sherbet glasses for $8 or an inexpensive 8mm film projector stowed away on a high shelf. There are sometimes a few examples of well-priced furniture on the sidewalk, like an antique school desk or a set of mission-style kitchen chairs for $20. You'll find a little area of keyboards, computer monitors, and electronics—even a few wigs. Don't miss the box of old scenic postcards for 50 cents each.

SECOND LOOK
Bay Forest Center
942 Bay Ridge Road
Annapolis, Maryland
Phone: (410) 263-3111
Hours: Mon–Fri 10–8, Sat 10–6,
   Sun 1–4

LUTHERAN MISSION SOCIETY'S
   COMPASSION CENTER
230 West Street
Annapolis, Maryland
Phone: (410) 269-5016
Hours: Mon–Sat 9–4:30

The **Goodwill Super Store** is a super place for clothes, records, and maybe kitchen items as well. The sign at the front notifies of the color tag sale of the day, or on some days the discount applies to everything in the store. You'll find sports shirts and men's ties, jeans and T-shirts, and fancy evening gowns. Dresses are $6—pick up a black satin ballerina-style frock, or a wavy-striped mod number from 1964. The housewares area is huge, with tons of silver, brass, crystal, and a few sets of china. For books, the selection is small, but intriguing—find out about area wildlife or home electrical repair. This Goodwill is also a record bonanza, with boxes and bins full of lounge tunes, 1980s pop and rap, and more contemporary choices.

GOODWILL SUPER STORE
1605 West Street
Annapolis, Maryland
Phone: (410) 269-1302
Hours: Mon–Sat 9–8, Sun 9–5

REGAL RAGS
Admiral Court Shopping Plaza
626 Admiral Drive
Annapolis, Maryland
Phone: (410) 224-3434
Hours: Mon–Fri 11–6, Sat 10–4

THE CLOTHES BOX
Anne Arundel Medical Center–Sajak
   Pavilion
2001 Medical Parkway
Annapolis, Maryland
Phone: (410) 481-5070
Hours: Mon, Wed, Thurs 10–6,
   Tues, Fri 10–4, Sat 10–1

Please send our regards to Miss Ricky, the tiny fluffy white dog that reigns supreme at **Regal Rags**, a consignment shop known as "the Rolls Royce of resale." Miss Ricky (aka Rotten Ricky, as in spoiled rotten) is an old pro at sniffing out the deals on Chanel, Lilly Pulitzer, and other well-known designers of women's clothing. Despite her highbrow taste, Miss Ricky and Regal Rags are both really fun and friendly. Try on long elegant gowns, beaded jackets, and other formal options as well as more casual clothes for the daylight hours. The racks are grouped according to size. Most items are in the $15 to $45 range; however, some exceptional garments may go as high as $100 or more. The color-tag discount system is usually in effect. Snack on little plates of dainty finger cookies at the counter while the clerk rings up your purchase.

The Clothes Box is a clean and cheery little thrift store located in the Anne Arundel Medical Center. To get there, turn into the Sajak Pavilion from Jennifer Road. Park on the ground floor level of the garage, which is free for the first hour. The Clothes Box carries many "mature" styles of clothing, along with some unique vintage garb and a few up-to-date finds mixed in. Choose from the classy selection of formal dresses. Expect most items to be inexpensive, with sweaters and tops priced from $3 to $6. There's more than clothes at the Clothes Box—find wall hangings and home decorations, luggage, linens, and a tiny bit of costume jewelry. If you're seeking anything in particular, a small army of volunteers can happily point you in the right direction.

The best stop for furniture in the area is probably **Annapolis Junque Boutique**, located northwest of the city on Route 450 (near the junction of Route 450 and Crownsville Road). The shop is a small house with a first floor packed with rarities and a front yard lined with furniture. Outside, find kitchen table and chair sets, a few bureaus, couches, and patio furniture, some stacked in large tents along the side of the property. Inside, navigate the skinny aisles of several rooms, all with shelves crammed full of nicknacks, kitchenware, china, and light fixtures. Snag a set of Blue Heaven patterned bowls and dishes, a vintage cake decorating set, or one of many funky table lamps. Prices are not always marked, but they are generally reasonable and almost always negotiable. Haggling is encouraged.

> **ANNAPOLIS JUNQUE BOUTIQUE**
> 520 Defense Highway (Route 450)
> Annapolis, Maryland
> Phone: (410) 573-1138
> Hours: Mon 10–dark, Wed–Sun
>   10–dark
>
> **ESTATE TREASURES**
> 17 Kent Town Market
> Chester, Maryland
> Phone: (410) 643-7360
> Hours: Mon–Fri 10–5, Sat 10–4

CHESTER, MARYLAND

On your way out of Annapolis, hop onto Route 50 to cross the Chesapeake Bay Bridge. **Estate Treasures** thrift shop is almost directly off the highway in Kent Town Market, a small shopping plaza in Chester. Everything in the shop is clean and neat. Housewares are displayed in the front windows and on shelves in the back. You can find some cool and unusual items here, like a sailboat-shaped bedside lamp for $12 or a set of daisy-patterned drinking glasses for around $10. A fancier item like a faux crystal lazy Susan could cost you up to $25. Estate Treasures is a marvelous place to pick up classy collectibles, silver platters, and lamps. There are clothes, too—men's and women's apparel at thrift shop prices. Look out for seasonal sales. All proceeds benefit the Hospice of Queen Anne's.

DENTON, MARYLAND

Divert to Route 404 toward Bridgeville. Along the way, find the **Samaritan House Thrift Shop** on the corner of 5th Avenue and Gay Street in Denton. Check the board for daily specials, although the prices are pretty good to begin with. Jeans or ladies' jackets might go for $2 or $3, and there are lots of clothes to choose from. Pick up a new-to-you tracksuit or polyester patterned dress. The shop has a small selection of household goods, including lamps, bowls, and dishes, and a back room with luggage and linens. Rifle through a basket of used videotapes and a book area in the front. Spend a few minutes poking around and see what you can find.

SAMARITAN HOUSE THRIFT SHOP
12 North 5th Street
Denton, Maryland
Phone: (410) 479-1251
Hours: Wed–Fri 10–2,
   Sat 9–12 noon

ART'S ANTIQUE ALLEY
Route 13 South
Bridgeville, Delaware
Phone: (302) 337-3137
Hours: Mon–Sun 9–6

BRIDGEVILLE, DELAWARE

Continue along Route 404 to Bridgeville. Here, find two excellent stops for good deals on antiques, collectibles, and other awesome junk: Art's Antique Alley and Bridgeville Emporium.

The first, **Art's Antique Alley**, is truly huge. Yellow arrows on the floor will guide you through the maze of rooms full of amazing stuff—you'll be surprised at both the quantity and the variety. There are tons of glassware items, from depression and milk glass to bright mixing bowls and Avon collectibles. Browse shelves of salt 'n' pepper shakers shaped like cactuses, rocket ships, or oranges. If you're looking for a sugar and creamer set, owl-shaped with rhinestone eyes, you're in the right spot. There are bazillions of framed pictures and paintings, odd pieces of furniture, and embroidered tablecloths and linens. Keep your eyes peeled for old cameras and used film equipment. Prices are generally good to moderate, and closer inspection will yield the occasional thrifty score.

Bridgeville Emporium is a shop of many moods. Turn left, and it's the land of many small dolls. Turn right, and it's a 1960s bachelor pad. Turn left again, and it's suddenly Christmas, 1982. Lots of small booths are curtained and sectioned off, and each has its own distinct flavor. Find tons of miniatures, a pair of ceramic geisha girl lamps, and a set of plastic souvenir coasters from Hong Kong. A few booths carry vintage clothes, scarves, bags and jewelry. Bridgeville Emporium is top-notch for random hidden deals, like an oak, drop-leaf table for a little over $100. Other furniture finds are scattered throughout. For unmarked items, consult owner Tim Curry, whose brain is a mental catalogue of prices for all the goodies you can find here.

BRIDGEVILLE EMPORIUM
105 Market Street
Bridgeville, Delaware
Phone: (302) 337-7663
Hours: Thurs–Mon 11–5, Tues or
  Wed by chance

SEAFORD'S THRIFT STORE
115 High Street
Seaford, Delaware
Phone: Unavailable
Hours: Mon–Sat 9–5

SEAFORD, DELAWARE

After Bridgeville, head south to Seaford on Route 13. **Seaford's Thrift Store** is sparse and doesn't carry large quantities of anything, but the prices are so dirt cheap that you really have to stop in. Lay your mitts on a denim jacket for 10 cents or a silky peach dress for 75 cents. Weirdly, all the clothing racks have Ralph Lauren signs over them. Cups, figurines, and other nicknacks line the window ledge, and more platters, bowls, and other housewares are spread out on a table. There are very few sets or pairs of anything, but the prices on these home items are also rock-bottom. A few shoe racks and some books round out the fare. Weird.

Because We Care has no sign out front, but the intriguing little shop can be found at the intersection of Pine and High streets. At first glance, you might think that wedding gowns and lawn statues are all it carries, but inside you'll find a horse of a different color. Small, dark, and cluttered are three words you might use to describe this weird-but-fun thrift extravaganza. Squeeze yourself into the narrow aisles of clothes and furniture, almost buried by miscellaneous junk. Here, you can find a few plaid couches, a bureau or two, or even some Cupid statues. Overflowing racks of memorable clothing are tightly squished into the back of the store, along with shoulder-high piles of random things. Take advantage of the permanent $2-per-bag clothing sale at Because We Care.

> **BECAUSE WE CARE**
> 323 High Street
> Seaford, Delaware
> Phone: (302) 628-8496
> Hours: Mon–Sat 9–5, Sun 10–4
>
> **CURIOSITY SHOP**
> 1100 Middleford Road
> Seaford, Delaware
> Phone: (302) 629-2650
> Hours: Mon–Wed 9–5, Thurs 9–2,
> Fri 9–5, Sat 9–3

Seaford's last stop is the **Curiosity Shop**, refreshingly more organized and easy to get around. Everything is a bargain, with most clothing items going for $1 or $2, and the very most expensive tagged at $10. Guys and gals will both find a good selection here. Nab some army pants or a crocheted shawl or raid the jumbled stash of leather accessories. Browse a wide array of both soft- and hardcover fiction for next to nothing or pick up some attractive curtains. Red, green, and blue suitcases line the top shelves of the housewares area, which is full of things like decanters, ashtrays, and eight-track tapes.

LAUREL, DELAWARE

If you're looking for a spacious and orderly place to thrift, wander into the **Good Samaritan Aid Thrift Shop** in Laurel, a family store with a wholesome feel. Search the shelves here for candy dishes, Pyrex bowls, and candlesticks galore. Don't miss the extensive selection of quilted coverlets, tasteful linens, and curtains. Decorative baskets are hung neatly on a rack. There are lots of clothes for everybody, including kids. Also find some usable sporting equipment, like footballs, bikes, and lacrosse sticks. Good Samaritan carries only a few pieces of furniture, but what it has tends to be quality.

GOOD SAMARITAN AID THRIFT SHOP
201 West Market Street
Laurel, Delaware
Phone: (302) 875-2425
Hours: Thurs–Fri 10–4, Sat 10–1

HARVEST MINISTRIES THRIFT SHOP
305 North Bi State Boulevard
Delmar, Delaware
Phone: (302) 846-3001
Hours: Mon 10–3, Wed–Sat 10–3

DELMAR, DELAWARE

Further down Route 13 in Delmar, **Harvest Ministries Thrift Shop** is the place to go. The shop is small but full of good clothing finds, such as a white knitted cape for $1 or a puffy winter ski jacket for $4. There is a varied selection of housewares and dozens of books on the shelves. Grab a macramé plant hanger, miniature figurines, old Tupperware, or needlepoint wall pictures. The back corner is stacked with furniture, most of which is just so-so. Score with the oddball find (a pair of green vinyl salon chairs) that may be lurking in the pile. The prices at Harvest Ministries Thrift Shop are always dirt cheap.

SALISBURY, MARYLAND

Zigzag along Route 13 in Salisbury and you'll find another town of busy multilane roads, strip malls, and, yet again, hard to pass up secondhand shops. Among the dirt-cheap finds is a nice mix of big to small thrift stores, antiques shops, and consignment boutiques. Choose your flavor or visit them all if you have the stamina.

First, stop at the **Opportunity Shoppe**, located steps away from the pedestrian mall in Salisbury where giant flowerpots overflow with blooms. The petite thrift shop is a great source for women's career ensembles and clothes for kiddies. In addition, it carries a very small selection of nicknacks, such as plates and vases, along with some quality costume jewelry and accessories like scarves and belts. Although the options are limited, drop a few dollars and exit with a bag full of goodies in hand.

Right next door, at **Feldman's Market Street Antiques and Collectibles**, shop to your heart's content for nice furniture and small collectibles. Feldman's is another of those big antique warehouses where destiny may bring you face to face with that creaky old rocking chair that you've been wanting. The rambling shop is full of booths offering all kinds of goodies at all kinds of prices. Take your chances on finding a bargain here.

Join the commotion at the popular **Goodwill Superstore**. Among the clothing racks, you'll spot many price tags at $2 to $6, with fancier items at $20 and up. Browse the glittery dress-up section and take home a fur-collar coat or leather jacket. Try on the eclectic styles of shoes that line the back wall and hunt through the many options for women's purses, wallets, and bags. Shop for half-price clothing on the last Saturday of every month. The enormous housewares area overflows with mugs, cups, and lots of baskets and

OPPORTUNITY SHOPPE
158 West Market Street
Salisbury, Maryland
Phone: (410) 749-9777
Hours: Thurs 10–3, Sat 10–3

FELDMAN'S MARKET STREET ANTIQUES AND COLLECTIBLES
150 West Market Street
Salisbury, Maryland
Phone: (410) 749-4111
Hours: Mon–Fri 10–6, Sat 10–5:30, Sun 12–5

GOODWILL SUPERSTORE
700 South Salisbury Boulevard (Route 13)
Salisbury, Maryland
Phone: (410) 219-9072
Hours: Mon–Sat 10–8, Sun 11–5

floral arrangements. If you want toys for the kiddies or plates for the cupboards, it's all here.

A few doors down from the Goodwill, dive into the confusion at **Henrietta's Attic**, just past the Wawa gas station. Inside Henrietta's, rummage through overflowing piles of great castoffs. Dig deep for old dolls, curio items, and other childhood favorites or find a prize or two among the stacks of books. Pick up an antique lamp or some retro kitchenware and check out the cascading strands of costume jewelry. You'll find yourself squeezing through cluttered aisles and narrow pathways to investigate the collectibles and bargains at this little shop.

If you're in need of a nice outfit, head over to **Classy Consignments**. This shop carries mostly women's clothing, plus a few racks for children. Find neat rows of carefully hung clothing, including designer styles and business suits. Pick up a chic ensemble to wear to your cousin's upcoming wedding. Classy Consignments also offers a noteworthy selection of flats and pumps. Expect to pay a little more than thrift store prices for these well-kept items.

HENRIETTA'S ATTIC
205 Maryland Avenue
Salisbury, Maryland
Phone: (410) 546-3700
Hours: Mon–Sat 10–5

CLASSY CONSIGNMENTS
1165 South Salisbury Road
   (Route 13)
Salisbury, Maryland
Phone: (410) 742-2727
Hours: Mon–Sat 1–5:30

CROSS STREET JUNCTION
503 Cross Street
Salisbury, Maryland
Phone: (410) 543-2822
Hours: Mon–Sat 10–6, Sun 12–5

Cross Street Junction, just over the train tracks from Route 13, is a comfortably cluttered antiques store offering home furnishings, garden objects, housewares, and other collectible items. Browse the numerous dealer displays to find plenty of dolls, jewelry, and other bargains. Spot a baroque tapestry couch and some fancy silver serving ware or take home a bright ceramic planter for less than $10. Nab a pair of bookends for your used book collection. You can expect to pay in the double digits for the nicer finds on the main floor. For cheaper

thrills, head upstairs to Sanford's Attic, where you can find miscellaneous items, haphazardly scattered about. Sort through these intriguing castaways and leave with an old
typewriter, a couple of nostalgic LPs,
or some doll parts for a few measly
bucks. Before leaving, stop in next
door at Chesapeake Center Antiques
for even more fun—wrought iron,
wicker, and more.

SALVATION ARMY
215 East Vine Street
Salisbury, Maryland
Phone: (410) 749-8146
Hours: Mon–Fri 9–4 and 5–8,
   Sat 9–4

UNIQUE FLEA
Three Bridges Road
Willards, Maryland
Phone: (410) 835-2580
Hours: Fri–Sat 10–3, closed Dec–Mar

Wrap up your Salisbury thrift adventure at the **Salvation Army** on
Vine Street, a great spot for oddball
furniture finds and great deals on
clothes. The store holds daily dollar
sales—on Mondays, snag $1 skirts,
on Tuesdays $1 shirts, and so on. Fridays are formal, with $1 suit jackets. Find belts, handbags, antiques, and finer household items near the
register at the entrance. Decorators will want to rummage through a
giant bin of baskets. Pick up some useful kitchen goods, books, and
records, too.

WILLARDS, MARYLAND

From Salisbury, head east on Route 50. Make a quick stop at **Unique
Flea**, a very out-of-the-way spot in the tiny town of Willards. You'd
never find this secret location unless you knew where to look for it—
turn north from Route 50 onto Main Street, then bear right on Three
Bridges Road. Navigate the tiny rural lanes to find Unique Flea, a
small cluster of tan cottages under a stand of tall and shady trees. Investigate this trove of old relics for shelves of antique nicknacks, colorful glassware, and assorted kitchen items. Pick up a few smaller
home furnishings and sift through a pleasant hodgepodge of weirdo
collectibles and fetching odds and ends.

OCEAN CITY, MARYLAND

Proceed east on Route 50. From the highway, you'll easily spot the big sign for **Edgemore Antiques**, which advertises "antiques, collectibles, treasures and trash." Pull around to the back of the circular drive to find this little house of curiosities. Find a fascinating postcard from the 1940s, a good-looking beaded necklace, or Ocean City memorabilia from the 1950s. Delve into the huge box of old bottle cap discs. Some scented candles, newish figurines, and collectible plates are included in the merchandise. Doll collectors will love this place, a good spot to find miniatures, Barbies, and dressed-up baby dolls. Check out the funky gift gazebo out in the front yard. Prices are moderate, so you'll have to dig a little deeper for any dirt-cheap bargains here.

Near the intersection of Route 50 and Stephen Decatur Highway, cool off from all the excitement at an Ocean City classic, **Dumser's Dairyland**, a 1950s-style ice cream stand. Make a roadside stop for decadent ice cream cones, thick shakes, sundaes, and Italian ices. Choose from a long list of hand-dipped gourmet flavors and toppings. Top off your order with Dumser's spectacular hot fudge topping, Chriss's favorite. Enjoy your frozen treat on the wooden benches out front before it melts.

> **EDGEMORE ANTIQUES**
> Visible from Route 50
> 10009 Silver Point Lane
> Ocean City, Maryland
> Phone: (410) 213-2900
> Hours: Mon–Tues 10–5, Thurs–Sat 10–5, Sun by chance
>
> **DUMSER'S DAIRYLAND**
> On Route 50 at Stephen Decatur Highway (Route 611)
> Ocean City, Maryland
> Phone: (410) 213-7106
> Hours: Mon–Sun 11–10
>
> **ATLANTIC COLLECTIBLES**
> 9625 Stephen Decatur Highway (Route 611)
> Berlin, Maryland
> Phone: (410) 213-0782
> Hours: Tues–Sat 9–4:30, Sun 12–4:30

Turn south onto Stephen Decatur Highway (Route 611) to get to **Atlantic Collectibles.** Weave your way through the shop, filled with funky dishes, interesting glassware, and small curios from decades past. Check out the collection of floral pitcher and glass sets. Classy antique furniture and vintage clothing are also part of the offering—don't miss ladies' fashions from the 1940s and '50s, including fur-trimmed coats, wool suits, and gorgeous hats of felt and tulle. Also find some great 1950s and '60s home furnishings—a stylish ottoman or some arty-looking lamps. Most items are in super condition and are beautifully displayed about the store. With plenty of tags marked from $15 to $30, find yourself some new home furnishings to take away.

The boardwalk in Ocean City can provide endless summertime entertainment. Hop from one arcade to the next for an afternoon of video games, ski ball, and other prize-winning ventures. Along with the amusing parade of humanity at the beach, you'll find many carnival attractions, like amusement parks with old time carousels, Ferris wheels, and roller coasters.

BOOKSHELF, ETC.
8006 Coastal Highway
Ocean City, Maryland
Phone: (410) 524-2949
Hours: Mon–Sun 10–8
  (summer hours)

A–Z USED FURNITURE
153 Market Street
Pocomoke City, Maryland
Phone: (410) 957-6600
Hours: Tues–Sat 8:30–5

Grab a hamburger on the boardwalk, then head over to the only thrifty spot in town, **Bookshelf, Etc.** Bookworms will adore this shop full of previously loved paperbacks and hardcovers in all genres. Investigate three crowded rooms of books on cooking, history, and more. In the front, find a box of comics, 45 rpm records, and a small craft section. Plan your next sewing project with a groovy 1970s needlepoint book or travel down memory lane with a 1950s children's book and record set. Make off with classics, sci-fi, and other budget literature. Expect to shell out $4 to $5 for these priceless finds.

POCOMOKE CITY, MARYLAND

From Ocean City, jet down Route 113 to Pocomoke City. On Market Street, prepare for a dig-deep adventure at the curious **A–Z Used Furni-**

ture. This enormous two-floor warehouse is not only a furniture mecca, but a thrift store and antique showroom combined. On the ground floor, you'll find nicer furniture in the front, along with an assortment of paintings, unique wall hangings, and collectible trinkets. The better deals are to be found in the back room and on the second floor. Find dressers, dinette sets, treadmills, and used carpets in the back room, along with heaped piles of very random items like greeting cards, old coffeemakers, and candles. Upstairs, browse through clothing marked at $1 to $3. A number of smaller side rooms are brimming with goodies—dig through the record room of wall-to-wall LPs and 45s. Meander into the book room for old favorites. Pick through a plethora of toys strewn about in the kids' room and dare to venture into the linen area. A–Z is very large and somewhat odd. The longer you stay, the weirder it gets. Avoid the bathroom at all costs.

Keep your eyes peeled for **Candy's Place**, on 6th Street between Market and Linden streets in Pocomoke City. Candy's is a fair-size shop in a sunshine yellow cinder block building, crammed full of good stuff. Inside, weed your way through the dim jumble of funky lamps, odd pieces of furniture, and some collectible items. Check out several racks of secondhand clothing and surfaces piled high with pots, pans, old dishes, and shoes.

CANDY'S PLACE
17 East 6th Street
Pocomoke City, Maryland
Phone: Unavailable
Hours: Mon–Tues 10–5, Thurs–Fri 10–5, Sat 8–3

FOODBANK OF EASTERN SHORE THRIFT STORE
24530 Coastal Highway
Tasley, Virginia
Phone: (757) 787-2557
Hours: Mon–Fri 9–4:30, Sat 9–4

TASLEY, VIRGINIA

Proceed south down Route 13 for a short stop in rural Tasley at **Foodbank of Eastern Shore Thrift Store**, a real thrift treat. The prices here are hard to beat, with most clothing items priced between $2 and $5. Find apparel here for men and women, plus a large section devoted to children in the back of the store. Peek through the orderly racks of household linens to find flowery or polka-dot sheets, gauzy curtains, and tablecloths, all at bargain basement prices. The bric-a-brac area is home to a bazillion glass bud vases and some utilitarian kitchen goods.

At the front counter, find a display of silver and costume jewelry and try some on for kicks.

THIS & THAT
24554 Coastal Highway
Tasley, Virginia
Phone: Unavailable
Hours: By chance

Not far away on Coastal Highway, pull over to investigate the merchandise at **This & That**. The title is an accurate description of what it carries—find a few "yard sale" items out front and a miscellaneous mishmash inside. This & That is a small, dusty junk-and-treasures shop with prices ranging from $1 to $25. Here you might find a sturdy lawn mower, a scenic painting, a slogan coffee cup, or a brightly colored plastic ceiling lamp. Look all around, because potential treasures may be found hanging on the walls and from ceiling beams as well. Haggling will get you nowhere with the colorful characters who run the store, but if you have the time they're eager to chat.

This & That, Tasley, Virginia

EXMORE, VIRGINIA

On sleepy Route 13 Business in Exmore, brake for a few good stops. Is it time for your afternoon milkshake? Consult the clock over the entrance to the **Exmore Diner** to find out. This 1950s shiny silver car diner serves up American road food at its finest. Open for breakfast, lunch, and dinner, the menu advertises "old fashioned food at old fashioned prices." Order a hamburger for $1.50 or a sandwich or sub for $3. Round it out with some fries, onion rings, or a thick and creamy milkshake. Sample the hot apple pie for dessert—out of this world and even better with a scoop of vanilla ice cream. Breakfast is served all day, for those of you who like to eat pancakes and eggs around the clock.

EXMORE DINER
4262 Main Street
  (Route 13 Business)
Exmore, Virginia
Phone: (757) 442-2313
Hours: Mon–Thurs 5am–8pm,
  Fri–Sat 5am–8:30pm, Sun
  6am–12pm

A–Z USED FURNITURE
4218 Main Street
  (Route 13 Business)
Exmore, Virginia
Phone: (757) 442-3991
Hours: Tues–Sat 8:30–5

From the Exmore Diner, take a short walk over to **A–Z Used Furniture**, another branch of that Pocomoke City oddity. Enter under the "Flea Market" sign, where a shopping cart full of 10-cent bargain mugs awaits you near the door. This gigantic dusty building contains a quirky mix of secondhand clothing and nicknacks, antique furniture, and new surplus goods. In the front room you'll find small mountains of linens, crocheted afghans, and bedding, along with yellow rain suits and army camouflage. Full shelves of bric-a-brac include old toasters, ceramic vases, and other random stuff. In the antique furniture area, exquisite Victorian couches and velvet lamps from the 1970s can be priced from $50 to $150. Imaginative thrifters may find some super treasures at rock-bottom prices amid the dusty chaos.

Pull over in front of the weathered store front of **Antique Addicts**. Around the side of the building, spot a lineup of vintage stoves and iceboxes. Step inside this antique wonderland of more than seventy dealer booths displaying furniture, housewares, and collectibles. Pick up some classy china, lemonade glass and pitcher sets, vintage dolls and figurines, or Christmas decorations from the 1950s. Curio collectors will have a ball here. Also find ornate lamps, rhinestone jewelry, and an entire book room. As for prices, many items are tagged under $20, though some high-quality furniture pieces can be marked into the triple digits.

> **ANTIQUE ADDICTS**
> 3515 Main Street (Route 13 Business)
> Exmore, Virginia
> Phone: (757) 442-5100
> Hours: Mon–Sun 10–5
>
> **ANGIE'S GUEST COTTAGE**
> 302 24th Street
> Virginia Beach, Virginia
> Phone: (757) 428-4690
> Office Hours: 11am–9pm

VIRGINIA BEACH, VIRGINIA

After Exmore, a long drive will transport you over fields of greenery to the Virginia Beach area. While meandering through the scenic landscape, drop in at one of the many fruit stands or fireworks shacks along the wayside. After leaving the terra firma of the Delmarva Peninsula, Route 13 alternates for many miles between the bridges and underwater tunnels that span the Chesapeake Bay, ending up in the seaside resort area of Virginia Beach.

Hoppin' in the summertime, Virginia Beach is a fun-and-games town full of entertainments like mini golf, boardwalk life, and carnival amusements. Sandy motels line the beachfront strip, and lively bars overflow with patrons every evening. Even if you aren't one of those spring break types, you can still find a good time in this town. Many of the thrift stores are on Virginia Beach Boulevard, the main drag that stretches all the way into Norfolk.

If you're seeking cheap digs in Virginia Beach, we can highly recommend **Angie's Guest Cottage**, a friendly hostel located just steps away from the enticing beachfront. You'll be warmly welcomed at Angie's, where affable staff are happy to point out their most beloved watering holes and other local nightlife favorites. The flowery backyard, complete with Ping-Pong table, is a social spot of its own. You might even make some new friends with the other riff-raff staying there (just kidding.) Accommodations include shared dormitory-style rooms at around $20 per night and even less during the off season. The office is open for check-in from 11 a.m. to 9 p.m. Be sure to make reservations in the summertime!

Get into the Virginia Beach groove by sampling the freshly made crab cakes or a huge platter of fried shrimp at **Big Sam's Inlet Café and Raw Bar**, a waterfront favorite. Enjoy this lowbrow dining experience, where the food is simply delicious. Specializing in just-off-the-boat seafood (and beer!), this lively restaurant is very popular with the natives and is almost always busy on weekends.

From Angie's Guest Cottage, it's only a short walk to **Pearl's Thrift Store** on Pacific Avenue. Forgot your bathing suit? Need a fresh pair of shades? How about a dashing beach umbrella? In that case, Pearl's your girl. Pearl's proximity to the waterfront means that it carries all necessary objects for fun in the sun; however, Pearl's is also a great source for nonbeach items as well. Load up on lampshades and oddball furniture, weird statues, and old socks, all on the cheap.

> **BIG SAM'S INLET CAFÉ & RAW BAR**
> 300 Winston Salem Avenue
> Virginia Beach, Virginia
> Phone: (757) 428-4858
> Hours: Mon–Sun 7am–2am
>
> **PEARL'S THRIFT STORE**
> 2301 Pacific Avenue
> Virginia Beach, Virginia
> Phone: (757) 437-0260
> Hours: Mon–Sat 11–6, Sun 12–5
>
> **SHELTER THRIFT**
> 1813 Virginia Beach Boulevard
> Virginia Beach, Virginia
> Phone: (757) 425-1220
> Hours: Mon–Fri 9–6, Sat 9–5

Meanwhile, for those tired of flip-flops and sunburns, **Shelter Thrift** offers clothes to suit your every mood. You'll find lots of practical and well-cared-for clothing at these super prices—ladies' slacks go for around $4, men's jackets can be had for under $5, and the odd fur coat might be sold for $20 or so. Pick up a Stevie Nicks-style dress or a satiny cummerbund. With all these great deals on the racks, don't become distracted from investigating the shelves. Those who do will be rewarded with heaps of silverware, dishes, china, and other homemaker goodies, in addition to televisions and a selection of working computers. Shelter Thrift also stocks refrigerators and other large appliances. A large wall of books and magazines provides reading material for all ages. Very lucky shoppers may even encounter the $6 Bag Sale, which happens once per month. The actual date is kept secret, but a little birdie told us that it is often held on a weekend toward the month's end. (Sorry, birdie, I guess we let the cat out of the bag!)

For a yummy eggs and bacon breakfast, stop into **Rick's Cafe** on Virginia Beach Boulevard. Rick's could be called short on sophistication, but it's also long on charm. We give Rick's the award for "Best Home Fries in the World," although we all know how subjective the matter of home fries really is. For freely flowing coffee or an extra-delicious piece of pie, drop by Rick's, open anytime day or night (that means twenty-four hours, baby.)

RICK'S CAFE
1612 Virginia Beach Boulevard
Virginia Beach, Virginia
Phone: (757) 425-1625
Hours: Open 24 hours

THINGS UNLIMITED THRIFT STORE
501 Virginia Beach Boulevard
Virginia Beach, Virginia
Phone: (757) 428-7841
Hours: Mon–Fri 10–6, Sat 10–5

There is, indeed, an unlimited number of things to be found at **Things Unlimited Thrift Store**. You'll find many household items at dirt-cheap prices, including dishes, platters, and drinking glass sets. Among the miscellaneous housewares are plenty of conch-shaped candles and seashell-encrusted frames and mirrors. Don't miss the "catch of the day" chalkboard for any daily specials. The selection here caters to those who love to play dress-up. Sift through the colorful costume collection, try on some funny wigs or fake jewels, and leave with a freaky Halloween outfit for next year.

Clothes, clothes, clothes, clothes, clothes! Welcome to the **Goodwill Super Thrift Store**, where you could easily revamp your entire wardrobe within twenty minutes. The prices are moderate, and the selection is wide, very wide. Ladies' suits sell for around $9, and men's button-up shirts are tagged at $3.50. The bounty of secondhand clothing is the main attraction here, from a pair of purple corduroy bell-bottoms to a froufrou Karen Carpenter evening gown, along with racks of kiddie clothes and playthings. A giant toy corner occupies a huge section of the sales floor, and shoppers seem happy to deposit their youngsters there before setting sail in the sea of clothing. The furniture selection is skimpy and mostly overpriced. Nonapparel goods of interest include a small bin of old vinyl as well as many shelves of cups, saucers, mugs, and plates for $1 each.

On most weekends, **DAV Tidewater Thrift Store** is packed to the gills with customers crowding the aisles and lining up at the dressing rooms and cash registers. Get ready to pick, poke, and push your way through the treasure-laden racks and shelves! If on your visit you encounter this pandemonium of thrifting, it's best to adopt the attitude of "search and destroy." The goods at Tidewater are not fancy, but most are truly cheap. In the rear of the shop, you'll find a small selection of useful furniture. Look closely to discover some great deals—a nightstand for $2 or a desk-with-potential, priced at $10. Home decorators will be pleased with the craft materials section as well as an exceptionally large array of baskets and fancy candles. For books, cheap paperbacks are practically a dime a dozen. Also check out the great deals on everyday clothing and ladies' handbags. We found many dirt-cheap deals in the $3 to $4 range, although the pricing can be unexplainably erratic, with the occasional $15 dress. Collectors should head toward the glass counters near the front to find lots of weirdo memorabilia, like a Freddie Kruger or Pee Wee Herman doll, among other things.

> **GOODWILL SUPER THRIFT STORE**
> 3838 Virginia Beach Boulevard
> Virginia Beach, Virginia
> Phone: (757) 463-0576
> Hours: Mon–Sat 9–9, Sun 12–6
>
> **DAV TIDEWATER THRIFT STORE**
> 5517 Virginia Beach Boulevard
> Virginia Beach, Virginia
> Phone: (757) 473-1987
> Hours: Mon–Sat 10–6

Almost directly across the street from Tidewater, you'll find an enormous **Salvation Army Thrift Shop**, probably the most organized resale store for miles around. A swarm of staff works to assemble furniture, restock the aisles, and tend the cash registers, all with the efficiency of a well-oiled machine. The huge space is dazzlingly clean and meticulously arranged, with red neon signs directing shoppers to specialized departments such as "Small Appliances" and "Bric-a-Brac." Electronics and books are housed in small separate rooms. Wander the acres of quality furniture, where you can find complete bed frames, couches, and bureaus from all eras. Drop into the "Sports and Fitness" department for an armload of tennis rackets or sort through piles of golf clubs and bicycles for kids and adults. Affordable options can be found on the hangers in the clothing departments for both men and women. Get some stylish clothes and name brands here. With men's suit jackets priced at $5 to $10, and women's full suits going for $6 to $15, the prices at this Salvation Army are a bit higher than other area thrifts, but the extensive offering more than makes up for it. The thriftiest shoppers show up on Wednesdays (Family Day) for special half-price sales.

> **SALVATION ARMY THRIFT SHOP**
> 5524 Virginia Beach Boulevard
> Virginia Beach, Virginia
> Phone: (757) 499-0032
> Hours: Mon–Tues 9–7, Wed 9–8,
>   Thurs–Sat 9–7
>
> **THRIFT STORE CITY**
> 1917 Victory Boulevard
> Portsmouth, Virginia
> Phone: (757) 485-5432
> Hours: Mon–Sat 9–7

PORTSMOUTH, VIRGINIA

The less beachy and more urban area of Portsmouth offers a wealth of thrifting opportunities. Sniff around for better bargains at a number of family thrift outlets.

Hit the jackpot at **Thrift Store City**! Located in a shopping center on Victory Boulevard, Thrift Store City is about the size of your average grocery store, complete with a multilane checkout. The consistently dirt-cheap price tags make this one of our favorite stops in the area. Probably the most expensive items we saw were furniture pieces tagged up to $50—bargain! The collectibles counter near the entrance stocks scads of cheap jewelry and doodads, plus specialty "antiques." This is a good spot for fake gems and other baubles. Score some oddball table lamps, along with tons of sheets, bedspreads, curtains, and crocheted afghans in bright colors, patches and stripes. From flowerpots to tea services, most of the houseware objects are inexpensively priced from $1 to $5. Thrift Store City is another local favorite, making it a lively scene.

For the ultimate experience of randomness, stop in at **P-Town Thrift,** a cluttered hodgepodge of secondhand goods located on a back stretch of Turnpike Road. This mishmash of urban refuse is barely organized, so be prepared to dig and sort. You can find anything here: baby toys, old tires, refrigerators, televisions, exercise records, vases, lamps, clothes, car seats, and wall mirrors. Wind your way through stacks of speakers and

> **P-TOWN THRIFT**
> 3935 Turnpike Road
> Portsmouth, Virginia
> Phone: (757) 397-8624
> Hours: Mon–Sat 10–6, Sun 11–5

mounds of mattresses and sort through the record collection of funk, disco, and soul music. Despite (or maybe because of) its almost total

P-Town Thrift, Portsmouth, Virginia

disorder, P-Town is full of charm, and an afternoon here will almost certainly yield some booty to cram into the hold.

Keep your eyes peeled for **Finders Keepers Unlimited**, which is marked only by a very small, easy-to-miss sign. In terms of quantity, this place has a hard time competing with the giant thrift outlets, but it's certainly worth a stop, especially for furniture bargain hunters. About half of the selection is newish low-quality furniture, but you'll also find a number of interesting retro pieces for $50 or less. Sort through several racks of clothing for men and women. The store's shelves, though sparse, contain dirt-cheap deals on weird nicknacks, toys, dishes, and random housewares for only 50 cents to $2.

FINDERS KEEPERS UNLIMITED
3107 Airline Boulevard
Portsmouth, Virginia
Phone: (757) 488-8882
Hours: Mon–Sat 10–6

GRANDMAW'S NIFTY THRIFTY
2874 Airline Boulevard
Portsmouth, Virginia
Phone: Unavailable
Hours: By chance

CHKD THRIFT STORE
2717 Airline Boulevard
Portsmouth, Virginia
Phone: (757) 465-5437
Hours: Mon–Fri 9–9, Sat–Sun 12–5

Grandmaw's Nifty Thrifty is a tiny quiet shop with a mysterious selection. Don't expect to be overwhelmed— when we visited, Grandmaw's contained one rack of clothes, two plates, and three records. Okay, this may be a slight exaggeration, but the point is that you will *not* find an enormous quantity of goods. That's not to say that you shouldn't drop in for a visit. Mostly you'll find some china, nicknacks, and a few pieces of furniture. What does it matter if Grandmaw's only carries two items, if you fall in love with one of them?

CHKD Thrift Store, on the other hand, is a bird of a different feather. CHKD (which stands for Children's Hospital of the King's Daughter) has a large and wide-ranging selection of clothing for men, women, and kids. Almost all the clothing items can be had for $5 or less, although trying them on might be difficult. No dressing rooms are available, but you might find a few wall mirrors scattered around. The store is sizable and is kept neat and tidy by the friendly staff (unlike the mean CHKD staff in Norfolk, see below). Aside from clothes there is a small smattering of furniture, and toys, and other items for babes.

NORFOLK, VIRGINIA

As you continue on Virginia Beach Boulevard toward Norfolk, the streets become more congested with strip malls. Norfolk may not be as fun to cruise around as Virginia Beach, but don't miss the great thrifting that it offers.

Super Family Thrift Store is located amid a cluster of over-size shopping centers. Even so, it's a really great place. Grab a cart and get to work. Wandering around this quiet thrift department store, you're bound to find some groovy clothes at great prices. Most items are $2 to $5, except for cold-weather coats, which may be priced as high as $10 to $30. One great thing here is the wide range of styles for both men and women, from fluffy lemon yellow dressing gowns to sports jackets to preppy sweater sets. Check out a table stacked with records, several aisles of shoes, and shelves in the back lined with china and assorted odds and ends. The kids' toy and clothing sections are full of deals as well. Ask at the register about the special daily sales.

> **SUPER FAMILY THRIFT STORE**
> 6035 Virginia Beach Boulevard
> Norfolk, Virginia
> Phone: (757) 455-3653
> Hours: Mon–Sat 9–9, Sun 11–6
>
> **THRIFT STORE CITY**
> 1760 East Little Creek Road
> Norfolk, Virginia
> Phone: (757) 583-6936
> Hours: Mon–Sat 9–7

Get down and get thrifty at **Thrift Store City**, where shoppers scurry back and forth among the aisles, and several speedy checkout lanes operate continuously. One large room holds racks of clothing, and another carries lots of housewares, linens, magazines, mattresses, and a few smaller pieces of furniture. Take a peek at the small book section and the few bins of records. Head over to the "Unique Boutique" counter at the front of the store for jewelry, collectible curios, and specialty items, still at reasonable prices. In the clothing aisles, the deals are also good, but expect to see higher prices for brand names and labels. In warmer weather, adventurous types might want to try a hot dog from the cart parked out front under the enormous Thrift Store cityscape mural.

Practically right next door, you'll get a warm welcome at the **Salvation Army**. This smallish shop has a hard time competing with its popular next-door neighbor. Find out about the 50 percent off discount of the day and shop around. There are some cute housewares, like funny planters and small bric-a-brac, and some questionable velour furniture. The clothes racks carry almost no vintage, but there are lots of goodies for the kids.

SALVATION ARMY
1736 East Little Creek Road
Norfolk, Virginia
Phone: (757) 480-7990
Hours: Mon–Sat 9–6

CHKD THRIFT STORE
1356 East Little Creek Road
Norfolk, Virginia
Phone: (757) 587-5437
Hours: Mon–Sat 9–9, Sun 11–5

GOODWILL
828 East Little Creek Road
Norfolk, Virginia
Phone: (757) 480-4053
Hours: Mon–Sat 9–7, Sun 12–6

The unfriendly staff at Norfolk's **CHKD Thrift Store** detracts from the overall thrifting experience, but all the same, you should drop by for a peek. If clothes are what you're after, check out the cheap and plentiful stash, with almost every item priced under $5. Find anything from a green zippered hoodie to a geometric or floral print scarf. Pick from the collection of *National Geographic* magazines and cheap paperback novels. The furniture selection is not great and is slightly overpriced, but the sizable housewares area contains plenty of options.

For still more new-to-you threads, head over to the mellow **Goodwill** on East Little Creek Road. The clothes are clean and in good shape, and a little investigation may reveal some good deals on oddball items. There are lots of table and desk lamps to choose from and some nearly new furniture that's worth a peek. Crafters can snatch up old-school dress patterns and colorful skeins of yarn for cheap. Also drop by the household items area, where you might find striped drinking glasses for $1 each, or a potpourri dish, if it suits your fancy.

We saved Norfolk's best for last—**Thrift Store USA** is one of our most beloved dirt-cheap stops. This gigantic, sprawling wonderland has many good deals on clothes, plenty of furniture, and in the far back, a bonanza for record buffs. The attentive staff is welcoming and can answer whatever questions you might have. Nudge your way through the clothes racks, where you'll find castoffs from every decade, very often at prices of $1 to $3. Don't miss the "Party Time" section with vintage and fancier

> **THRIFT STORE USA**
> 875 East Little Creek Road
> Norfolk, Virginia
> Phone: (757) 588-2900
> Hours: Mon–Sat 9–7, Sun 12–4

clothes. Laze around on a small sea of couches that range from low-end quality to eye-catching vintage styles, a steal at $25 to $75. You can also find living room chairs for $20 or less. Flip though the stacks and bins of inexpensive vinyl, which could take hours. There is also an extensive toys and games area, mattresses galore, and an array of TVs and other working electronics. Don't miss this grand finale of the Norfolk area, an overflowing treasure chest of cheap fun.

FAVORITE STOPS

A list of our favorite stops, in alphabetical order:

Favorite Thrift Stores:

Bargain Cellar, Pennsboro, West Virginia
Bargain Thrift Center, Philadelphia, Pennsylvania
Georgia Avenue Thrift Store, Washington, D.C.
Gift & Thrift, Harrisonburg, Virginia
Life Line Outreach Center, Henderson, North Carolina
Red White & Blue, Pittsburgh, Pennsylvania
Search Thrift Shop, Mount Jackson, Virginia
Teen Challenge Flea Market, Laurel, Maryland
Thrift Store USA, Norfolk, Virginia

Places for Furniture:

David's Used Furniture, Baltimore, Maryland
Whosoever Gospel Mission, Philadelphia, Pennsylvania

Antiques and Junk:

Crystal Dove Gift Shop, Arlington, Virginia
Everything But Grannies Panties, Raleigh, North Carolina
Lee Jewelree & Thrift, Marcus Hook, Pennsylvania
Monongah Auction, Monongah, Virginia
National Pike Flea Market, Boonsboro, Maryland
Ruff & Ready Furnishings, Washington, D.C.
Somewhere In Time Antique Mall, Nitro, West Virginia

Vintage Clothing:

Dreamland, Baltimore, Maryland
Takoma Underground, Takoma Park, Maryland
Untidy Museum, Durham, North Carolina

Pit Stops:

Beehive, Pittsburgh, Pennsylvania
Little Grill Collective, Harrisonburg, Virginia
Traveler's Rest Motel, Everett, Pennsylvania

Weirdness:

American Dime Museum, Baltimore, Maryland
Gravity Hill, Bedford, Pennsylvania

INDEX

ABOUT THE AUTHORS

Chriss Slevin is a bona fide pack rat. On her numerous road trips and cross-country escapades, she has accumulated a collection of highway souvenirs and thrift oddities. She also collects roadside kitsch such as vintage postcards, messages from Chinese fortune cookies, and squished pennies from truck stops.

Chriss studied painting at the Rhode Island School of Design. She uses thrifted textiles, yarns, papers, and other materials in her artwork. When she is not squishing pennies or painting, Chriss works at an arts foundation in New York City, where she organizes and promotes public arts projects and large-scale exhibitions across New York state.

A dedicated thrifter, an expert bargain hunter, and a staunch advocate of dirt-cheap living, Chriss currently lives in a totally thrift-furnished apartment in Brooklyn.

After many years of dusty ventures, **Leah Smith** has officially attained the status of Thrift Guru. She has been known to travel far and wide to get the goods and has worked up an unrivaled collection of the odd and the unusual. She has a passion for faded objects and the stories that come with them. These days she enjoys hunting for old exercise LPs and bizarre vintage clothing.

Leah studied new media and visual arts at the School of the Museum of Fine Arts, Boston, and continues to pursue artistic interests across the northeast coast. When thrifting isn't on the agenda, she can often be found collaborating on new masterpieces or crafting out in her sewing studio in Boston.

Leah and Chriss adore fan mail and presents, especially with exciting postage.

Address love letters to:

Chriss and Leah
Dirt Cheap, Real Good
c/o Capital Books, Inc.
22841 Quicksilver Drive
Sterling, VA 20166